Construc
Architec

Natascha Meuser
Born in 1967, studied architecture at the Illinois Institute of Chicago and interior design at the Rosenheim University of Applied Sciences. Course-related placements and scholarships in Greece (set design) and Italy (painting). In 1993 she was awarded the *Art Institute of Chicago's Harold Schiff Fellowship*. 2000–2005 research assistant at the Technical University of Berlin. Columnist and illustrator (*Der Tagesspiegel* and *Cicero*). Numerous publications on topics such as building typologies and designs.

Klaus Jan Philipp
Born in 1957, studied art history, history and archeology in Marburg and Berlin; 1996 habilitation; 2003–2008 Professor of History of Construction and Municipal Construction, University of Fine Arts of Hamburg; since 2008 Professor of Architectural History at the University of Stuttgart. Numerous publications on topics at the interface between history of art and architectural history.

Augusto Romano Burelli
Born in 1938 in Udine. Architect and Professor at the Department of Architecture of the University of Venice, where he has also been the Director of the Department of Drafting since 1991. Research in the field of architectural design and urban planning as well as numerous publications. He has designed residential buildings, town halls and churches. Currently lives and works in Udine, Venice and Berlin.

Hans-Dieter Nägelke
Born in 1964, studied art history, medieval and contemporary history and literary studies. Doctoral thesis on the construction of universities of the Kaiserreich Empire. From 2001, founding director of the Schinkel Centre for Architecture, Urban Studies and Maintenance of Monuments at the Technical University of Berlin; from 2003 Director of the Design Collection; from 2007 Director of the Design Collection of the Museum of Architecture of the Technical University of Berlin.

Sergei Tchoban
Born in 1962, studied architecture at the Russian Academy of Arts in Saint Petersburg, managing partner of the architectural studio nps Architekten BDA; from 1996 Head of the Berlin-based office and SPEECH Tchoban & Kuznetsov 2006, another company of his own with offices in Moscow and Saint Petersburg. In 2009 he founded the non-profit Tchoban Foundation which in 2013 established the Museum for Architectural Drawing on the Pfefferberg, the premises of a former brewery in Prenzlauer Berg, Berlin.

Fabrizio Avella
Born in 1968, he is a Professor of Drawing and Measuring and Digital Drafting at the Faculty of Product Design of the University of Palermo and at the Faculty of Architecture at the University of Agrigento. In 2000 he was awarded his doctorate by the University of Palermo.

Construction and Design Manual
Architectural Drawings

Natascha Meuser

With additional contributions by
Fabrizio Avella, Klaus Jan Philipp, Augusto Romano Burelli,
Hans-Dieter Nägelke and Sergei Tchoban

Content

History and Theory

6   **Foreword**
Natascha Meuser

11   **The History of Architectural Drawing**
Klaus Jan Philipp

21   **Architecture for Keyboard Instruments Only**
Augusto Romano Burelli

26   **Collecting Architectural Drawings**
Hans-Dieter Nägelke

38   **The Art of Architectural Drawing**
Sergei Tchoban

Freehand Drawing

53   **School of Perception: Freehand Drawing Exercises**
Natascha Meuser

56	Exercise 1	Point and Line
57	Exercise 2	Proportion and Order
58	Exercise 3	Geometry and Space
59	Exercise 4	Perspective and Space
60	Exercise 5	Composition and Space
61	Exercise 6	Man and Space
62	Exercise 7	Light and Colour
63	Exercise 8	Nature and Design
64	Exercise 9	Two-minute Sketches
65	Exercise 10	Freehand Drawing

67   **Freehand Drawings by Contemporary Architects**

- 68   Yadegar Asisi
- 76   Paul Böhm
- 80   Massimiliano und Doriana Fuksas
- 84   Zaha Hadid
- 88   Zvi Hecker
- 94   Rob Krier
- 98   Wolf D. Prix
- 102   Alexander Radoske
- 106   Christoph Sattler
- 110   Sergei Tchoban

Technical Drawing

119 **An Introduction to Technical Drawing**
Natascha Meuser

121 **Working Tools**
122 Analogue Drawing Tools
129 Digital Working Tools

133 **Basics**
133 Standards
134 Paper and Drawing Sheets
135 Drawing Sheet Sizes and Sheet Folding
136 Headers
138 Drawing Sheets
140 Drawing Scales
142 Line Types and Line Widths
144 Dimensions of Architectural Drawings
146 Labelling Architectural Drawings
148 Shading
150 Stairs
152 Doors and Windows
154 Recesses
156 Roofs
158 Symbols

160 **Architectural Drawings in Practice**
160 Types of Architectural Drawings

Discussion

180 **Drawing between History and Digital Innovation**
Fabrizio Avella

181 The Plan
185 Orthogonal Projections and Flat Section
194 Perspective
206 The Axonometric Projection
212 Paper
214 Techniques
227 Permanence and Variations in Computer Science Design

Appendix

232 Index
234 Sources

Foreword
Natascha Meuser

The drawing architect – for centuries, this term was just as tautological as the *baking baker* or the *gardening gardener*. Nevertheless, in this design manual one has to begin with the fact that the doctrine of signs is by no means a minor field of study for architects. Design methodology, also referred to as methodology of space and the representation of the human body, plays an important role in the current field of activity for architects – once more. While in the post-war period architectural representation developed increasingly into the design plan and no longer served as an architectural consultant, a counter-tendency can be observed in the meantime. Elaborate perspectives and architectural consultants are an essential feature when securing the business of the architect. Yet, as with a lot of specialisations, a professional outsourcing also takes place in the fine-grained, diverse architect's profession. That is to say, the designing architect is not simultaneously the drawing architect. The authors Burelli and Philipp pursue this question in various ways. It is still the case that, in addition to practical instructions for the developer, architectural drawings must have an aesthetic quality which is consistent with the architectural quality. This book is primarily devoted to the history of architectural drawing in order to address the issue of the role it currently plays and which parameters are both indispensable and are of importance for the qualifications required for architects.

Architectural training always begins with vision. Immersing oneself in the history of architectural representation is an integral component of almost every architectural theory. Theoretical ideas in the true sense of the word – concerning the image and drawing – are always clear, even to a non-specialist. Thus, in the course of the training programme, point and line enter the perception of students and develop into the foundations of constructive ideas. In the best case scenario these are implemented, but sometimes are also intended to abstract an idea or illustrate a design. Using the medium of drawing, the guild of planning, building and vision present the remaining unbuilt aspects. In a digital age whose virtual spaces dissolve the boundaries between image and reality, there is a high risk to indulge in a fascinating technology without a measure of sentiment and beauty. Let us not deceive ourselves: even the untrained eye can detect the quality of a beautiful drawing – whether in ancient times, the Renaissance or the digital era.

Quite indisputably, new media and drawing techniques enable an unexpected diversity of new fields of research and creativity. However, the technical means required must be developed. There is no alternative to classical architecture theory with its building typologies and the systematic consideration of the environment created by humans, as well as its architectural, historical derivations and the visualisation of architecture based on architectural drawings. The technical drawing remains a practical basis and form of communication for architects, artists and engineers. Therefore, for these professions it is vital to become familiar with both the methods and tools of this form of representation, as well as its history and the larger contexts of architectural theory. The following areas are important in the representation of architecture: the doctrine of signs, colour and proportion theory, spatial thinking and perspective. This book addresses both the presentation options and contemporary practice of architectural representation. Therefore, only partial aspects of colour and proportion theory are examined. The doctrine of signs is based around the following three topics: history and theory; freehand drawings and technical drawings. An essay by Fabrizio Avella concludes the book by examining the contrasts between tradition and innovation to be found in the world of architecture.

> »Oh Writer! With what words will you describe the entire congfiguration with the perfection that the illustration here gives?«
>
> Leonardo da Vinci

1. History and Theory

In his contribution, Klaus Jan Philipp covers a wide spectrum of the history of art and architecture. He approaches the current discussion on the use of digital technologies in the representation of architecture with an informative brief history of architectural drawing. The Italian architect Augusto Romano Burelli addresses the issue of how the proliferation of digital representation forms leads to a decline in the sensual side of the architectural profession – a high price to pay for the extremely precise and rapid architectural representations of the computer. Hans-Dieter Nägelke, a curator at the Technical University of Berlin and the adjoining Museum of Architecture, conducts a situation analysis in the current (re)discovery of historical architectural drawings. Sergei Tchoban, the renowned Berlin-based architect, has devoted his own address to his passion: Tchoban established his own museum in 2013 to gather his extensive collection of valuable and unique architectural drawings. These partly belong to the Tchoban Foundation.

2. Freehand Drawings

Ten contemporary architects who embody various architectural designs and stylistic elements also rely on distinct drawing and presentation techniques. The selection of architects represents the contemporary presentation of freehand drawings and the elective affinity between drawing and the architectural concept of the offices concerned. As the editor, I have taken the liberty of examining the subject of this book in the most practical way possible. By means of ten exercises on freehand drawing, I would like to demonstrate that spatial perception can be learnt by everyone – namely on the basis of communicating the technique of architectural drawing in a challenging format. In separate chapters, I focus on two basic types of drawing using an educational and instructive method: freehand and technical drawing. The brief theoretical part is complemented by practical exercises and illustrative examples for the benefit of the reader.

3. Technical Drawings

Construction projects undergo different levels of planning and phases of work in their development and implementation. Depending on the status of the project, various methods of presentation are sought after. Since architecture always emerges from the interaction between art and construction, a suitable creative handcraft is also needed. First, an architect must be able to put an idea or a vision down on paper. However, on the other hand, they then must operationalise this idea of a building by using technical drawings and plans in a manner that enables all other construction parties to play a part in the implementation of the project. By means of a technical drawing, an architect becomes a great translator who must master the various languages of both the crafts and expert planners. Thus, this involves nothing less than the communication and permanent reconciliation of utopia and reality.

4. Discussion

Fabrizio Avella, an Italian-based Professor of Digital Drawing Science, subsequently discusses in depth the relationship between tradition and innovation in architecture on the basis of architectural drawings. In his informative essay he has chosen to address the complex problem of two-dimensional representation by distinguishing the representation methods from the techniques of construction. His contribution is intended to provide an outlook on a future discussion on the theory of architectural drawing.

Appendix

The appendix presents a list of carefully selected exhibition catalogues, textbooks and reference books which have formed the basis of the chapter related to technical drawing. These are not only listed but are commented in detail for the benefit of teachers and learners.

»Art holds out a hope for the future if we will allow our cities to be designed by artists instead of by engineers – if we will take into our calculation's the artist's conception of space and line.«

Sir Yehudi Menuhin

History and Theory

11 **The History of Architectural Drawing**
Klaus Jan Philipp

21 **Architecture for Keyboard Instruments Only**
Augusto Romano Burelli

26 **Collecting Architectural Drawings**
Hans-Dieter Nägelke

38 **The Art of Architectural Drawing**
Sergei Tchoban

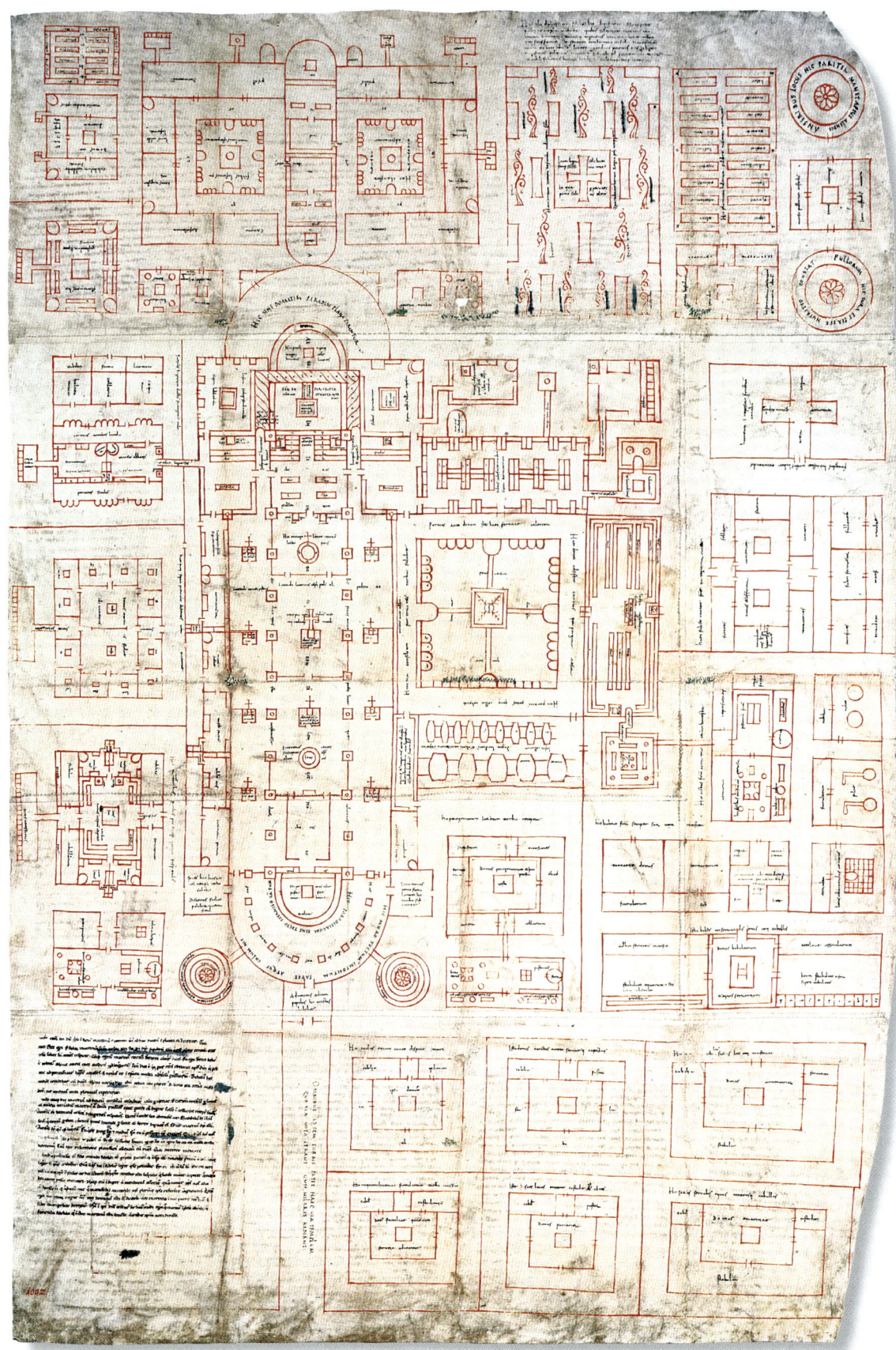

Abbey drawing of St. Gallen, c. 820
Parchment, 77.5 × 112.0 cm
Source: bpk / Hermann Buresch

The History of Architectural Drawing
Klaus Jan Philipp

Outlining the complex history of architectural drawing in a few pages, and placing modern-day digital presentation techniques in their historical context, is a major, if not impossible, challenge. This attempt should therefore be seen as a prologue to a history as yet unwritten – surprisingly, since architectural historians since the Middle Ages have based their researches on architects' sketches, studies and other drawings. These are a rich source of information on how buildings were designed and what they looked like at a given time, and can help us to reconstruct those that no longer exist.

Architectural drawings have always attracted interest as what Josef Ponten calls *unbuilt architecture*.[1] Apart from their documentary value, researchers over the past thirty years have focused on them as a form of artistic expression, with numerous detailed assessments of the drawings of the ancient Greeks and Romans,[2] the Middle Ages,[3] the Renaissance,[4] Baroque[5] and Classicism,[6] and the nineteenth and twentieth centuries.[7] Some are comprehensive assessments of individual collections,[8] many of which can now be viewed online.[9] Other studies have considered the drawings of individual architects as oeuvres in their own right.[10] However, overviews of this subject – which do not concentrate on specific collections – are few and far between: one example is given by Helen Powell and David Leatherborrow's 1982 book *Masterpieces of Architectural Drawing*.[11]

There have been many definitions of what constitutes an architectural drawing. It is an umbrella term covering works as varied as sketches, finished artwork, presentation and working drawings, copies, tracings, reproductions, travel sketches, academy drawings, and illustrations.

Of these, the most important to historians of art and architecture are sketches, which record the architect's first tentative ideas, and presentation drawings, the means by which they communicate with their clients and the public.[12] If we see drawings purely as a means of representing architecture on a two-dimensional surface, technique becomes more important than purpose. With the exception of medieval paintings, where architecture was used to provide narrative context for human figures,[13] this has changed little since classical times. As two-dimensional representations of architectural objects, these drawings combine highly abstract icons into an easily understandable, geometrically based code. Because they convey so much information and are universally understood, they are superior to language as a form of description, and are in theory easy to read, regardless of their historical provenance.[14] Architects use three ways to explain their work to others: plan, section, and elevation. Of these, the plan is undoubtedly the most important. The oldest surviving medieval architectural drawing is the famous ninth-century *Plan of St Gall*, depicting an unbuilt ideal monastery. Werner Jacobsen has shown that this was not simply a factual record, and the plan was worked out by trial and error on the parchment.[15]

The compass holes are visible, and the draftsman scored out various ideas with a sharp object, rejecting these before eventually drawing the final version in red ink. Jacobsen also shows that the dimensions on the plan correspond to those of the completed building, so the drawing was very much a construction plan, serving as a pars pro toto of the whole building.

The importance of the plan as a description of the design and its execution is apparent in later medieval drawings.[16] The rough line drawings in the sketchbook of the thirteenth-century travelling architect Villard de Honnecourt were records of existing buildings, though he and his colleagues also used schematic plans to design new ones.[17] Compared to the *Plan of St Gall*, which includes many inscriptions detailing the contents and functions of the various rooms, Villard's plans concentrate solely on the architecture: his drawing of Meaux Cathedral, for example, uses crosses to represent the vaulting of the bays, together with the outer walls, buttress and diaphragm arches, and pillars. It would have been very clear to the architect and his colleagues and patrons that this plan showed a church and its elevation,[18] and an educated medieval viewer would have had no difficulty in deciphering and reconstructing the three-dimensional spaces represented by this abstract drawing.

Late medieval plans of important church towers were the culmination of these orthogonal parallel projections. One example is the design for the north tower of the Stephanskirche in Vienna,[19] where more than sixteen sections through the steeple are arranged so that a knowledgeable observer could mentally superimpose the plans to visualise the tower's elevation and three-dimensional form. Because they entailed a degree of abstraction, the plans assumed a reasonable familiarity with the building or part of a building they depicted, and an ability to knit together countless lines into a solid shape.

Apart from plans, Villard de Honnecourt's sketchbook includes interior and exterior elevations and sections. He did three drawings of Reims Cathedral: the interior and exterior elevations of a

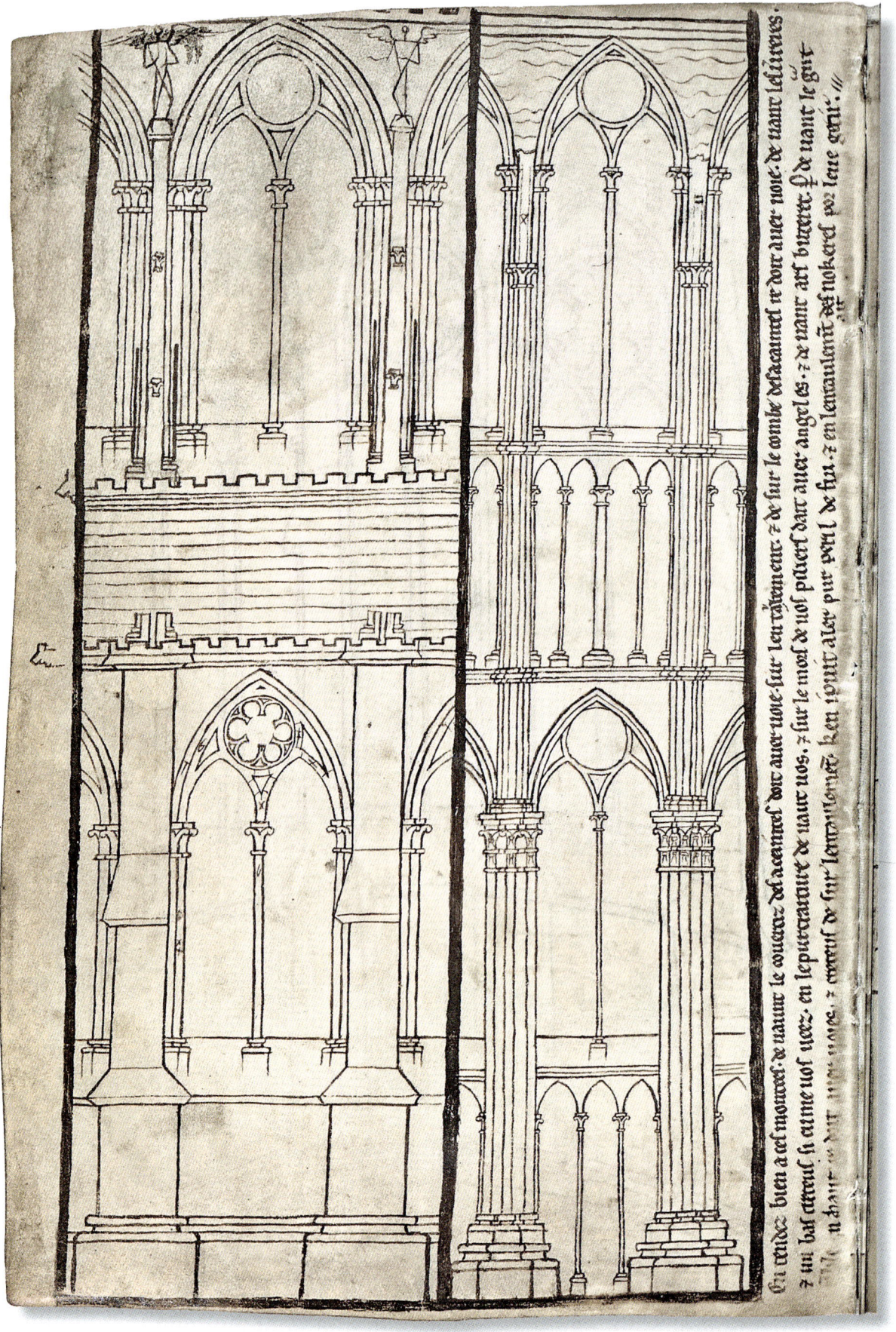

Villard de Honnecourt: Interior and exterior elevations of a bay in the nave of Reims Cathedral, c. 1230
Source: Bibliothèque nationale de France, MS Français 19093, fol. 31v

Villard de Honnecourt: Plan of Meaux Cathedral (bottom),
Imaginary plan (top), c. 1230
Source: Bibliothèque nationale de France, MS Français 19093, fol. 15

Villard de Honnecourt: Section through the buttress of the choir,
Reims Cathedral, c. 1230
Source: Bibliothèque nationale de France, MS Français 19093, fol. 32 v

bay in the nave, and a section through the buttress of the choir.[20] None of these attempts to explain the spatial relationships between components, and the elevations do not show that some of these components, such as pillars, are arranged at specific distances from others, such as the wall of the side aisle. Rather, Villard is interested in the measurable relationships between them. His purpose is not to create a perspective view of the space occupied by the cathedral,[21] and he avoids any attempt at reproducing depth, for example by using undulating lines to show a section through the curved cells extending into the space. This denies any sense of space, and says nothing about the position of the section, as it is not clear from where Villard drew the side or interior elevations. In this way, his views have the same objectivity as that of the plan.

In contrast, the *perspective* drawings of the choir chapel at Reims Cathedral and the spire of Laon Cathedral are subjective depictions of architecture, with no measurable and objective depth. Those in Villard de Honnecourt's sketchbook are unusual among medieval architectural drawings, which were almost always orthogonal. In his treatise opposing the use of perspective drawing in architecture, Leon Battista Alberti supports this practice: 'While the painter uses fine shadows, lines and angles to create relief on the flat surface of the picture, the architect is not interested in shadow, but uses the plan to show the verticals. He wishes his work to be judged not on the appearance of perspective, but on the true divisio (the wall), based on the ratio (in other words, measurable relationships).'[22]

The *untrue* nature of perspective architectural drawing was a constant subject of theoretical debate. Even today, we see a continual succession of new techniques and technologies – central perspective, photography, cinema, CAD, Photoshop, 3D animation – which expands the space that can be experienced by the senses. For the purposes of presenting architectural designs, however, the elevation and section in parallel orthogonal projection and the plan, defined as a 'view from above of the lower part of a building cut through horizontally,'[23] are defined in the German standard DIN 1356-1. The standard does not cover perspective, axonometric, isometric or other forms of representation,[24] although graphic representation uses them. It ultimately employs the same types of projection as those which were commonly used in the Middle Ages, in some ways justifying the provocatively ambitious title of this article – though it would not be true to say that this continuity has remained unbroken to the present day.

13

Cologne Cathedral: Elevation of the completed western facade. Etching from: Hermann Crombach, Primitiarum gentium seu historia ss trium regum magorum, tomi III. Cologne, 1654, p. 800
Source: Kölnisches Stadtmuseum – Rheinisches Bildarchiv

Strasbourg Cathedral, western facade, facade plan 5, between 1341 and 1371
Source: Musée de l'Œuvre Notre Dame, Strasbourg

The history of architectural drawing would indeed be brief if artists and architects had not continually sought out types of projection that went beyond the objective and schematic. Even in the Middle Ages, they knew that construction drawings need not be simple depictions of planned or existing buildings. Bruno Klein, for example, has argued convincingly that the famous Strasbourg Cathedral *Facade Plan 5* is not a real architectural design.[25] This impressive parchment drawing, probably dating from between 1341 and 1371, and measuring 4.1 m high by 82 cm wide, was produced when the clock tower on the western facade was being built. It was intended to convince the cathedral's masons' lodge of the need for the tower, and of the beauty of the structure.

The rise of architectural drawing in the thirteenth century probably resulted partly from the fact that building projects involved a growing number of decision-makers. It was therefore important that the plans be easily understood by laypeople, so that they could see what the architect wanted to build. In *Facade Plan 5*, for example, the complex filigree architecture of the belltower could not have been constructed in real life – but practical feasibility was not the greatest of the architect's concerns: he wanted the plan to impress his patrons, and was not averse to a little artistic licence. The unusually ornate plan and its beautifully coloured figures served to distract laypeople from the issue of whether the tower was actually possible, and impress them with its beauty. Probably for the first time in the history of architectural drawing, *Facade Plan 5* was a work of fiction. Its purpose was to seduce, and it was a forerunner of the many drawings produced largely for persuasive purposes during the seventeenth and eighteenth centuries. Even in the fourteenth century, before any theories were set down in writing, architectural drawings included fictitious elements. The Gothic

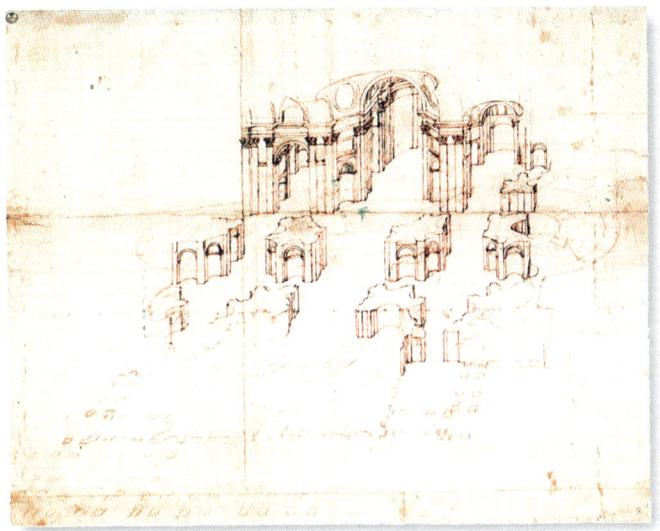

Baldassarre Peruzzi, Rome, St. Peter's, Florence, Uffizi 2 A r
Source: Soprintendenza Speciale per il Polo Museale Fiorentino, Gabinetto Fotografico

Andrea Palladio, Corinthian Hall, 1570
Source: Andrea Palladio, I quattro libri dell'architettura, Venedig 1570

and Italian Renaissance periods produced the earliest professional architectural drawings of structures intended to be built, containing all the key elements of their modern counterparts, including orthogonal projection, scale, and concordance between plan and elevation.[26]

The rediscovery of Vitruvius' *Ten Books on Architecture* resulted in many innovations. As in many other cases, his definition of the different forms of *dispositio* played a fundamental rolepart in subsequent discussion of architectural drawing: 'The forms of *dispositio*, which the Greeks call ideas, are *ichnographia*, *orthographia*, and *scaenographia*. *Ichnographia* is a reduced-scale plan, made with a ruler and compass, used to show the outlines of the different parts of the building on the ground. *Orthographia* is an upright frontal view, again a small-scale version of the future building's dimensions. And *scaenographia* is the perspectivist, illusionistic depiction of the facade, the receding sides, and the lines converging on a point.'[27]

But Vitruvius' original text is not always easy to understand, and the concept of *scaenographia* was the subject of lengthy dispute, with many translations and interpretations being proffered.[28] Other new forms of representation were also debated by the masonic lodge of St Peter's, as we can see from the letter on the protection of ancient monuments, probably sent by Raphael to Pope Leo X.[29] These included Leonardo da Vinci's bird's-eye views of central-plan buildings, Raphael's visually distorted depiction of the interior of the Pantheon, and the idea, probably advanced by Bramante, of projecting the dome of St Peter's such that the interior and exterior structures are visible simultaneously. Just as Leonardo sectioned the human body for analytical purposes in his anatomical drawings, so the planned dome was sliced up like a living organism to show the correspondence between its inner and outer elevations.

Architects even experimented with new forms of plans: that of the new St Peter's by a member of Bramante's circle (UA 20 recto) combines those of the Basilica of Constantine with Pope Nicholas V's and Bramante's plans, and the various possible crossing and nave layouts. Interior perspectives of the side chapels are also sketched at the top of the page.[30] The overlap between the various sections, dating from different times, is discernible using a grid. To the modern eye, the result resembles the plan of an archaeological excavation, combining past and future by documenting the existing and the anticipated.

Baldassare Peruzzi's drawing in central perspective of his design for St Peter's (U2A) resembles an axonometric view. It dramatically combines the plan with the physicality of the pillars, which are shown as though under construction, and the elevation and perspective view of the crossing and the main apse of the central-plan building.[31] The drawing is a record not of an actual stage in the building of St Peter's, but rather of the ongoing process of constructing the crossing. The vaulting and dome have yet to be added, and the porch is shown only in plan.

Even if this interpretation is incorrect, these three drawings go one step beyond the orthogonal projections of medieval times. They incorporate narrative elements into an otherwise purely architectural record by overlapping different layers separated by space or time, either orthogonally architecture described by Vitruvius [32] or in perspective. Some authorities reacted against this painterly approach, which Alberti had already described as un-architectural. In his *Quattro libri dell'architettura*, for example, Andrea Palladio uses only orthogonal projection in his designs and precisely measured depictions of ancient Roman architecture. One example is his reconstruction of a *sala di quattro colonne* (Vol. II, p. 37), described by Vitruvius, where quite different planes are brought together on the page and it is

15

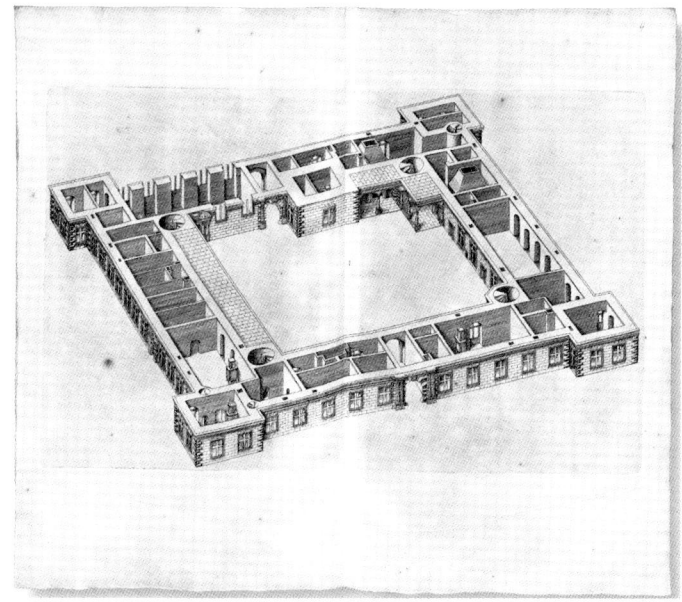
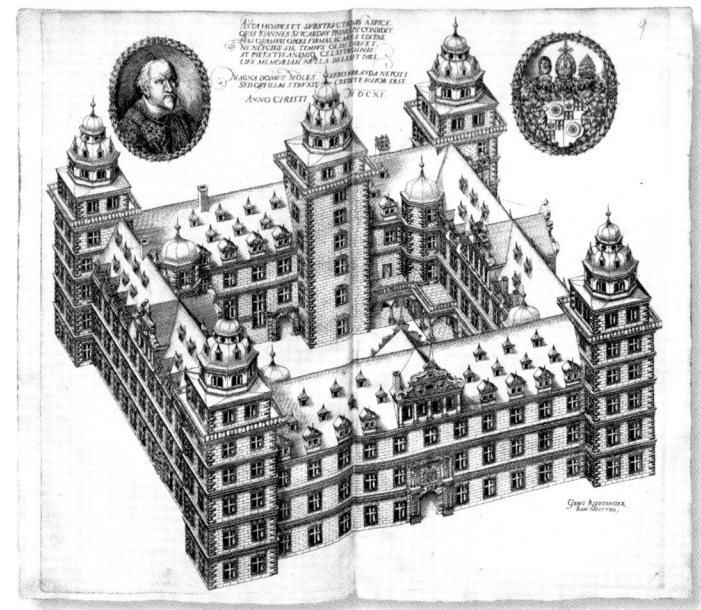

Georg Ridinger: Aschaffenburg Castle, 1616
Source: Bayerische Staatsbibliothek München, Res. 2/A. civ 157m

hard to orient oneself at first. The top third is a section through the niched vertical walls and coffered ceiling. We also see the Corinthian columns with their bases, swelling shafts and capitals, and the entablature divided into three fascia.

The surface hatched from left to right represents the inner wall: only the hatching betrays the fact that this is a different space to that of the columns. The elevation (*orthographia*) at the top of the page and the vertical section (*profilo*) of the space are followed at the bottom of the page by the plan as a horizontal section through the plane of the niche. The ceiling panels and their surrounds, together with the rosettes, are incorporated into the plan. By cross-hatching it from left to right, Palladio makes it clear that this is a different spatial plane to that cross-hatched in the opposite direction in the elevation. Like Villard's drawings, those of Palladio deny the sensory experience of space as a category of architecture. There is no suggestion that we could enter, use or in any way subjectively interact with this interior, and the drawing banishes any sense of illusion, focusing solely on the architectural idea and the timelessness of the ancient architecture described by Vitruvius.[32]

Orthogonal parallel projection, rooted in the medieval tradition and perfected by Palladio, is a constant theme in architectural drawing. The schematic grid-based illustrations in Jean-Nicolas-Louis Durand's *Précis des leçons d'architecture* (1801–1803) influenced architects in the nineteenth century: Durand believed that it was not only wrong for architectural drawing to strive for painterly effect, but also dangerous, because it promised more than it could deliver. Nothing beyond plan, section and elevation was required to develop architectural ideas.[33] At the opposite end of the spectrum were those drawings, from the Middle Ages onwards, that went beyond the idea itself and included non-architectural elements to impress a lay public.

Between these two opposites, of course, everything was possible, such as the shadowless perspectives of Karl Friedrich Schinkel, combining the objective qualities of orthogonal projection with perspectivist, illusionistic representation.[34] But axonometry, a hybrid of orthogonal and perspectivist projection, was of greater importance: since it has none of the foreshortening effect of central perspective, it combines the measurable dimensions of orthogonal projection with the didactic, communicative function of perspective.

Axonometric perspective had its forerunners in mechanical and technical drawing, drawings of military fortifications (which introduced the idea of cavalier perspective), cartography[35] and the writings of various French theorists.[36] But theory apart, I believe one of the first truly axonometric representations of an architectural subject to be contained in Georg Ridinger's 1616 publication on Aschaffenburg Castle, which he built. He includes axonometric projections of the castle itself, and full plans of the four storeys, all of which are presented both plane-parallel and axonometrically.[37] To the best of my knowledge, it was another hundred years until this process, which heralds the axonometric and isometric perspectives of the early modern period, acquired any theoretical underpinning. In 1699, for example, Leonhardt Christoph Sturm criticised orthogonal projection and, citing Ridinger, emphasised the greater descriptiveness of axonometric perspective.[38]

In his *Anleitung zur Bürgerlichen Baukunst* (1744), Johann Friedrich Penther showed an axonometric projection of a house in every conceivable elevation, section, plan and perspective.[39] Penther, like Ridinger and Sturm, was not familiar with the theory and practice of axonometric and isometric depiction, which were developed during the nineteenth century.[40] Instead, he referred to this mode of presentation as *horizontaler Durchschnitt*,

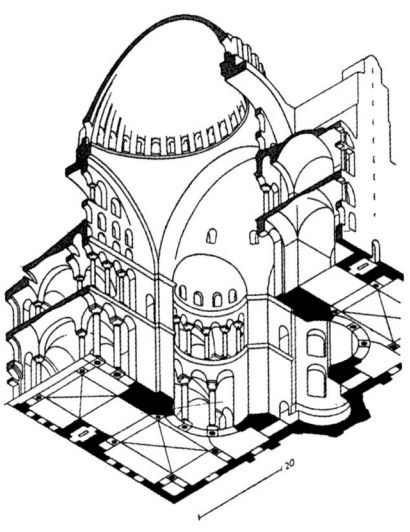

Auguste Choisy: Istanbul, Agia Sophia, axonometric view, 1899
Source: Auguste Choisy, Histoire de l'architecture, Vol. II, Paris 1899

horizontal section, and wrote: 'This shows all parts of the building sectioned horizontally to a certain height, but also some of each part from a perpendicular side, so that one can quickly see from where each section is taken.'

Penther believed that this form of representation had two advantages: 'This view is useful in giving a beginner an idea of what a draft means, and also in giving a patron a conception of what his future house will look like, the locations of and connections between rooms and so on, while a mason can use it to understand the positions of chimneys, secret passages etc.'[41] This means that an axonometric projection has greater didactic value than an orthogonal plan, and offers the practical benefit of helping construction workers to imagine the finished building. Much later, the clarity of axonometric projection compared to plan, elevation and section was affirmed by Walter Gropius in his teachings at the Bauhaus in 1923.[42]

During the last quarter of the nineteenth century, axonometric and isometric projection were increasingly used as a means of expressing technical and architectural relationships.[43] The architectural historian and engineer Auguste Choisy, who used them to the exclusion of all others in his books, exerted a major influence on modern architecture. He justified the didactic value of axonometric projections of historical buildings on the grounds that they combine clarity of perspective with measurable dimensions, so that foreshortening does not cause distortion. Also, Choisy pointed out, axonometry shows a building's plan, section and interior and exterior elevations at a glance. Most importantly, however, it creates 'a single image, as animated and full of movement as the building itself, replacing the abstract figuration of plan, section and elevation.'[44] Without wishing to over-interpret Choisy, I see this as the point where the aspect of virtual representation finds its way into the two-dimensional depiction of architecture. Significantly, Le Corbusier chose to illustrate the *Plans* chapter of his book *Vers une architecture* with axonometric drawings by Choisy. The caption reads: 'The plan affects the whole structure of the building, revealing every aspect of its geometric laws and changing relationships.'[45] It would be going too far to draw connections between, on the one hand, Choisy's axonometric projections and Le Corbusier's dictum that everything begins with the plan, and, on the other Le Corbusier's *Promenade Architecturale*, but my brief history of architectural drawing does describe what could be seen as a continuous transition towards modern virtual methods of depiction.[46] Even before the first theories on the subject were articulated, plan, elevation and section constituted the foundations of architectural drawing. The invention of fictitious design dates back to the Middle Ages, and pre-perspective representation is used to clarify space. Vitruvius' teachings on architectural drawing and the introduction of *scaenographia* created problems of definition and depiction that took pure architectural drawing into the realms of painting, a subjective and non-measurable medium. Ridinger's parallel-perspective axonometric representations provided a balance between the two extremes of the geometric and schematic on the one hand, and the perspectivist and painterly on the other. Auguste Choisy and others carried this process of reconciliation forwards into the modern area of virtual depiction.

»There is a rumour that I can't draw and never could. This is probably because I work so much with models. Models are one of the most beautiful design tools, but I still do the finest drawings you can imagine.«

Jørn Utzon

Drawing: Augusto Romano Burelli, 2009
Technique: Red pencil, red ink and sepia wash on card

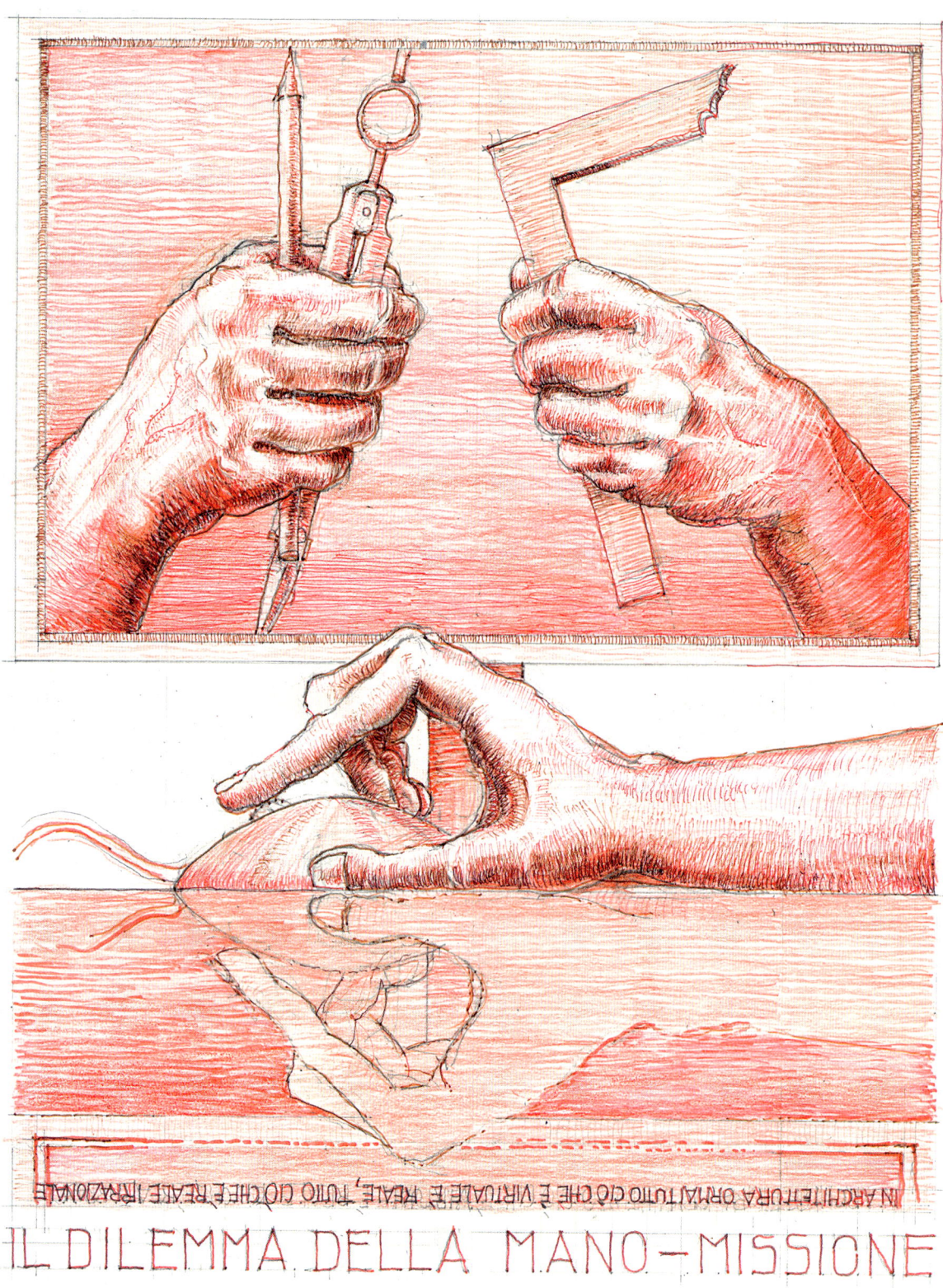

The dilemma of the *mano-missione*
Today architects are hamstrung by the dichotomy between the traditional role of the hand in the arts, and the disappearance of hand drawing in architecture. They believe that all virtual architecture is real, while the real appears ever more irrational.

Drawing: Augusto Romano Burelli, 2009
Technique: Red pencil, red ink and sepia wash on card

Architecture for Keyboard Instruments Only
Augusto Romano Burelli

The rise of computer-aided design in architecture has been unpredictable and dramatic. It has marched imperiously into the world of design and changed its roles: where once the computer merely contributed to the drawing, now it plays an active part in the creative process. It has freed architects from the slavery of hand drawing, but has imposed less obvious yet equally direct restrictions on our liberty. Computers allow architects to achieve absolute precision, requiring them to add endless detail and leaving no room for uncertainty or vagueness. The thought itself and the detail must be taken into account at the same time, and the once drawn-out process by which ideas gradually took shape has been brutally curtailed.

Another problem is that there is no longer any demand for quick, simple ideas; instead, the building must be *right* from the outset. Electronic drawings can be transformed with amazing speed into plans, sections and perspective views, but this speed and level of detail have spawned a dependence on computers which is spiritually comparable to the medieval belief in witches. Some advocates of electronic design claim that critics of the computer are simply ducking one of the major challenges of our time. This medium has been so profoundly and overwhelmingly successful that it has destroyed individual style and authenticity, and yet architects seem to pervasively view this violence as an act of liberation.

The endless manipulation of form is a logical consequence of what Heidegger called the question of technology.[1] 'Technology is no longer simply a resource, an instrument which modern man uses to achieve his objectives. Because technology has already changed us inwardly, the objectives we can set ourselves are themselves technologically determined.'[2] Architects have been seduced by the absolute precision of electronics, which offers an attractive paradox: only some of you will be capable of making use of all the subtleties I offer, and yet all of you can be a part of this elite.

At a seminar in Berlin fifteen years ago, I said that in the old days, incompetent architects with useless ideas were given away by their bad drawings. Today, their ideas are just as useless, but now they can present them in a dramatic, or at least attractive way, and they enjoy this so much that they keep churning out bad ideas. Many mediocre architects reach the age of fifty and rediscover themselves almost overnight as artists. They think they are part of an elite, but they are simply a big group of incompetent architects whose careers have been saved by computer graphics. This is similar to the situation described by the philosopher Hans-Georg Gadamer, who said that the internet had created a huge *intelligentsia* with very little in the way of intellect.

At the same time, all those wonderful German drawing-machine factories closed down. Principal among these was Kuhlmann, whose products offered the precision required for hand-drawn circles and parallelograms. And electronic reproduction technology has radically changed the whole process from initial draft through to final details, making architects subservient to their keyboards, creating a perverse synecdoche by slyly suggesting that if they feed in the basic outlines, the computer will do the whole design for them. This quick, simple process dilutes the initial idea, swamps it with technical minutiae, and encourages the repetition of detail even in the first draft – perhaps even recycled from earlier projects. Thus, truly the devil is in the details.[3]

I remember the very intricate and realistic eagles, originally the work of Karl Friedrich Schinkel in 1825, which the architect Hans Kollhoff reproduced on the fascia of the Altes Museum in his competition design for Berlin's Museum Island in Berlin. I was hugely impressed by the eagles themselves, and by the intricacy of the capitals and cast-iron balustrades, but then I thought sadly of all the time and effort expended by the original artist, whose only resources were pen and paper. I began to realise that computers had infected architecture, and the only cure for this epidemic was to build things.

The fact that details can be designed separately on the computer monitor, regardless of the floor plan or the whole facade, made me think that electronic drawing technology was a serious assault on the basic principle of humanistic architecture. This principle, adopted in Greek art and bequeathed to us by Vitruvius, asserts that the part is inseparable from the whole, born of the same genetic inheritance.

In the old days, would-be architecture students simply had to pass a drawing test – but this was still too difficult for Albert Speer and his friend Rudolf Wolters when they sought admission to the Berlin school of Poelzig, Gropius, and Mies van der Rohe. What kind of test would today's students have to take? How can we remind ourselves that hand drawing is by far the best and quickest way of turning ideas into reality, and of

Hypnos, or the sleep of memory

Hegel suspected that the word *erinnern* (to remember) implies *to internalise* because it contains the root inner. Art serves memory.

Photography brought a radical transformation by freeing us from the obligation to reproduce images from memory. Today, in the age of computer technology, we manage these images in digital archives, but the technology is changing so fast that current data formats will be illegible to future generations. So everything we do not keep in our minds, we throw away.

Heidegger said, as he watched tourists photographing the ruins of Delphi: 'They are throwing away their memories in images manufactured by technology.' (Martin Heidegger, *Aufenthalte*, Frankfurt, 1989)

Drawing: Augusto Romano Burelli, 2003
Technique: Red pencil, red ink and sepia wash on card

Descartes' belief that the hand was the one part of the body in direct contact with the brain? The new Cassandras of contemporary architecture tell us there is nothing to be gained from idealism, and we should simply accept these changes. They also inform us that ugliness has a great aesthetic future, though Theodor Adorno said that there is no continuum from ugliness through mediocrity to beauty; the things in the middle are always ugly.[4] The Cassandras invite students to focus on the middle ground – in other words, on the ugly. They have no difficulty with such teachings: if beauty is banned in architecture as a relic of the past, we can all achieve distinction with ugliness.

So, is computer drawing destroying the previously immutable principle of learning by imitation, or simply shaking it to its foundations? All artistic education is built on this principle: just as we learn a language by repeating the words we hear from other people, so we learn about architecture which, as a collective art form, is itself a language.[5] Even with the computer, we learn by imitation, and using it simply to copy the work of others is the ultimate imitation.

Until Le Corbusier came on the scene, architects honed their imaginations by drawing ancient buildings, using quick sketches in their travel journals as reminders of what they had seen. They continued to use this learning technique even after the advent of photography, so when Heidegger watched tourists taking pictures of the ruins of Delphi, he remarked: 'They are throwing away their memories in images manufactured by technology.'[6] Egocentric architects complain that because they all use the same software to turn their sketches into computer drawings, this creates a sense of sameness. They want to achieve a style of drawing that has never existed and is unattainable, because the keyboard does everything for them, and the software provides little scope for creativity. Some architects working to American standards of productivity and cost control subcontract their renderings to specialist companies. As a result, talented architects can no longer be distinguished from mediocre ones by the excellence or extravagance of their designs. Leafing through an international architecture journal, you could be excused for thinking that all the drawings are by the same graphic artist working for the same editor, so similar are they.

At this point, we need to answer three strategic questions:

> What can we not manage without?
> What can we learn from all this?
> What do we have little control over?

What can we not manage without?

Electronic drawing has been successful because it is a fast and accurate way of working on and replicating a project. From this standpoint, its usefulness cannot be disputed.

Because of the huge amount of information contained in building plans, the computer is the only way of carrying the design to the site, and as such it has become irreplaceable. It is thanks to the computer that different firms of architects in different European countries can work together on a project like the complex on the corner of Unter den Linden and Friedrichstrasse in Berlin, which consists of five adjoining buildings.[7]

It is hard to say whether an architect drawing on a computer is following a consistent analytical logic at any given moment. They spend a lot of time copying and pasting, which reduces planning times, so there is no gradual run-up to the construction phase, especially since the computer allows overwhelming precision, ease of repetition, and fast, easy changes and corrections to the design. All this was a real chore for anyone drawing by hand, and this revolutionary transformation appeals to something deep in the architect's soul: a combination that includes greed and laziness.

Spolia et memoria! The restitution of the opisthodomos at the Heraion of Olympia

In the second century AD, Pausanius entered the prytaneum of the opisthodomos and discovered an oak pillar which had survived from the original temple. Over a period of eight centuries, the wooden columns had been gradually replaced by stone ones, financed by donations from the faithful.

The most recent of the sixteen capitals unearthed by the German Archaeological Institute are archaic in style, and were rebuilt at some time around the first century AD. This is a good example of how reconstruction is a job not for architects, but for a community that wants to remember itself.

Drawing: Augusto Romano Burelli, 2006
Technique: red pencil, red ink and sepia wash on card

Given the importance of copying and learning by imitation in architecture, what can we learn by studying current building projects on the computer? In the past, the slow, laborious process of hand drawing, with its complex axonometric perspectives and redrawings whenever a change was made, meant that drawings were the only authentic documents we could use to reconstruct the development of a project. With electronic designs, we immediately get the *right* building, albeit a virtual one, even though we are many steps removed from the site and the construction process. This *right* building is not the original, but a copy of all the rapid, high-speed changes, corrections, manipulations and deletions made by the computer. It is a triumph of alteration, with no original to serve as a point of reference. We could almost say that each new altered version of the electronic design is another print of a photograph with no original negative, or one whose initial version has been lost.

What can we learn from this?

Apart from the important principle of copying and pasting, there is another which I have already mentioned: that of synecdoche, the need to isolate a detail of the work as though it were separable from the project as a whole. It is synecdoche that forces us to fill the entire screen with a single detail and focus our full attention on it. Isolated in this way, the detail can be configured before being copied and incorporated into the facade of which it forms only a small part. It could be said that this process has always existed in architecture – and this would be true if this detail, for example a capital, were not already part of an architectural whole. The individual parts of this arrangement were connected to one another by fixed proportions. Within certain limits, this arrangement could become larger or smaller without changing the ratios between individual parts. We should use this system of fixed dimensions when drawing with the computer keyboard, but instead, we design building details with no precise scale. Precision is no longer determined by the scale we choose. We can achieve the same level of detail at any scale, except that the design looks darker at larger scales and sharper at smaller scales. I have never seen an architect computer-designing all or part of a building with a human figure on one side of the picture, helpful though this would be, because it would immediately show us the sizes of the individual details. The computer has given us a world without scale, in which we design buildings with no thought for their relationships with the site or with the human beings who will live or work in them. This lack of a specific frame of reference makes the architectural work tangible. It highlights the paradox identified by Peter Eisenman in the late 1970s in his planning design for the site of the former Saffa factories in Venice, when he drew the same pavilion on the same area of the same drawing, but at scales of 1:50, 1:100, 1:200 and 1:500.

What do we have little control over?

Computers allow us to reproduce the same plans, sections, components and details at a rapid rate. Some architects rebel against this lack of freedom and choose another route, one which is itself made possible by computers: that of distorting, twisting, stretching and compressing Euclidean spaces. They believe that this escape mechanism will save them from the eternal recurrence of the identical, because all parts of the design are constantly changing and the details become increasingly numerous.
To put it more directly, this phenomenon, known as deconstructivism, is simply the freedom to design a space or a solid so complex that only a computer can recognise, remember and reproduce it.[8] Complexity is one way in which architects can respond to the new technology. Adorno said that each successful

The Olympieion of Akragas and the sin of hubris

Extinguish your hubris before you extinguish the fire in your house. Diogenes Laertios (9, 2), after Heraclitus

Zeus is the law, the need for the existence of a boundary, a benchmark, something which cannot be surpassed. But where does this unsurpassability begin? For the Agrigentians, it was directly manifested in their attempt to build the biggest temple in the Hellenistic world and dedicate it to the Olympian Zeus, to avoid the sin of hubris, the presumption that offended the gods. They tried to maintain a sense of proportion, based on the golden section and interwoven with a harmonic series which preceded the Fibonacci sequence by sixteen centuries.

The Greeks had reached the boundary, but they did not know exactly where it was. They added something of their own to the sin of hubris: arrogance and excess. Setting a boundary and then trying to overcome it are one and the same thing: both follow the same impulse. And so the architects of the Temple of Zeus at Akragas took a risk by subjecting their materials to huge forces. Although Zeus was deeply moved by the sheer size of his future residence, he allowed the temple to collapse around its builders' ears.

All of the temple's dimensions are based on the Agrigentian foot, equivalent to 31.5 cm. The building blocks of the peristasis were 2 ft, or 63 cm; the stylobate was 116.5 m by 53.5 m, and the sima 34.65 m high. The word *hubris* engraved on the tablets is written in the Agrigentian version of the Greek alphabet.

Drawing: Augusto Romano Burelli, 2005-2006
Technique: Red pencil, red ink and sepia wash on card.

work of architecture must also be a successful building. But this assertion is called into question by architecture's detachment from the building process, the antidote which makes it less error-prone than other less structured visual art forms.
The deconstructivists' renderings are created long before the building is constructed, and seemingly in defiance of the laws of gravity: these are someone else's problem, to be dealt with at a later date. Alternatively, the architect decides that these laws do apply to the first element of the building, but then hides it behind cladding. Cladding is not a facade, or at least only to the extent that it separates the interior from the exterior, and the unity of structure and facade, of what is load bearing and what supported, is broken. This is not a new phenomenon, but it has undoubtedly become more widespread as a result of computer graphics, and has increasingly served to separate architects from their place of work, the building site.

The result is a radical movement which has nullified the role of building, the specific purpose of architecture, and replaced it with an architecture of arrogance and excess, one which cannot be turned into constructed reality. This is no longer the architect's role. Just as Christian heresy leads to hell, so architects' lack of interest in building creates an aesthetic hell. Architects have always been tempted to indulge in the sin of hubris. The desire to impose boundaries on this art form, and the desire to overcome these boundaries, are two sides of the same coin.[9] The total freedom promised by CAD systems is the ability to manipulate complex geometric figures, a very time-consuming process when done by hand. For this reason, today's so-called avantgarde architects content themselves with virtual drawings of dimensionless, statically indeterminate and impossibly complex structures which can only be built using lightweight, flexible materials offering little resistance to the vagaries of nature.

Today's hubristic architecture liberates the building from the cladding which envelops it and places the two in conflict. The building follows its own rules, and may end up as a mass-produced prefabricated structure, so the architect and developers are interested only in the cladding at this stage. The architect is guided by the surface layer, the appearance of which distinguishes their work from that of other architects and creates a relationship between them and a technology which has long since lost any connection with durable construction. This architecture has little future prospect owing to the fact that its tectonics are weak.

So great are the conceptual, methodological and practical contradictions in such projects that they could actually be carried out by different architects and different construction companies. Clients welcome this split in architects' minds, because this makes it easier to award contracts: big, prefabricated boxes concealed behind cladding, which has imposed itself as an artistic style. As the public part of the building, it can now be freely used to convey an advertising message. This style is a prostitution of art that says to all and sundry: 'I don't mean anything, or represent anything. My sole message is come and buy. If this message comes across sufficiently aggressively, I have achieved my aim.'

When Johann Sebastian Bach copied a Magnificat by Antonio Caldara, he saved it: as it transpired, the original disappeared. Bach may have adapted it, and probably even made some improvements.

Collecting Architectural Drawings
Hans-Dieter Nägelke

There are many reasons to collect architectural drawings, perhaps the oldest being to preserve the original idea of a building in the form of a plan: the building itself may change over time, possibly decaying and/or being redesigned, but the plan never does. It tells us how the building was conceived, designed and built, and this is the main reason (rather than nostalgia, for instance) why the oldest surviving architectural drawings are plans of monasteries and cathedrals.From the Renaissance onwards, royal courts had their own record offices for this purpose. Whenever a building was extended, rebuilt or repaired, it was useful to base the work on the original plans. The more complex the building, and the more sophisticated its construction and technology, the more essential the plans. Churches and planning authorities still have their own record offices as so do large companies' construction departments, though here there is always a risk that historically important drawings which have lost their practical value are neglected or thrown away. Public archives have an important role to play as a repository for plans from all these sources, and also from individual bequests of architectural material – and, indeed, this is where the majority of such drawings are to be found.

Architectural drawings are not collected solely for the practical or historical information they contain. They may be records of buildings and construction ideas, but they often have great artistic value, particularly if drawn by the architects themselves. Although they did not become highly marketable commodities until the 1970s, they have been privately collected since the Renaissance. Giorgio Vasari's (1511–1574) *dei Disegni* became the basis for the Uffizi's architecture collection, while the private collections of Inigo Jones (1573–1652) and Sir John Soane (1753–1837) were acquired in turn by the Royal Institute of British Architects. The private collection of the renowned Parisian architect Hippolyte Destailleur (1822–1893) was acquired in 1879 by the Berlin Art Library, and in 1979 another private collection became the nucleus of the Canadian Centre for Architecture.

Not surprisingly, architectural drawings have always been collected mainly by architects, who appreciate this genre's special artistic qualities and its importance for their own work. Sketches and design series often record not only the solution that was finally reached, but also all the wrangling that preceded it.

This is another reason to collect drawings (and, for that matter, other items bearing witness to the design and construction process and the completed building): apart from their practical, cultural, historical and technical interest, they have considerable educational value. The most important public collectors of architectural drawings are archives, museums, libraries and universities. When architectural training was formalised and professionalised from the mid-eighteenth century onwards, the drawings were collected as teaching aids, along with plaster casts of building components and ornaments, models, books, prints, engravings (and later photographs), and hand drawings from architects' bequests or other sources. Alongside its sister universities in Karlsruhe and Munich, the Technical University of Berlin houses one of Germany's most important architectural collections. When the architect and design professor Julius Raschdorff (1823–1914) opened the university's architectural museum in Charlottenburg, he drew on the older collections of the Bauakademie in Berlin. These included prominent bequests such as that of David and Friedrich Gilly, a model collection, designs from the Prussian construction administration, and countless studies produced at the academy itself. The collection also incorporated that of the Schinkel Museum, run personally by Raschdorff, and established in 1844 in the former apartment, located in the academy, of the architect, city planner and painter Karl Friedrich Schinkel. This was Germany's first public architectural museum.

Raschdorff ran the museum as a collection of examples intended to serve as sources of inspiration for architecture students and members of the public. It contained drawings by masters from Langhans to Martin Gropius, which were displayed in frames and behind glass, while everything else was made available in folders and drawers in the exhibition spaces. Raschdorff continued to collect older architectural items, but increasingly acquired contemporary items of monumental architecture that matched his tastes, obtained in Berlin, the Reich, and beyond. The museum was a historical collection in two senses: it comprised historical items, and leading examples of historical buildings. However, its contents were increasingly sidelined by the rise of Modernism after the First World War, and a similar fate befell its sister collections in Karlsruhe and Munich: these were not closed, but were gradually transferred to the universities' architectural history faculties. As a result, small numbers of bequests and other material were added between the 1920s and 1960s. A new beginning occurred in the 1970s, which saw a growing interest in architectural drawings on the part of universities, archives, museums and, ultimately, the art market. A wave of architectural museums opened around the world, from Stockholm in 1969 to Frankfurt in 1984, and universities began collecting again, produced academic analyses of their holdings, acquired new material and opened to the public. The Berlin museum has increased its stocks more than eightfold since 1945, and now has some 160,000 objects, including 30,000 photographs. Karlsruhe has 270,000 plans and 500,000 photographs, and Munich 500,000 plans and 100,000 photographs. Germany still has its archives, along with library, museum and academy collections; a number of new institutions have opened in Hamburg, Schleswig-Holstein and elsewhere in recent years, as a result of cooperation between professional bodies and public institutions.

Close cooperation has helped institutional collectors to carve out their own specialist niches, avoid rivalry, and share information on bequests. But collecting is not much easier. In the 1970s, collectors began to realise just how many bequests had been destroyed by a combination of war and ignorance, and today's collections are often swamped by the sheer quantity of material emerging both from bequests and from architects shutting down their offices. Before the Second World War, architects' bequests rarely comprised more than a few thousand pages. Today, firms that have operated successfully for decades dispose of material by the truckload. Coping with these requires not only files, cupboards, space and time but also, more importantly, people: architects and historians of art and architecture, who are sufficiently qualified to evaluate the material and preserve the most important and interesting items. Collectors must make careful choices to ensure that their collections do not become dumping grounds.

An end is in sight to this flood of paper, created partly as a result of new copier technology in recent decades. While valuable sketches and hand-drawn designs will continue to serve as the core of the architectural museum of the future, digital media will also play an important day-to-day role. Although most bequests still consist of paper, CAD has been in use for more than thirty years, and it can only be a matter of time before people bequeath data storage media instead. Many collections in Berlin, Munich and elsewhere are carrying out high-resolution digitisation of their historical stocks – not to replace them with digital images, but to make them more easily available, protect valuable originals, and create an infrastructure for this new material. This is creating a virtual architecture collection, bringing together documents in different places to realise the long-held dream of a universal, central repository for plans, a treasure trove of the finest examples of architecture.

Further Reading: On the history of the collection and preservation of architectural drawings see, most importantly, Ursula Baus: *Zwischen Kunstwerk und Nutzwert. Die Architekturzeichnung, gesehen von Kunst- und Architekturhistorikern seit 1850*, dissertation, Stuttgart 1999. For another overview of the history of collecting, see Eva-Maria Amberger: 'Von der Kunst- und Wunderkammer zum Architekturmuseum. Architektursammlungen im Spiegel der Zeit', in: *Westfalen und Italien. Festschrift für Karl Noehles*, Petersberg 2002. There is a considerable literature on the history of individual companies' collections: for those in Berlin, see *Die Hand des Architekten. Zeichnungen Berliner Architektursammlungen*, exhibition catalogue, Berlin 2002 (*Schriftenreihe der Berliner Bauakademie Vol. 1*). For Munich, see Winfried Nerdinger (ed.): *Die Architekturzeichnung. Vom barocken Idealplan zur Axonometrie. Zeichnungen aus der Architektursammlung der Technischen Universität München*, Munich, 1987, and ibid. (ed.): *Architekturschule München 1868–1993. 125 Jahre Technische Universität München*, Munich 1993. For Karlsruhe, see: *Querschnitt. Aus den Sammlungen des Südwestdeutschen Archivs für Architektur und Ingenieurbau*. Published by the Südwestdeutsches Archiv für Architektur und Ingenieurbau, Karlsruhe 2006. For the Museum of Architecture of the Technical University see, most recently, Hans-Dieter Nägelke (ed.): *Architekturbilder. 125 Jahre Architekturmuseum der Technischen Universität Berlin*, Kiel 2011.

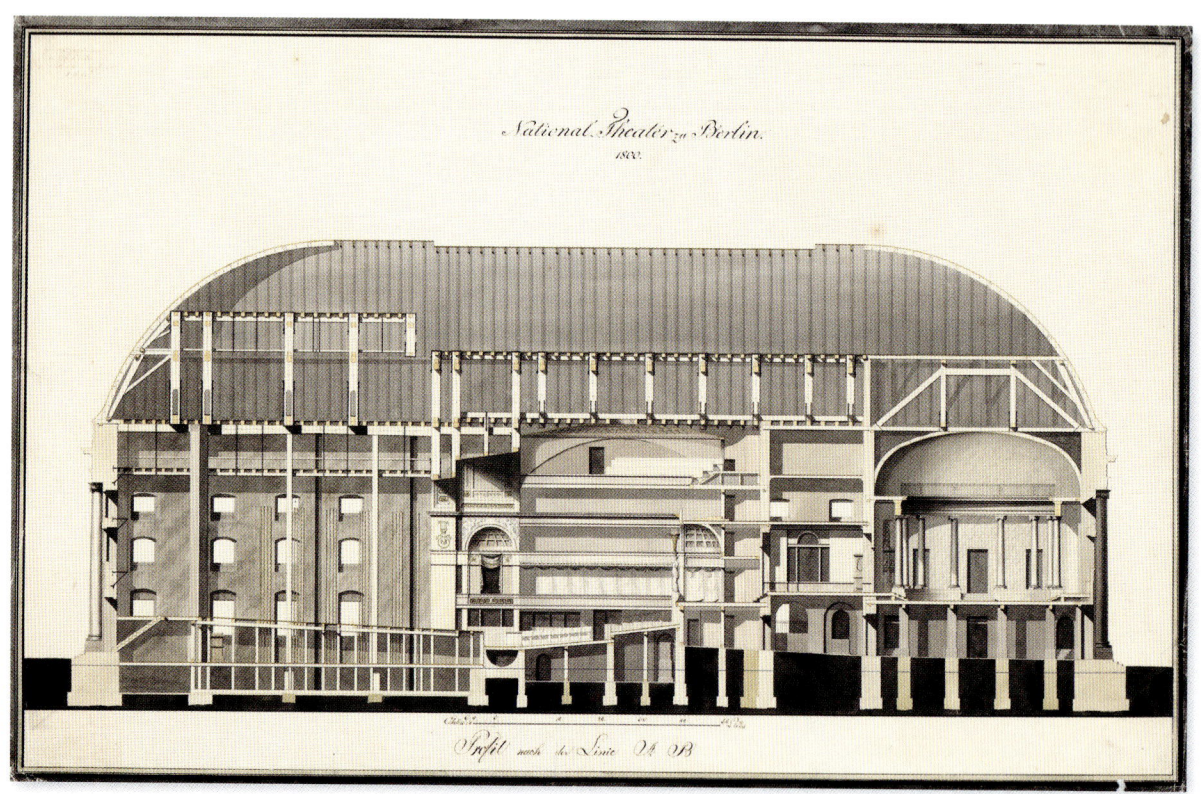

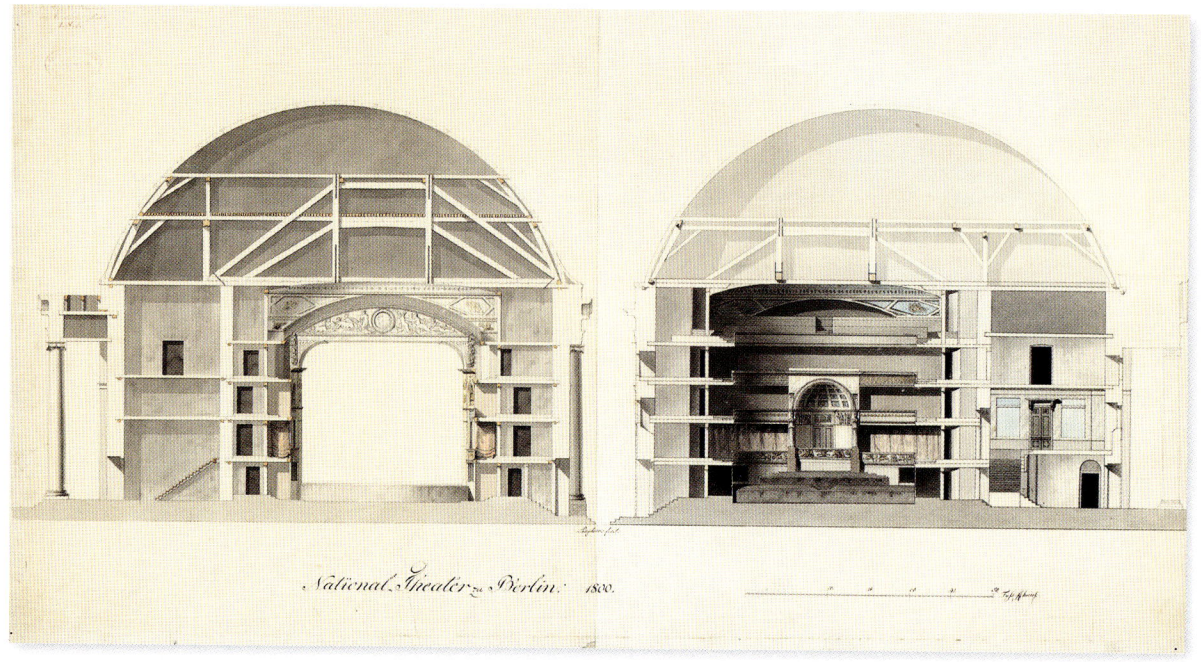

Carl Gotthard Langhans (1732–1808)
Nationaltheater, Berlin
Indian ink and watercolour on card
Longitudinal and transverse sections
61 × 95 cm / 53 × 97 cm
1800

Museum of Architecture of the Technical University of Berlin, Inv. No. 5978 und 5982

Karl Friedrich Schinkel (1781–1841)
Theatre on the Gendarmenmarkt, Berlin
Indian ink, pencil and watercolour on paper
Details of the stage area
105.5 × 69.3 cm
1818

Museum of Architecture of the Technical University of Berlin, Inv. No. 15417

Friedrich August Stüler (1800–1865)
Travel sketches: factory in Liège
Pencil on card
Perspective view
16 × 9.2 cm
1829

Museum of Architecture of the Technical University of Berlin, Inv. No. 17176

Martin Gropius (1824–1880)
Villa Bleichröder, Berlin-Charlottenburg
Pencil and watercolour on paper
View of the garden side
23.5 × 33.4 cm
1863

Museum of Architecture of the Technical University of Berlin, Inv. No. 1608,2

Otto Kohtz (1880–1956)
Design for a building at Königsplatz, Berlin
Pencil and watercolour on paper
Perspective view
54.5 × 69 cm
1920

Museum of Architecture of the Technical University of Berlin, Inv. No. 9049

Ludwig Scheurer
Competition design for the redevelopment of Unter den Linden, Berlin
Indian ink, charcoal and watercolour on card
Perspective view
63 × 67.6 cm
1925

Museum of Architecture of the Technical University of Berlin, Inv. No. 7852

Johann Emil Schaudt (1871–1957)
Planning competition for Alexanderplatz, Berlin
Charcoal on tracing paper
Two perspective views
66 × 52.5 cm
1929

Museum of Architecture of the Technical University of Berlin, Inv. No. 42533

Hans Simon (1909–1982)
Study project for Hans Poelzig: cinema
Pencil and coloured chalk on card
Perspective interior view
74.6 × 10 cm
1931

Museum of Architecture of the Technical University of Berlin, Inv. No. HS 008,006

Hermann Mattern (1902–1971)
School building for Kassel-Wahlershausen
Indian ink on tracing paper
Perspective view
65 × 9 cm
1955

Museum of Architecture of the Technical University of Berlin, Inv. No. 26021

KARL FRIEDRICH SCHINKEL MUSEUM · BERLIN 1981

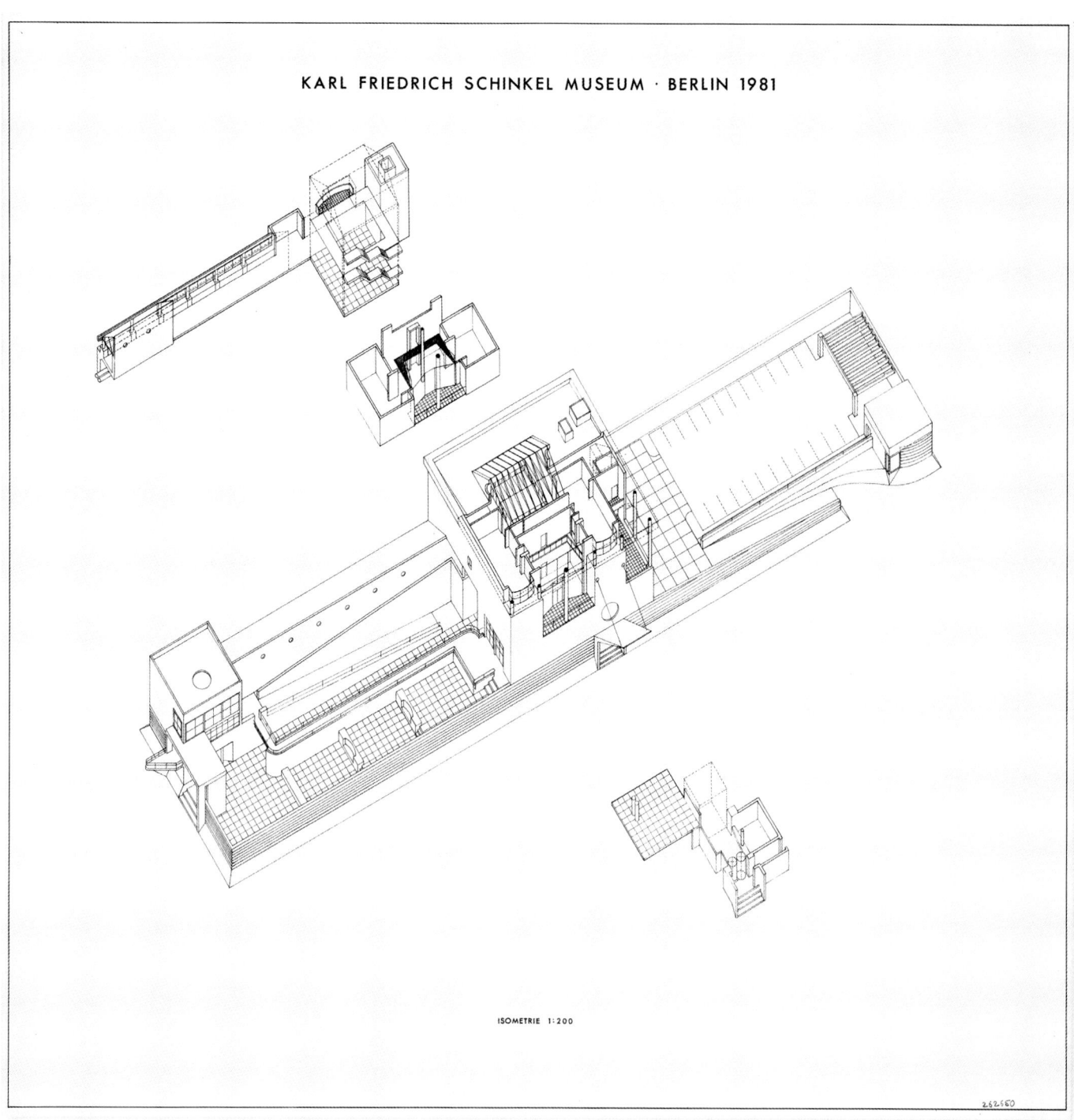

David Chipperfield und Roger Huntley
Schinkel competition: architecture archive, dedicated to Friedrich Karl Schinkel
Photocopy on paper
Isometric perspective
84 × 84 cm
1981

Museum of Architecture of the Technical University of Berlin, Inv. No. SW-A 1981,01-02

The Art of Architectural Drawing
Sergei Tchoban

What do we understand by an architectural drawing? Is the drawing an independent genre or can it rather be understood as a sketch for built architecture?

Originally, the architectural drawing in the form of the Trias ground plan, section and elevation served as a tool for representing a future building or scenery on paper. At the same time, the veduta – a landscape painting with architectural representation – developed into a special type of architectural drawing. One of the founders and best-known representatives belonging to this genre is Giovanni Antonio-Canal, referred to as Canaletto (1697–1768).

A new chapter in the history of the evolution of the drawing as an independent artistic movement began with the dispute that broke out in the late Renaissance. This revolved around whether drawing can ever be deemed equal to painting, illustrated in the famous speech by Federio-Zuccari (c. 1542–1609) to the Accademia del Disegno in Rome. Zuccari takes the view that the drawing is the expression of a divine idea (*concetto*) which God himself lent to the artist – thus, drawing is an autonomous genre. During that period, this understanding was by no means considered natural, since architectural drawings were seen solely as sketches or plans for architecture to be built later – or as preparatory drawings for etchings. Zuccari's speech and his work *L'idea de'scultori, pittori e architetti* (1607) led to a turning point in the general view. Previously regarded as a tool of, and precursor to, other *higher* art forms, drawing was now able to establish itself in its own right in addition to painting and increasingly found its way into art collections; many textbooks on the art of drawing were published.

A special situation arose in the middle of the eighteenth century in Rome, where many talented architects, artists, collectors and art connoisseurs worked during this period. The world inside papal Rome was a unique one, seeking its role models and inspiration in the ruins of ancient worlds, and it gave rise to the birth of the architectural fantasy as a genre of architectural drawing. From this period – which can best be described as a *second Renaissance* – the works of Giovanni Battista Piranesi (1720–1778), Giovanni Paolo Panini (1691–1765) and two Frenchmen Charles-Joseph Natoire (1700–1777) and Charles Michel-Ange Challe (1718–1778) were of particular importance for future generations of architects and artists. With his architectural fantasies – including his prisons (*carceri*) in particular, Piranesi has had a significant influence on generations of architects and stage designers, right up to the makers of the Harry Potter films. His drawings of the temples at Paestum are also widely known, and were displayed at the first exhibition in the Museum for Architectural Drawing on the site of a former brewery, Pfefferberg, in Berlin. These were loaned from Sir John Soane's Museum in London. The fantastical preparatory drawings for the later etchings are not exact architectural representations, but are rather fantasies in terms of architecture and archaeology.

Drawings by British neoclassicists such as Joseph Gandy (1771–1843), Robert Adam (1728–1792), Sir William Chambers (1723–1796) are renowned the world over, as are those main members of the *Rossica* group, those foreign artists who worked in Russia in the eighteenth and nineteenth centuries such as Giacomo Quarenghi (1744–1844), Thomas de Thomon (1760–1813) and Pietro di Gottardo Gonzaga (1751–1831), whose works were also rooted in the study of ancient forms. The twentieth century and new art movements such as art déco, art nouveau, expressionism, futurism, the Russian avant-garde, constructivism and Bauhaus have not only had a significant influence on architectural style but also, of course, architectural drawing. They have also primarily characterised modern architecture. Architectural drawing increased in importance following the nineteenth century – artistry in drawing has become a benchmark for artistic and architectural abilities. That is one of the reasons why the art of architectural drawing has established itself as an integral part of architectural study, such as for example at the Russian Academy of Arts in Saint Petersburg, a tradition-oriented school which also shaped my graphic work. Development of and training in determining form and proportion provide a guiding light over one's thoughts and to the hand that draws – a line emerges which acquires form, the form takes shape and becomes architecture. I find it regrettable that manual drawing is no longer given the same importance at architecture schools, as was still the case twenty, thirty years ago: talent and training in drawing were the foundation stones on which art in architecture was built, until the arrival of the development and proliferation of CAD systems. This is also the starting-point of the Tchoban Foundation, which was founded in 2009 and which promotes young architectural talent and presents for public view my extensive collection as well as the collection of the foundation.

The idea of building a Museum for Architectural Drawing developed over the past few decades in the course of which I personally produced and later collected architectural drawings by other architects with great passion. Thus, over time I ascertained that the art of architectural drawing does not only represent for me an independent genre, leaving behind a deep impression, but it is also of considerable significance to the majority of its beholders, having a stimulating effect. People are increasingly interested in their built environment – they argue vigorously over it, fight for their interests, and not least, discuss with the architect the origin, intent and purpose of buildings and designs. Thus, architectural drawing not only helps to develop a better understanding of the ideas and thoughts of the architect, but opens up an inimitable and fascinating world – sometimes even the long-awaited environment or an ideal place which is the case in architectural fantasies and utopias. During the construction of our museum, we wanted to create a place where conditions are ideal for the display and preservation of graphic works of art in all respects. In the case of individual rooms, we decided to install private booths for the graphic arts. These allow the visitor to observe undisturbed individual pages and, in a way, to enter into private dialogue with one particular work of art. Furthermore, the rooms are not only a repository for the collection of the foundation, but also offer a place suited for study and temporary exhibitions of renowned institutions, as well as ideally becoming an institution itself at some stage.

The appearance of the building aims at arousing interest and curiosity among those visiting for the first time, people who are not aware of its content or want to look at it in a new light. In its facade there is a silent interplay between the elegant, dynamic and occasionally fragile method of drawing and the large-scale, robust method of construction. Poured and solidified concrete, as well as the flowing, sculptured motifs on the facade and in the building's interior emphasise this interplay. Just as the architectural illustrator develops his sheet of paper down to the last detail, so too does the museum demonstrate its creative outpourings – right down to the door handle – and thus embodies its purpose in an unmistakable way.

The collection of the foundation comprises over 2,500 pages which are presented to the public during changing exhibitions. Furthermore, we offer joint projects over and above those of our own institution at borrowing exhibitions and together with other insitutions such as Sir John Soane's Museum in London, the École nationale supérieure des beaux-arts in Paris, the State Tretyakov Gallery in Moscow, the State Hermitage in Saint Petersburg, the Pushkin Museum of Fine Arts in Moscow and the German Museum of Architecture in Frankfurt am Main.

Giovanni Battista Piranesi (1720–1778)
Architectural Capriccio with a Palace and Rostral Columns
(also known as Forum with a Palace)
Paper, quill, brush, brown inks and traces of sanguine
17.5 × 20.3 cm
Mid-eighteenth century

Giovanni Paolo Panini (1691–1765)

Architectural Fantasy. Baroque Palace with an Obelisk
and the Farnese Hercules
Paper, quill, grey and brown inks
24.5 × 36.9 cm
Mid-eighteenth century

Jean-Francois Thomas de Thomon (1759 – 1813)
View of the Temple of Hadrian in Rome (Roman Customs House)
Paper, quill, dry brush and watercolours
35.8 × 45.1 cm
1788

Charles Michel-Ange Challe (1718–1778)
Architectural Fantasy with Obelisks and an Arched Bridge
in Front of the Imperial Palace on the Palatine in Rome
Paper, quill, brown ink, pencil
37.8 × 57.0 cm
Third quarter of the eighteenth century

Joseph Michael Gandy (1771–1843)
Design for a Cenotaph (also known as the Tomb of Agamemnon)
Watercolour
75.0 × 130.0 cm
1804

Charles Percier (1764–1838)
Palais, Maisons et autres édifices modernes dessinés à Rome (Paris, 1789)
Paper, quill, ink, watercolour
30.4 × 23.9 mm
1786–1792

Yakov Georgievich Chernikhov (1889–1951)
Perspective with Spherical Elements
Paper, quill, ink, heightened with white
30.8 × 24.8 cm
c. 1933

Yakov Georgevich Chernikhov (1889–1951)
Architectural Fantasy
Gouache over a preparatory pencil drawing on yellow paper
29.4 × 23.5 cm
1929–1933

Steven Holl (*1947)
Composition of Different Intersecting Forms
Paper, watercolour over a pencil drawing
12.3 × 17.4 cm
1997

*Sergei Tchoban (*1962)*
Fantasy with a Design for the Museum
for Architectural Drawing in Berlin
Charcoal on paper
32 × 41 cm
2010

>»For in truth, art lies hidden within nature; he who can wrest it from her, has it.«

Albrecht Dürer

Freehand Drawing

53	**School of Perception**
	Ten Freehand Drawing Exercises

56	Point and Line
57	Proportion and Order
58	Geometry and Space
59	Perspective and Space
60	Composition and Space
61	Man and Space
62	Light and Colour
63	Nature and Design
64	Two-minute Sketches
65	Freehand Drawing

67	**Freehand Drawings by Contemporary Architects**

68	Yadegar Asisi
76	Paul Böhm
80	Massimiliano und Doriana Fuksas
84	Zaha Hadid
88	Zvi Hecker
94	Rob Krier
98	Wolf D. Prix
102	Alexander Radoske
106	Christoph Sattler
110	Sergei Tchoban

Natascha Meuser

School of Perception
Ten Freehand Drawing Exercises
Natascha Meuser

What is beauty? A few years ago, a group of international researchers sought to unravel the mysteries of human beauty. They used state-of-the-art, totally impartial computer technology and a huge dataset to establish once and for all why particular faces are perceived as beautiful, and whether beauty exists independently of ethnic, social and cultural background; in other words, whether it can be calculated mathematically. The scientists input countless photos of faces from all over the world, each described by survey respondents as particularly beautiful, into a powerful computer. The resulting information, they believed, could be used to generate a face that would be recognised by any human being as possessing absolute beauty. But what the computer eventually spat out was a picture of an ordinary face, neither beautiful nor ugly, devoid of both life and character. It left most viewers cold. The accumulated data had created not superhuman beauty, but a statistically correct average.

But that is precisely what you would expect of a computer. Here, I want to examine the relevance of this anecdote to architectural beauty, and discuss whether drawing by hand, a skill fast disappearing from everyday practice, is one worth preserving. It would appear to be a relic of the past – but does that mean that computer-generated images are the future? Thanks to modern design and display software, the intention of this book may seem quaintly anachronistic. Would any architect today think of presenting a client with a building detail drawn in Indian ink, or a perspective in pencil?

Clients often expect designers to produce pixel-perfect images right from the beginning of the design process, looking not unlike photographs at first glance. And even before the ground is broken, a virtual idea has already acquired the authority of a tangible reality that serves as the benchmark during the construction process. Often, the client is disappointed because a detail bears no resemblance to the initial plan. Sometimes, poor-quality rendering ends up provoking a protracted legal dispute: was the balcony supposed to be made of reinforced concrete, or just brightly painted steel? Like it or not, the computer is a handy desktop tool, a creativity machine that translates the most outlandish fantasies into physically realisable, fully costed designs that can be altered at a click of a mouse. The resulting photorealistic printout gives form to an idea that has not really even taken shape in the architect's own mind.

It is easy to forget that, for all its apparent creative talents, the computer is just a machine. The image that emerges from the printer is like that of the perfect face in the experiment, shaped by complex, soulless programs. Paradoxically, the tool we use in an attempt to make it look less soulless is also the computer. After all, animation means adding life and soul to an otherwise lifeless object, creating a realistic, perhaps even moving image using infallible, invisible and incomprehensible computer code. The spaces inhabited by avatars in computer games are not greatly different to the standard CAD output used by architects to persuade developers, contractors, clients, and competition juries.

Precision is the death of thought

Anyone looking for soul in a building or interior design will not find it in these colourful animated digital images. Their impressive perfection is artificial and deceptive, their precision a challenge to the viewer's imagination. To put it bluntly, architects who rely solely on the design skills of their computers are neglecting what was once one of their profession's core skills since time immemorial: the connection of eye, head and hand to create sketches, drawings, designs and plans.

In the old days, prospective architects had to start by learning to use a pen, analysing structure, proportion, cubature, light and shade to break down the world into its component parts and reassemble them on the paper. To do this, their eyes and hands had to be trained. This can be an enjoyable and intuitive process: as my drawing teacher Heinrich Pittner once said, 'What counts is not knowledge, but inspiration.' His methods were based on clear principles, and he was not only a teacher but also a poetic artist with a philosophical turn of mind, who used simple exercises to teach the complexity of architecture. He made his students feel that they were both artists and architects. The next person I encountered who displayed this passion for architectural education was Alfred Caldwell, a legendary lecturer at the Illinois Institute of Technology in Chicago. His personality alone made his lectures worth the metaphorical price of admission, and he used to say: 'The individuality of architecture is always based on personal experience.' The following chapter is devoted to Pittner's methods, which teach the basic principles of freehand architectural drawing in nine steps. The exercises can be carried out in any order, and are anything but comprehensive, but their aim is to introduce trainee architects and other interested readers to one of the most creative areas of architecture. Even experienced draftspeople should find the exercises an enjoyable reminder of their own training. This is also a reminder that the drawing marks the architect's

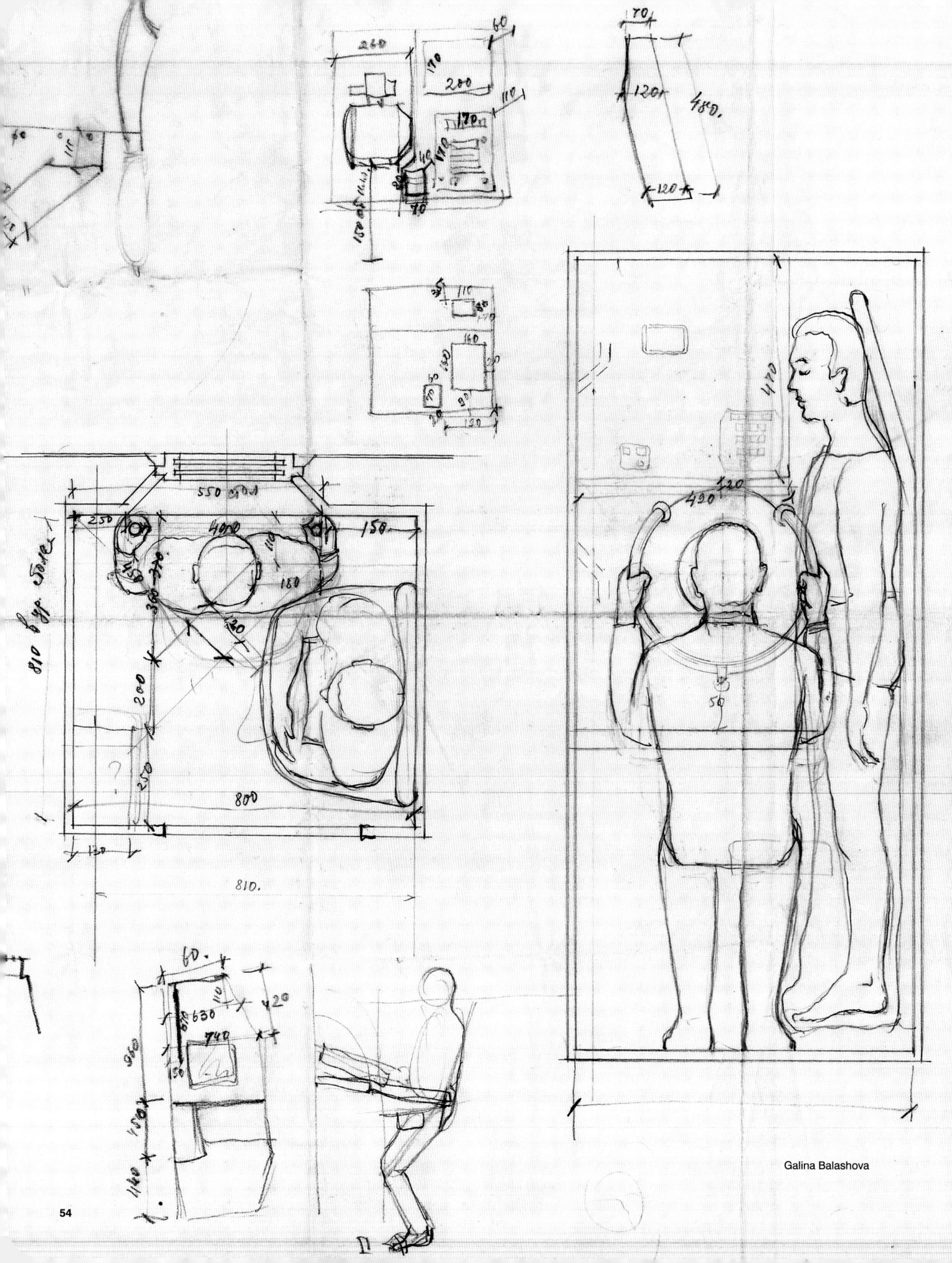

Galina Balashova

Natascha Meuser

emergence as creator, giving visible expression to a unique idea without the help of computer programmes. While many would say it is an outmoded pictorial technique, drawing transforms the idea into the intangible basis of the entire design process. In this context, and at this stage in the project, the image is not a mirror of reality, but it gives the idea credibility.

A decision that only the architect can take

Architectural drawing is like photography: it is no good having a high-end, feature-packed camera if you lack the ability to compose images and to capture the essence of the subject. Having the technology to generate preliminary architectural and design ideas does not necessarily mean that the final result will be convincing. The choice of medium, be it 6B pencil, drawing pen or watercolour brush, is no guarantee of good architecture, which demands a basic understanding of proportion, perspective, form and colour. The ability to connect the eyes, mind and hand when designing details, buildings and cities also requires familiarity with a wide variety of architectural cultures, periods, and styles. It entails knowing, based on practical experience, that ideas build on one another, and being able to absorb and develop traditions and use one's own outlook and ideas to create distinctive buildings for clients that can be highly valued.

Such is the nature of architecture: it is very rarely created in a vacuum, and is usually part of a context of variety and difference. Take away the sharp edges of architectural space, and you are left with nothing. The architect's penstroke brings it together and gives it form, which assumes an ability to imagine the space and give it proportion, structure and beauty. Only the architect can take these decisions. Like all talents, architectural imagination and creativity are God-given, but born of practice and experience. People who have seen, understood and adapted other people's ideas are more easily able to come up with ideas of their own, drawing on a rich menu of visual and spatial ingredients. A person who uses drawing to explore the built environment sees its variety in a different light, and perhaps with greater respect, than someone who can imagine nonexistent space only by donning 3D spectacles. Architecture and the art of drawing are inseparable – and people who are good at drawing usually make good architects.

Exercise 1:
Point and Line

Points, lines and planes are the architect's means of expression, and are combined to create the three-dimensional spaces of architecture. This exercise uses only points and lines to build, first, basic geometric shapes, and then landscapes and places. Compression and changes of direction are used to create the identifying outlines of forms and spaces, define distances and clarify spatial depth. Our approach to architectural space begins with an excursion into art, with a quotation from the painter and Bauhaus teacher Paul Klee: 'I begin wherever the pictorial form itself begins: with the point that moves.'

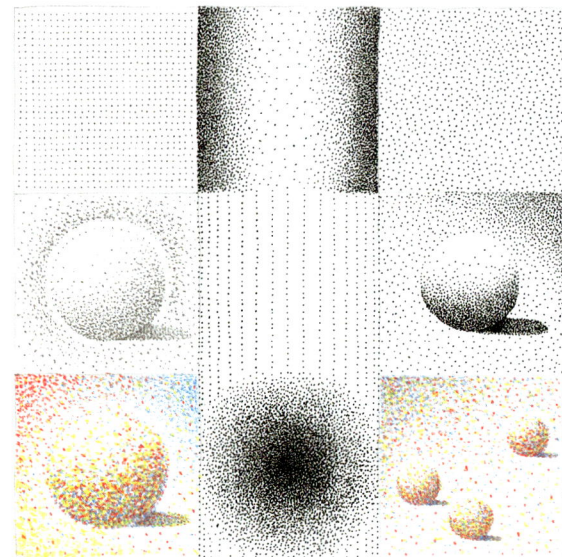

Heidi Reibl

Susanne Kraft

56

Exercise 2:
Proportion and Order

Every building project begins with a simple exercise: draw, measure, think. Finding harmonious relationships between the parts of a building, and between the parts and the whole, helps to order the elements of the design. The basic principles of proportion are dependent on finding relationships between measurements, and have remained almost unchanged since the ancient Greeks and Romans. The golden section, Renaissance theories and Le Corbusier's *Modulor* are all based on the proportions of the human body and describe a line divided into sections, the shorter of which stands in the same ratio to the larger as the larger section to the whole. These laws and relationships allow architects to create meaningful, harmonious connections, and are a key moment of creative inspiration. This drawing exercise trains the eye by analysing the dimensional relationships between geometric solids, and also provides a basic introduction to architecture with relation to elements, construction and composition.

Unknown example: Practice is essential to finding the right proportion and lines

Adelheid Kraut

Basilica of Santa Croce, Florence (Photo: Liz Leyden)

Exercise 3:
Geometry and Space

All variety of form depends on identifying measured relationships. This exercise, too, is based on simple geometric forms: the triangle, square, circle, pyramid, cube and sphere, cutting them up and reassembling them in new ways. Architecture derives its endless variety from combinations of two- and three-dimensional shapes, and from projecting two-dimensional surfaces into the third dimension. In the words of Heinrich Pittner, 'If you want to achieve an outcome, you must see abstraction and reality as a unity. We are architects, not artists, but abstraction is the basis of our designs.'

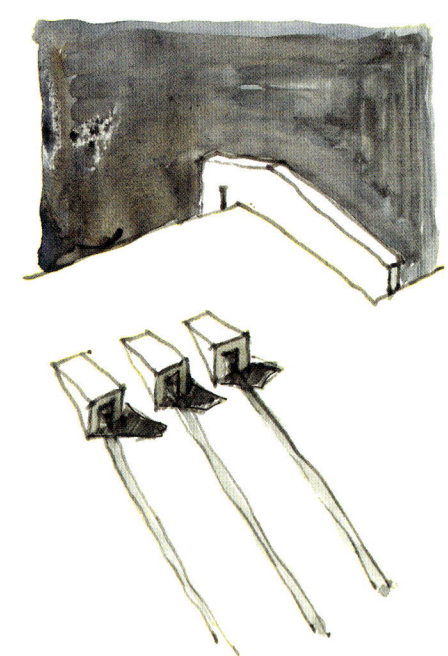

Natascha Meuser

Jochen Spiegelberger

Exercise 4:
Perspective and Space

Freehand drawing can be used to learn and practise the *right way of seeing*, but also requires a basic knowledge of perspective construction methods and their history. In the Middle Ages, space was still seen as a plane, but the Renaissance discovery of vanishing-point perspective brought major changes in the visual arts. This form of perspective remains an important medium of communication for today's architects, whether they draw by hand or use a computer. The purpose of this exercise is to learn the principles of freehand perspective and spatial construction. Each point has a measurable position in the space, and the exercise involves drawing two or more simple objects turned or shifted in relation to each other. It takes only a small number of lines to create a three-dimensional representation. The exercise teaches the artistic and technical aspects of drawing, using an enjoyable artistic approach to such simple principles of construction as horizon, viewpoint and vanishing point. It also entails identifying, absorbing and analysing dimensions and proportions, because drawing is ultimately about not just knowledge, but the inspiration born of individual perception.

Natascha Meuser

Exercise 5:
Composition and Space

Architectural drawing always involves composition and the abstraction of the depicted space. To draw spatially is to see spatially. The purpose of this exercise is to build up a composition step by step, creating tensions using hierarchies of detail and whole, centre and periphery, front and back, top and bottom, dark and light. This brings out complex spatial relationships and makes visible the forces that form space. In the exercise, simple forms and gradual abstraction are built up and composed on the picture surface. 'Architecture is an artifice, an appearance of inner movement. It goes far beyond issues of construction. The purpose of construction is to create durability, and the purpose of architecture is to stir our inner selves. As soon as specific relationships are created, we grasp the work.'
Le Corbusier, Vers une architecture (1923)

Natascha Meuser

Exercise 6:
Man and Space

The theory of proportion dates back to Vitruvius and thus the early days of architectural theory. Up and into the time of the Renaissance, theories of art focused on the notion of human scale and determined the continuity of a harmonious design and proportioning. Vitruvius also factored the proportions of the human body into the tectonic system of a building and placed these in a proportional context. In particular, studies on the human body can be gleaned from Leonardo da Vinci, who was a pioneer in the understanding of human anatomy. Alberti had already demonstrated that each regular shape can be constructed from circles and squares. Le Corbusier in turn discovered a harmonious design of the human figure according to the golden ratio. He named the human figure *Modulor* which he based on the height of a man with his arm raised and integrated into his spaces for emphasis. This art figure is still today synonymous with a style of architecture adapted to suit the human environment. The relationship between man and space will form the content of this exercise. In the process, the aim is not only to analyse the proportions of the human body but also its proportionality in space. Here it is less significant honing drawing techniques but developing a feeling for a composition of man and space that matters.

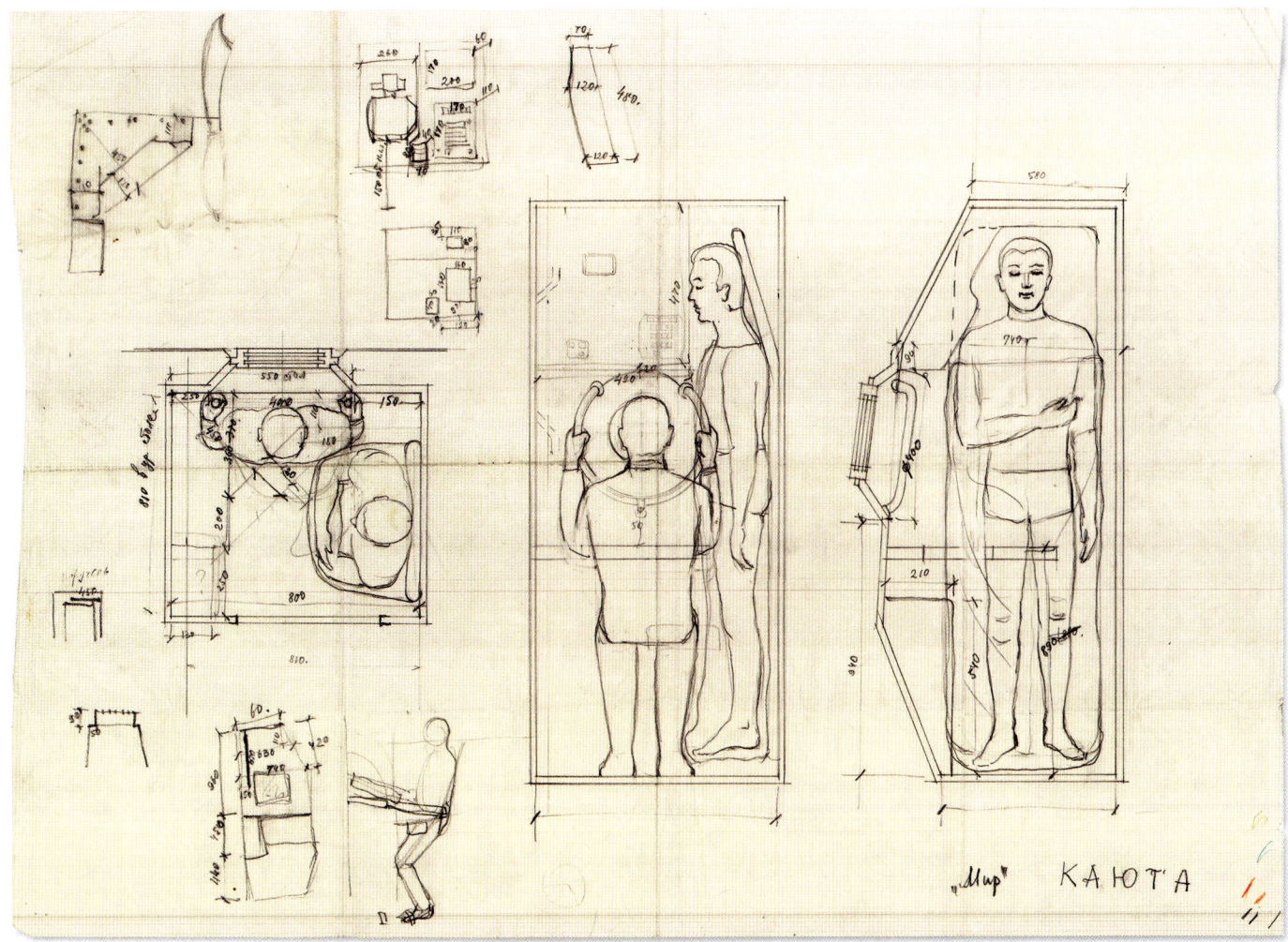

Galina Balashova

Exercise 7:
Light and Colour

Light and colour are closely related, and play a mutually reinforcing role within the design process. The purpose of this second exercise is to discover the basic elements of colour theory, and learn the main colour mixes. The primary colours red, blue and yellow can be used to create any other colour except black – mix all three, and the result is brown. Colour theory is also the theory of harmony, which deals with the interaction of colours and tones. The purpose of the exercise is to understand the phenomenon of colour as a whole, based on the theories of Johann Wolfgang von Goethe.

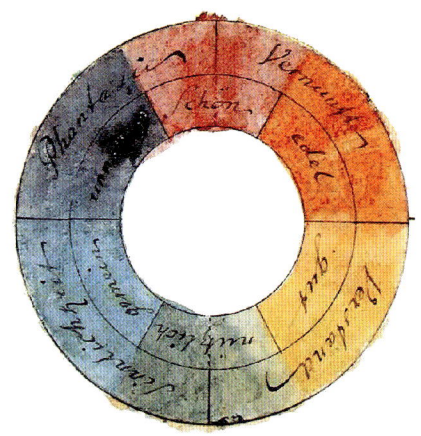

Ink drawing by Goethe, 1809
Source: Goethe-Museum, Frankfurt

Rita Ahlers

62

Exercise 8:
Nature and Design

This exercise, in which nature provides the inspiration for the design process, involves drawing an open flower at the final stage of growth, and then using its geometry as the basis for various floor plans. The purpose of the exercise is to design architectural structures using natural forms, so nature herself is the inspiration. It highlights the origins and theory of design: in the words of Albrecht Dürer, 'Art is hidden in nature. If you can tear it out, you have it.' *Albrecht Dürer*

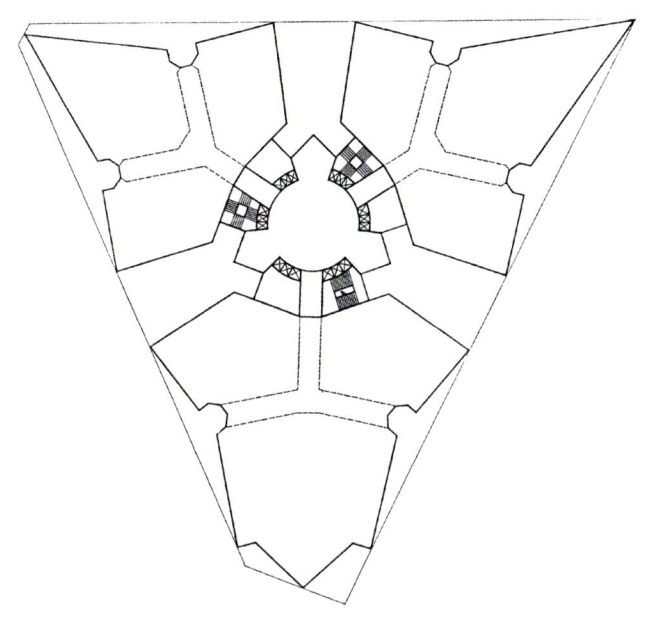

Ludwig Mies van der Rohe: Design of an office building, 1919

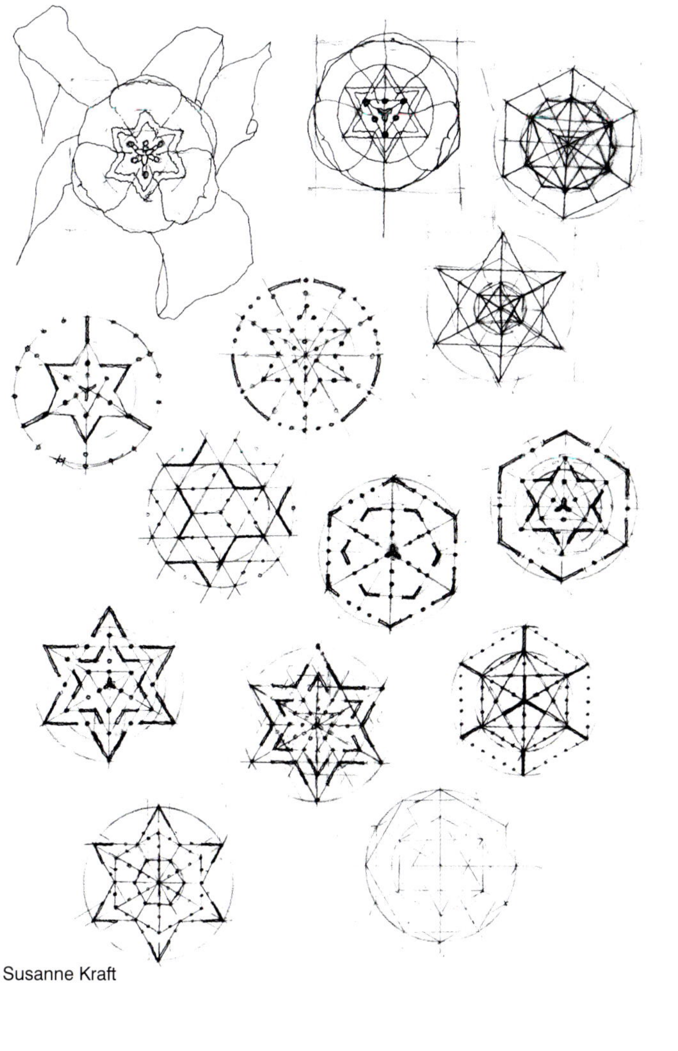

Susanne Kraft

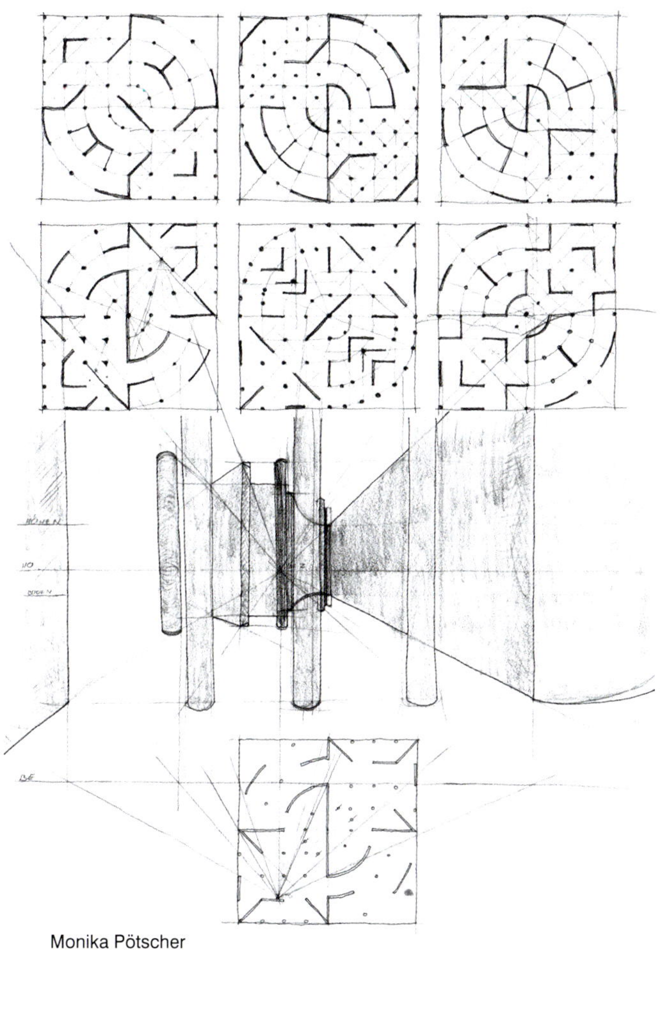

Monika Pötscher

63

Exercise 9:
Two-minute Sketches

Learning to draw means learning to see, as the eye seeks, observes and understands. This exercise aims to encourage spontaneity by imposing a time limit; the act of producing a rapid initial sketch forces us to decide how much visual information we want to convey. The sketches are a way of experimenting without needing to produce a complete or perfect result. The aim is to develop a strong sense of expressiveness by being confident from the first penstroke. 'When I went to see Matisse one morning, he was still in bed, but he had his drawing board in front of him and was drawing the same head with great concentration and rapid strokes. Each time he finished one, he threw the piece of paper onto the floor beside the bed and began another, so he was surrounded by a pile of paper. Seeing my surprise, he laughed and said: "I'm like a dancer or a skater. I practise every morning so that when the moment arrives, I'm completely in control of my jumps and pirouettes."'
Werner Haftmann, Documenta III (1964)

Natascha Meuser

Exercise 10:
Freehand Drawing

A good plein-air drawing is not simply a depiction of nature under a cloudless sky. It leaves space for inspiration, using the model and natural objects and forms, to practise line and composition. In this exercise, a single motif is depicted using a variety of techniques, with the choice of drawing medium and colour playing an important role. The intention is to encourage visual thinking, design variations, and drawing as a process. If freehand drawing is what we learn from seeing, sketching is an aid to thinking like a designer. Architects use sketches to test out, change and add to their ideas. Many students do not realise how much creative wealth lies hidden inside them, and freehand drawing reveals the secret of design.

Natascha Meuser

Freehand Drawings by Contemporary Architects

Yadegar Asisi

The architect and artist from Berlin has mastered perspective drawing and uses the visual spectacle of an architectural image to create spectacular panoramas.

Rob Krier

The Dutch architect and artist combines the traditional craft of drawing and classical imagery to create vedute modelled on the Old Masters.

Paul Böhm

The Cologne architect combines contrasting elements to produce subtle drawings in course chalk, rich in detail and scenically animated to behold.

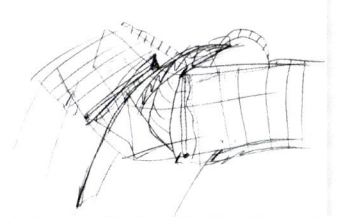

Wolf D. Prix

Anarchy and architecture: the Austrian architect is counted among the originators of the deconstructivist architecture movement.

Massimiliano and Doriana Fuksas

The elegant displays of art by the Italian architect duo forcefully anticipate architectural qualities and unfurl their impact, especially in combination with drawing and models.

Alexander Radoske

His artwork is a sober, stark rejection of an illusionism which is characteristic of drawings.

Zaha Hadid

As the founder of Parametricism, she also plays with the visuals of a cool, prismatic computer representation in her freehand drawings.

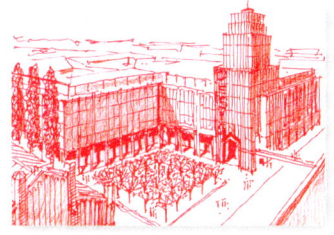

Christoph Sattler

Even his drawings leave no doubt of his superb architectural ambition. Classic mastery at the highest level.

Zvi Hecker

Analytical geometry makes his drawings clearly distinguishable – shapes taken from a solid-state physics building set on paper.

Sergei Tchoban

The fact that the Russian architect attended a strict art school cannot be overlooked. His depictions masterfully sound out the fantastic potential of this form of representation.

Yadegar Asisi

World Trade Center competition, New York
for Daniel Libeskind
Oil on colour plot, digitally edited
Revised draft sketch
90 × 42 cm
2002

*World Trade Center competition, New York
for Daniel Libeskind*
Pencil and acrylic on paper
First draft sketch
100 × 70 cm
2002

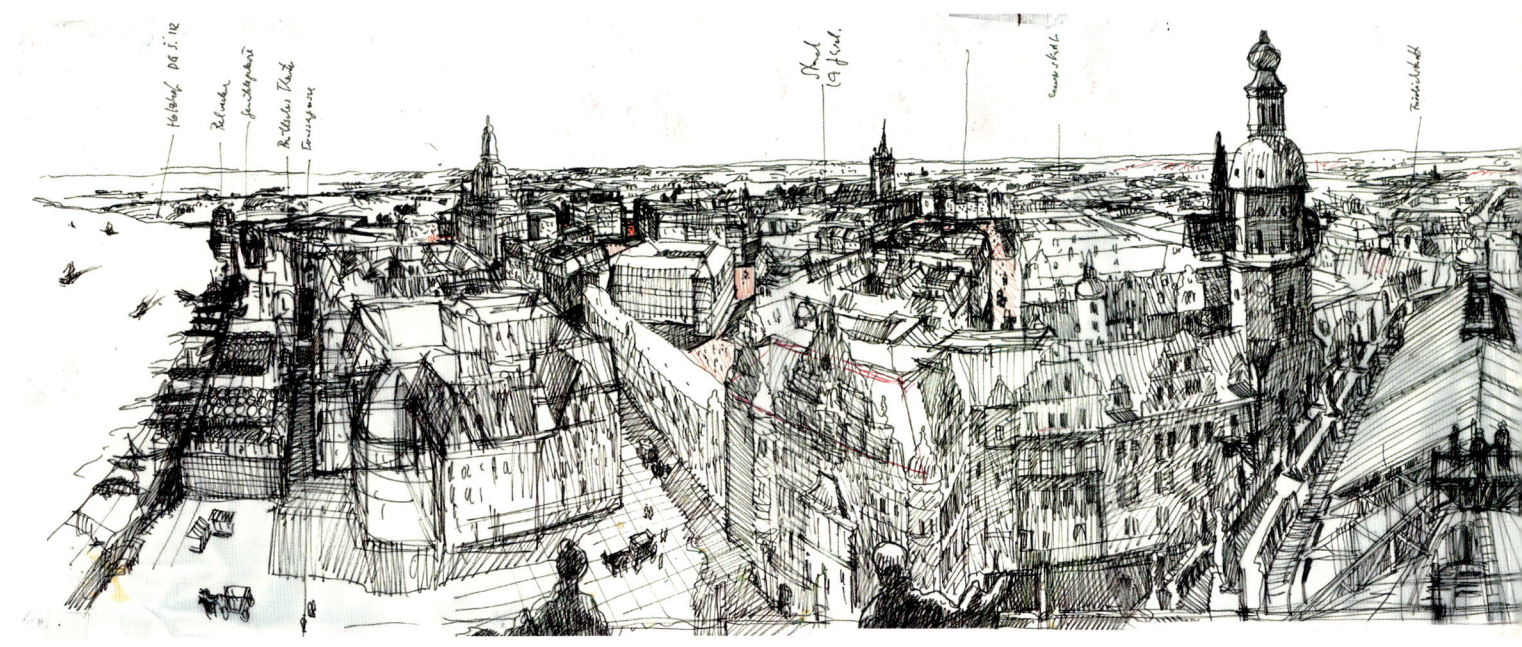

'1756 Dresden' panorama project, Asisi Panometer Dresden
Oil Indian ink on tracing paper
First sketch with areas marked as examples for three detail sketches
165 × 33 cm
2005

'1756 Dresden' panorama project, Asisi Panometer Dresden
Photoshop
Extract, state of digitally edited panorama based on detail sketches
207 × 95cm (at 300 dpi)
2005

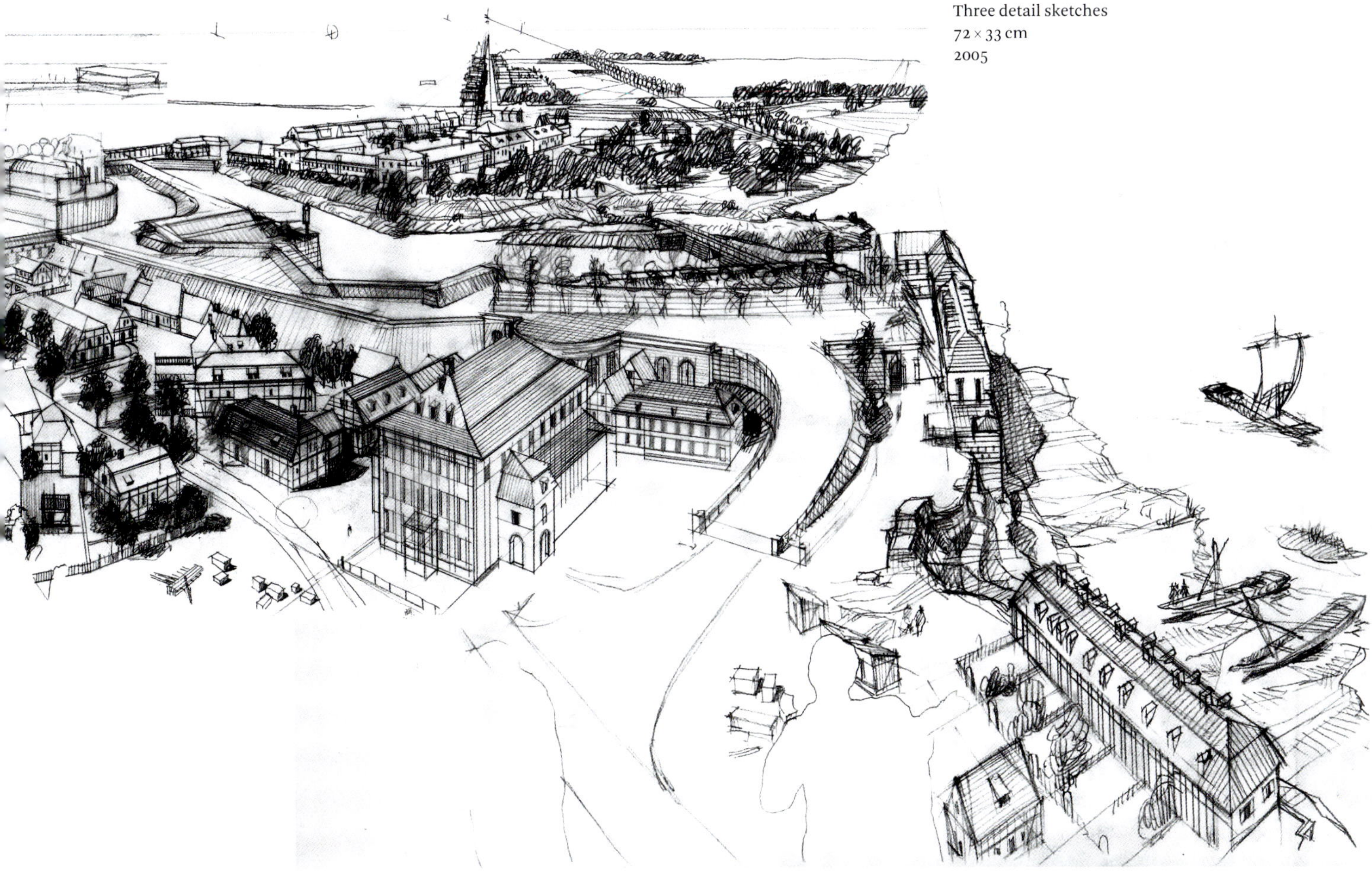

'1756 Dresden' panorama project, Asisi Panometer Dresden
Pencil on tracing paper, digitally merged
Three detail sketches
72 × 33 cm
2005

'1756 Dresden' panorama project, Asisi Panometer Dresden
Extract from a current panorama of the tower and roof of the Hofkirche, Gemäldegalerie, Semperoper
2005

'1756 Dresden' panorama project, Asisi Panometer Dresden
Photo
Visitors on the platform with view of panorama
2006

'1756 Dresden' panorama project, Asisi Panometer Dresden
Photo
View of the panorama interior from above, with the visitors' tower in the foreground
2006

'1756 Dresden' panorama project, Asisi Panometer Dresden
Photo
View of the panorama interior from above, with the visitors'
tower in the foreground
2009

'Amazonia' panorama project, Asisi Panometer Leipzig
Indian ink on tracing paper
Second detailed sketch, first digital sketch behind
98 × 33 cm
2007

Yadegar Asisi

Born Vienna 1955, grew up in Saxony. Studied architecture at the Technical University of Dresden and painting at the Berlin University of the Arts. Co-founded the Berlin architecture firm Brandt-Asisi-Böttcher and won the Mies van der Rohe prize in 1988. His architectural graphics studio carried out pioneering simulations and 3D animations for leading architects, including a panorama of the Ground Zero development for Daniel Libeskind in 2003. Asisi lectured at HDK Berlin from 1985 to 1991 and was Professor of Architecture at Beuth University of Applied Sciences in Berlin from 1996 to 2008. In the 1990s, his experience of architectural simulations, stage scenery and painting led him to the medium of the panorama, which he used as a means of artistic expression to turn the act of seeing into experience. His two *Asisi Panometers* (panoramas set inside former gasometers) have attracted 2.5 million visitors since 2003. The Asisi Academy offers a series of events to promote drawing as a key means of communication that follows the rules of perspective and composition.

Paul Böhm

New Islamic cultural centre, Cologne
Charcoal on paper
Section
29 × 51 cm
2009

New Islamic cultural centre, Cologne
Charcoal and red chalk on paper
Elevation
70 × 89 cm
2009

Office block competition, Halle
Charcoal and chalk on paper
Front views
52 × 110 cm
1996

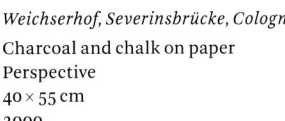

Weichserhof, Severinsbrücke, Cologne
Charcoal and chalk on paper
Perspective
40 × 55 cm
2000

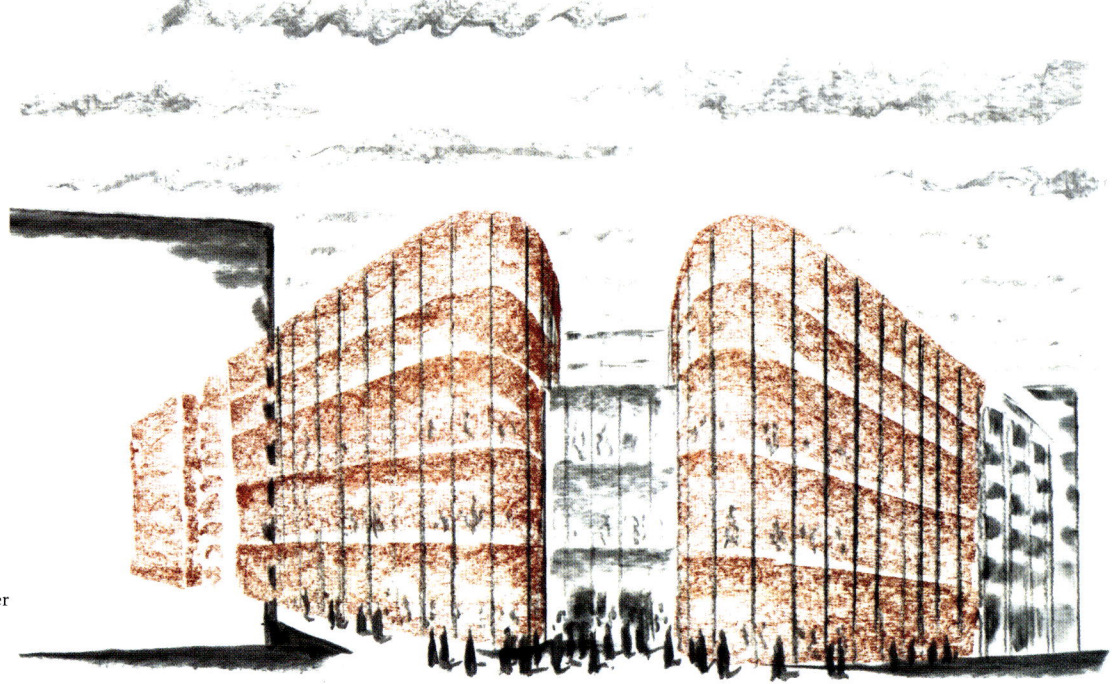

Peek & Cloppenburg, Wuppertal
Charcoal and red chalk on paper
Design variant
36 × 64 cm
2005

Clemens-Sels-Museum competition, Neuss
Charcoal and red chalk on paper
Perspective
41 × 74 cm
2003

Paul Böhm
Born Cologne 1959, son of the architect Gottfried Böhm. After his Abitur, he worked for two years with, among others, the landscape architect Gottfried Hansjakob in Munich. Studied architecture at the Technical University of Berlin and the Vienna University of Technology from 1983 to 1990. After graduating, worked for the firm of Bernhard Strecker and Jürgen Eckhardt in Berlin, and then for Richard Meier in New York. From 1992 onwards, he was involved in a variety of projects at Büro Böhm, including the employment office in Trier and the parish church of St. Theodor in Vingst, Cologne. In 2001, he founded Architekturbüro Paul Böhm. Held various teaching posts in Germany and abroad from 2005 to 2009. Founded Böhm & Partners Architects FZC, Dubai in 2007. Visiting professor at Cologne University of Applied Sciences since March 2009.

Massimiliano and Doriana Fuksas

Scenery for 'Oedipus at Colonnus', Siracusa
Idea sketch
29 × 22 cm
2009

Photo: Moreno Maggi

80

Photo: Archive Fuksas

New trade fair centre, Milan
Idea sketch
23 × 34 cm
2002

Massimiliano Fuksas
Born Rome, 1944. Graduated in architecture at La Sapienza University in Rome in 1969, and in the same year founded Massimiliano Fuksas Architetto in Rome, with other offices following from 1989 onwards. From 1998 to 2000, directed the 7th International Architecture Biennale in Venice. Was a visiting professor at various universities, including the École Spéciale d'Architecture in Paris, the University of Fine Arts in Vienna and Columbia University in New York City. Lives and works in Rome and Paris.

Doriana Fuksas
Born Rome. Graduated in architecture from La Sapienza University in Rome in 1979, and was a board member of the National Institute of Architecture in Rome, Italy. Has worked with Massimiliano Fuksas since 1985, and has been head of Fuksas Design since 1997. Curated the 7th International Architecture Biennale in Venice in 2000. Lives and works in Rome and Paris.

Peres Peace House, Tel Aviv
Idea sketch
29 × 20 cm
1999

Photo: Amit Geron

Zenith, Strasbourg
Idea sketch
25 × 14 cm
2003

Photo: Philippe Ruault

Zaha Hadid

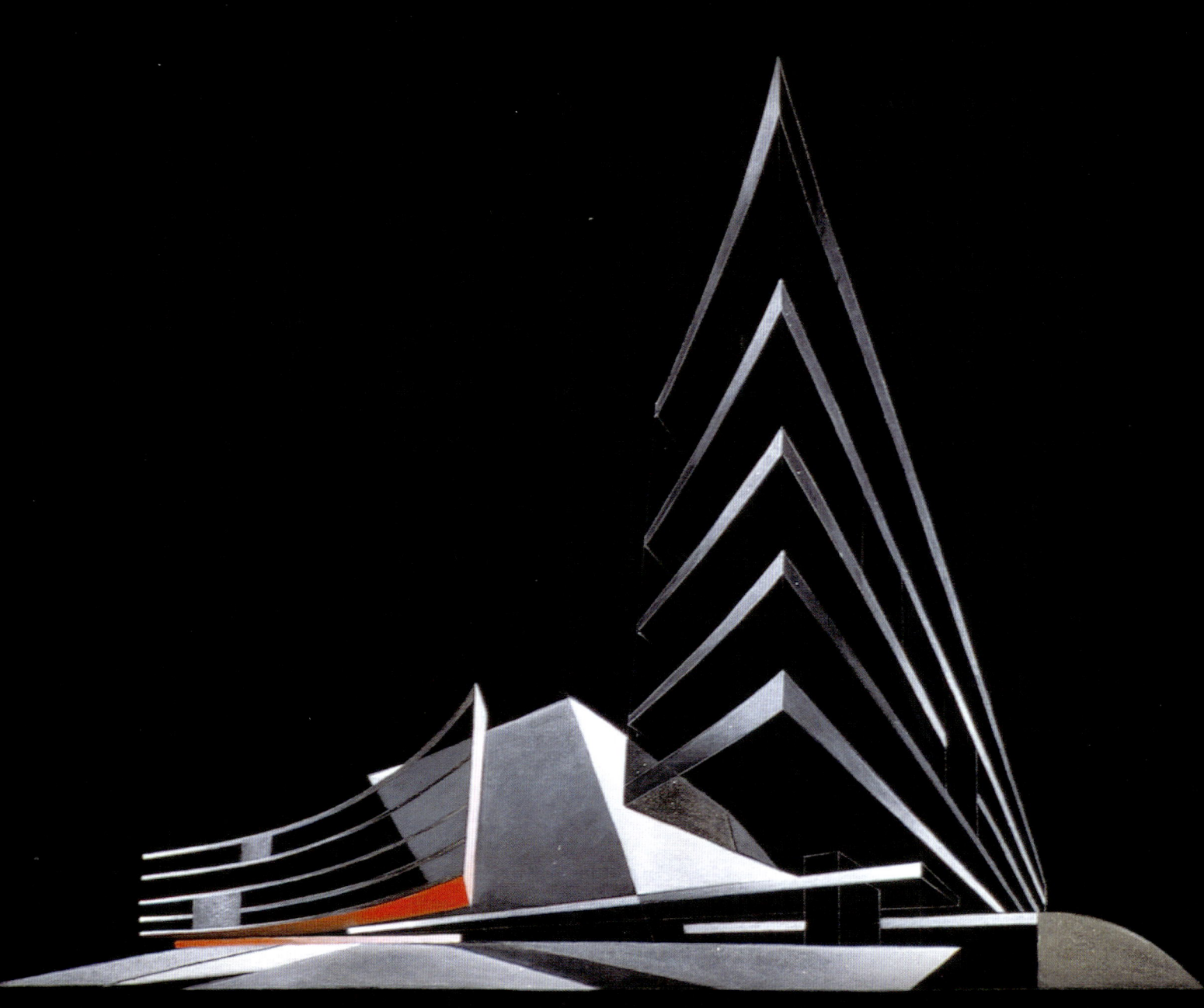

Cardiff Bay Opera House, Cardiff
Acrylic on black card
Perspective
25 × 15 cm
1994

Photo: Zaha Hadid Architects

Cardiff Bay Opera House, Cardiff
Acrylic on black card
Perspective
17 × 18 cm
1994

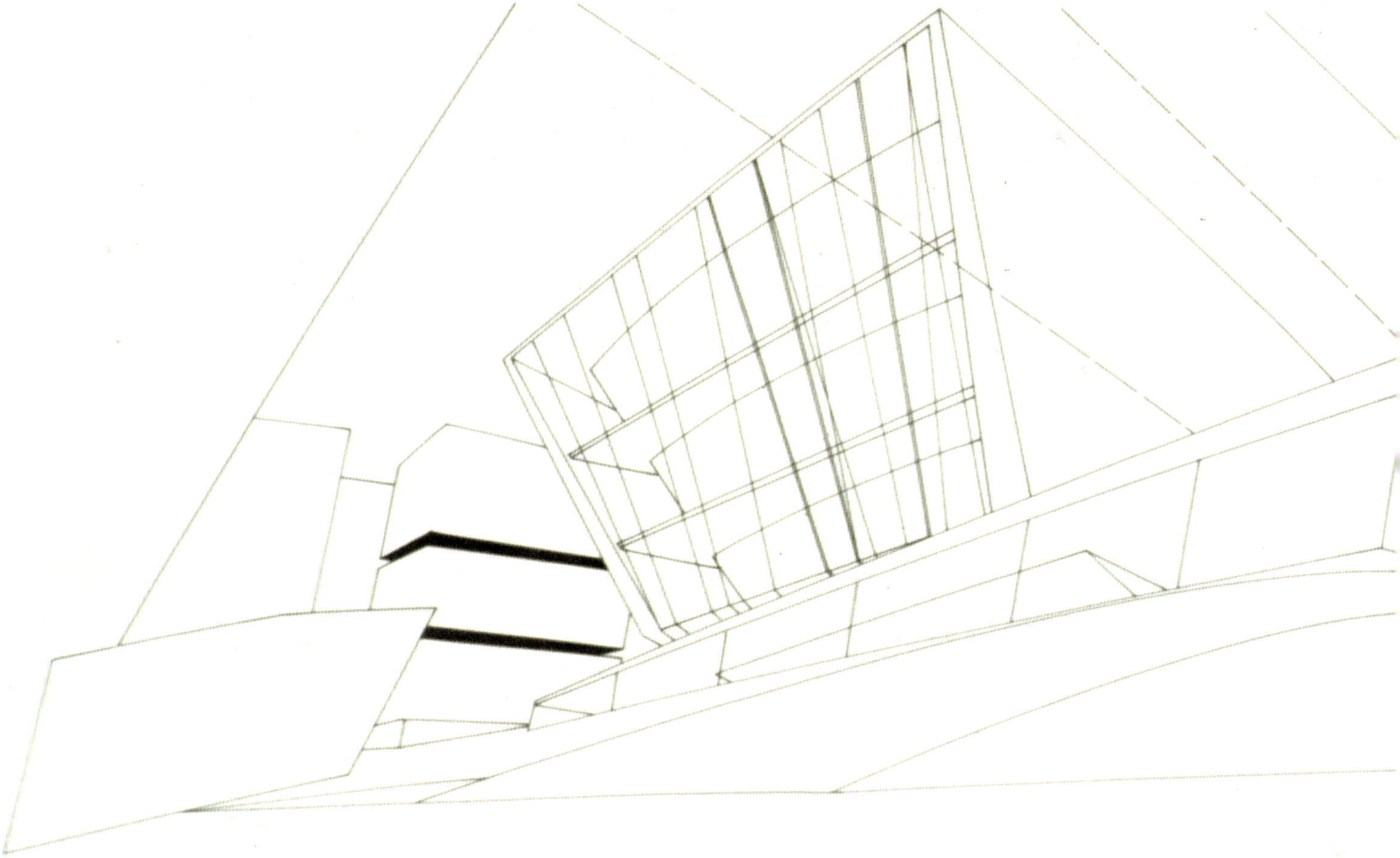

Floor plan, ground floor

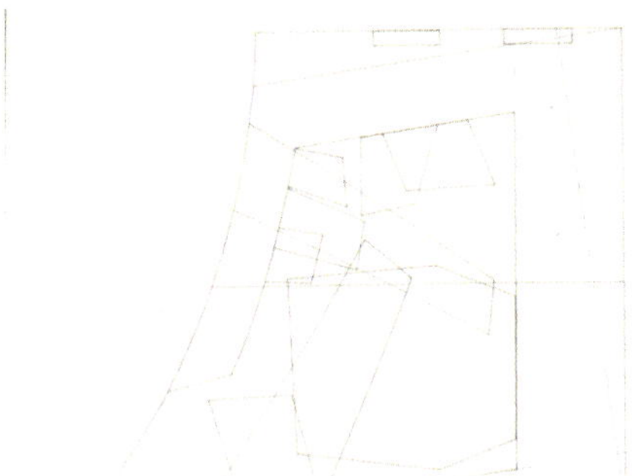

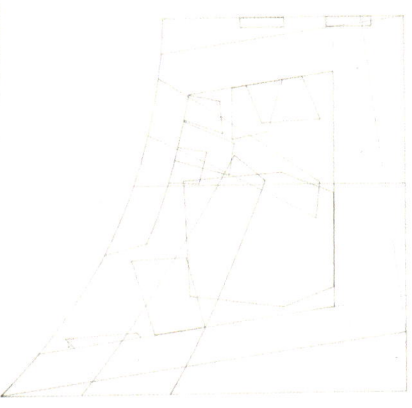
Floor plan, first floor

Floor plan, second floor

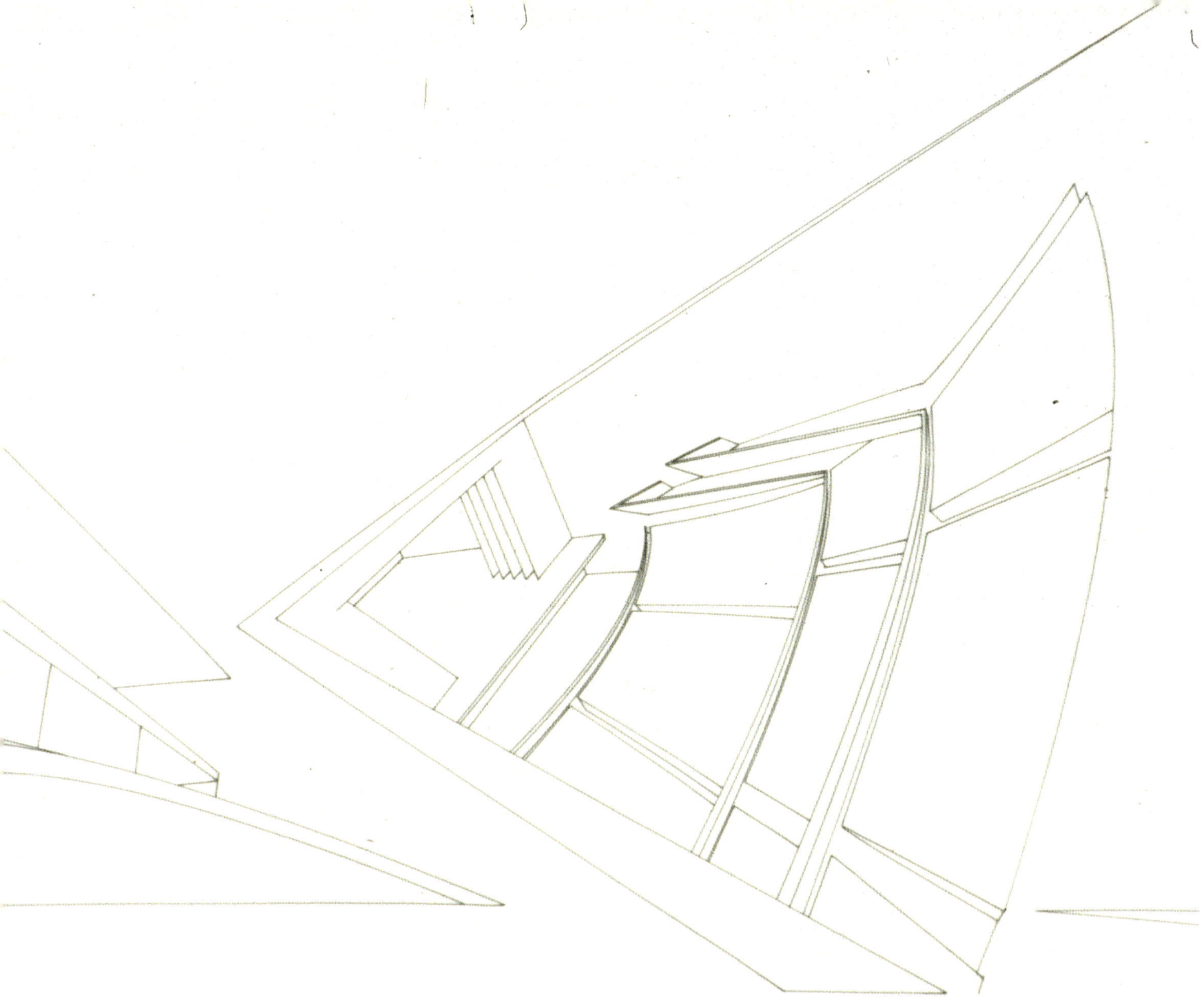

Zaha Hadid

Born Baghdad, 1950. Studied at the Architectural Association in London from 1972 to 1977, and then worked with Rem Koolhaas at Office for Metropolitan Architecture. Gained international recognition in 1983 with her design for the Peak Leisure Club in Hong Kong. Another career milestone was her participation in the 1988 deconstructivism exhibition at New York's Museum of Modern Art. Hadid completed her first major project in 1993 with the fire station in Weil am Rhein. Since then, her oeuvre has been a long list of architectural superlatives, and in 2004 she became the first woman to be awarded the prestigious Pritzker Prize, often referred to as *architecture's Nobel*.

Zvi Hecker

Spiral Apartment House, Tel Aviv
Crayon on technical drawing
Floor plan and details
70 × 50 cm
1987

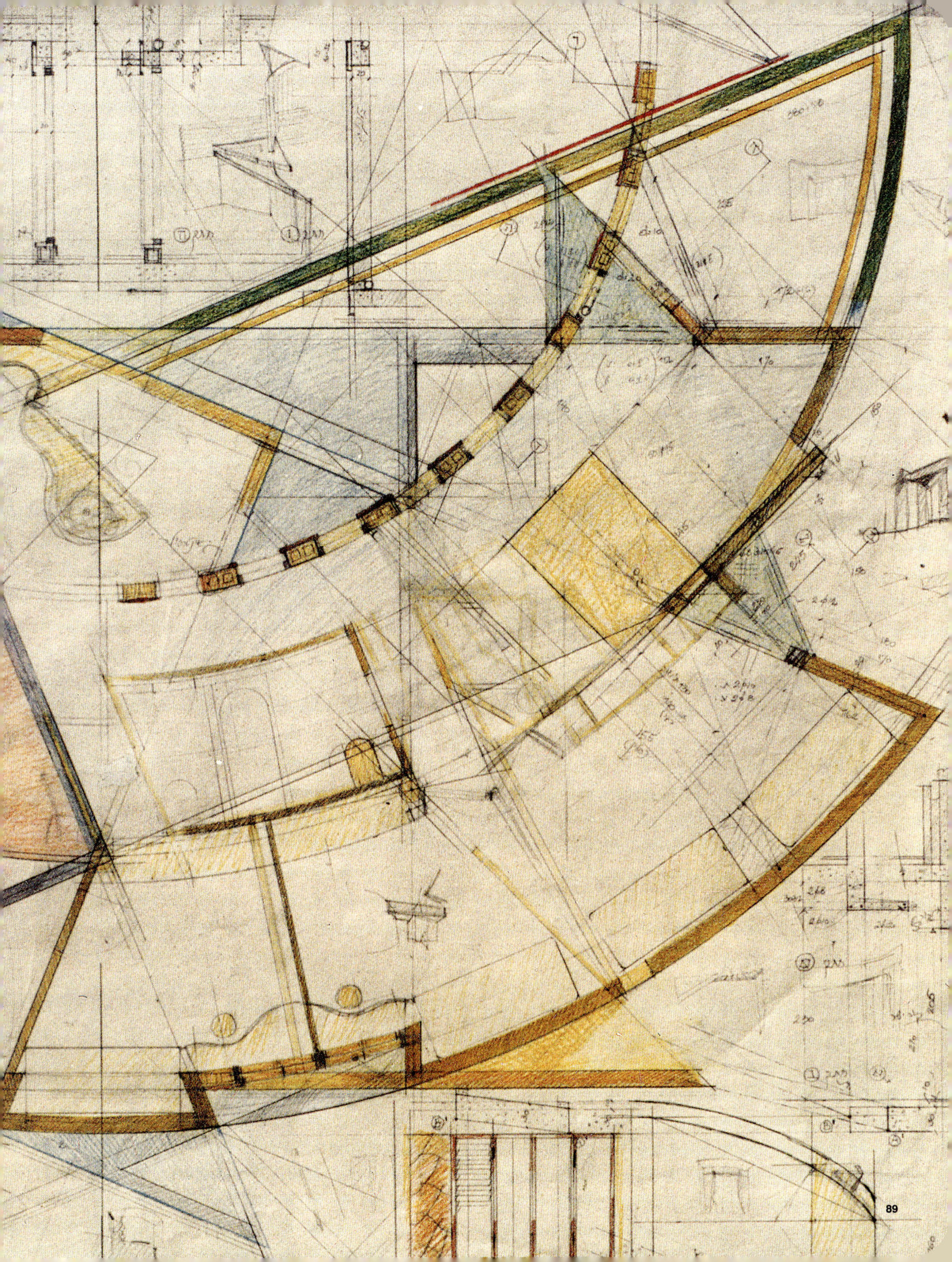

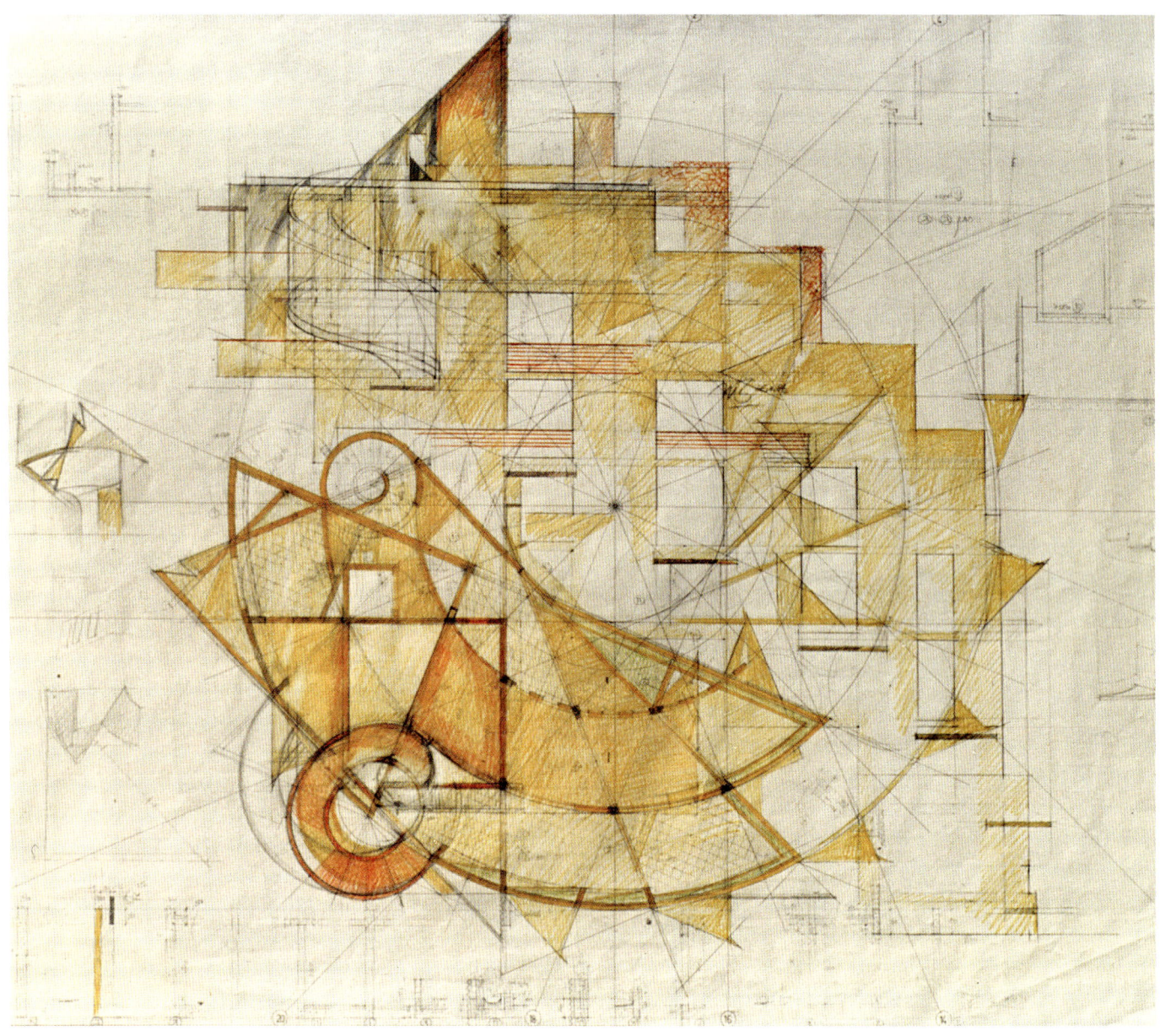

Spiral Apartment House, Tel Aviv
Crayon on technical drawing
Floor plan and view
70 × 50 cm
1985

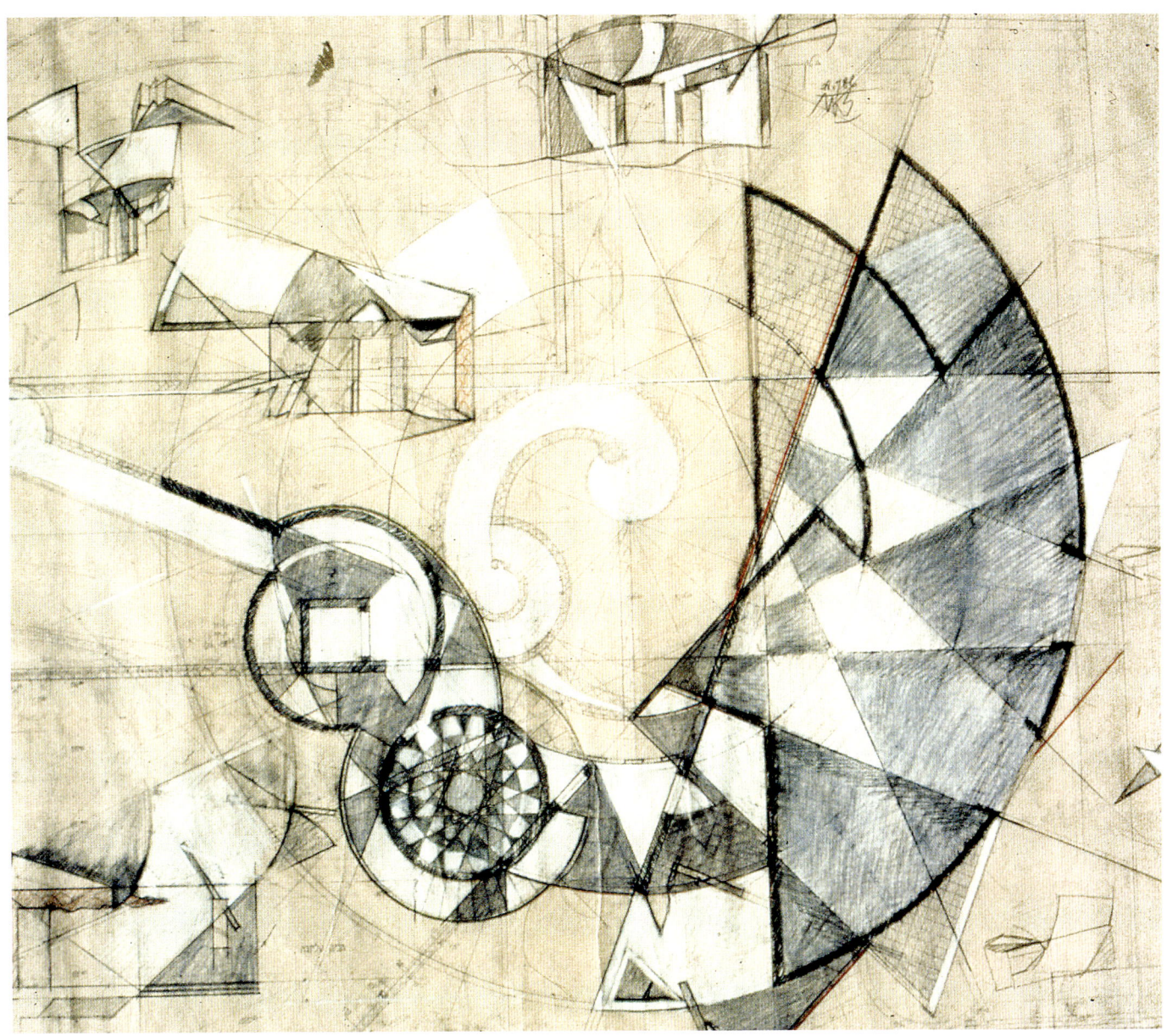

Spiral Apartment House, Tel Aviv
Crayon on technical drawing
Floor plan and details
70 × 50 cm
1986

Spiral Apartment House, Tel Aviv
Crayon on paper
Perspective
30 × 50 cm
1985

Spiral Apartment House, Tel Aviv
Crayon on paper
Perspective
30 × 50 cm
1985

Zvi Hecker
Born Kraków, 1931. Studied architecture at Kraków Polytechnic from 1949 to 1950 and the Israel Institute of Technology in Haifa from 1950 to 1954, and painting at the Avni Institute of Art and Design in Tel Aviv from 1955 to 1957. Hecker was Professor of Architecture at Laval University in Québec and the University of Applied Arts in Vienna, a partner in the firm of Alfred Neumann from 1958 to 1968, and worked with Eldar Sharon from 1965 to 1968. In 1968, after Neumann's death, Hecker opened his own architectural practice. He designed mainly government buildings and shopping centres, primarily in Israel, but also in the Netherlands, Iran and Canada. He now lives and works in Berlin.

Rob Krier

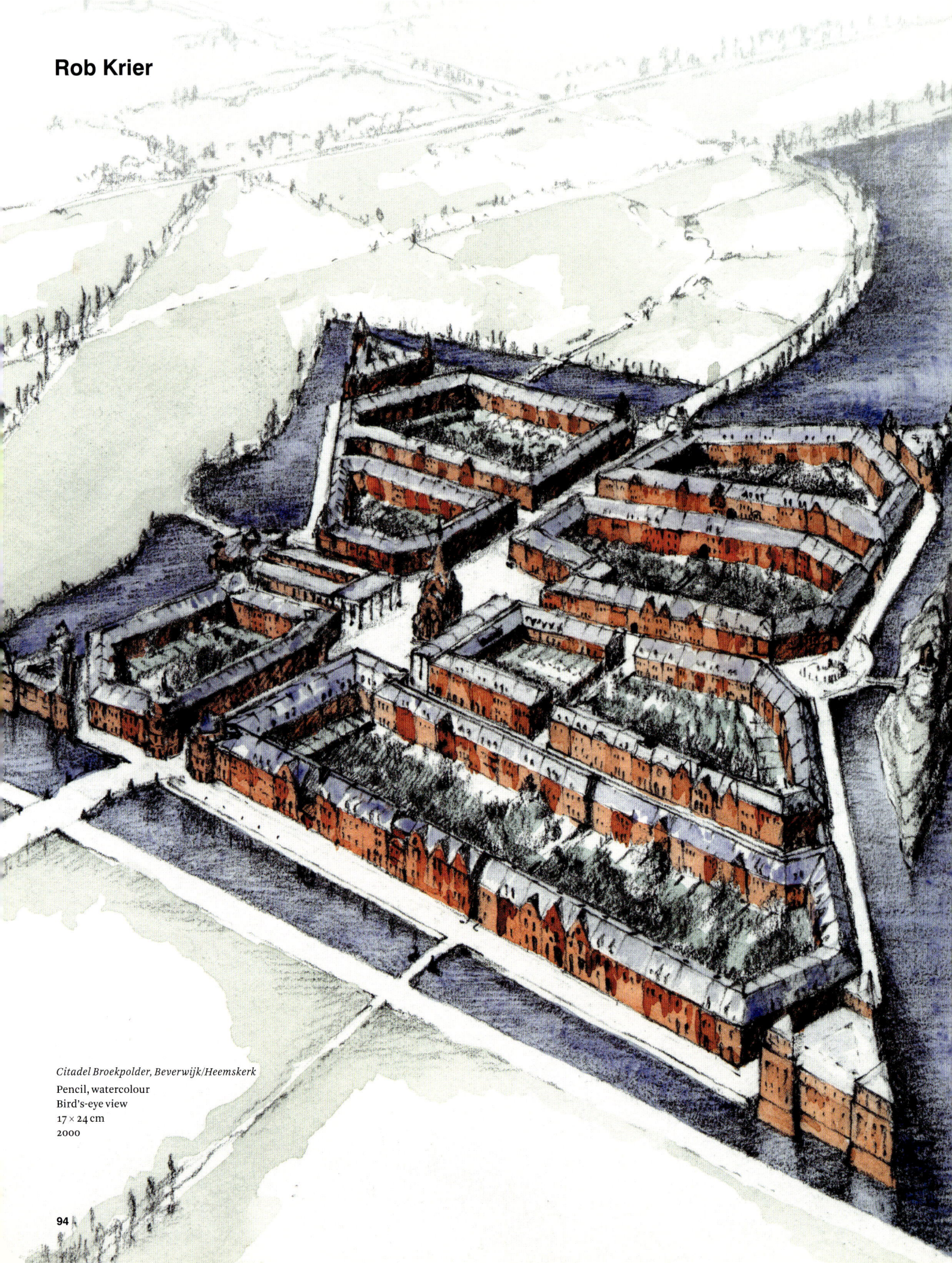

Citadel Broekpolder, Beverwijk/Heemskerk
Pencil, watercolour
Bird's-eye view
17 × 24 cm
2000

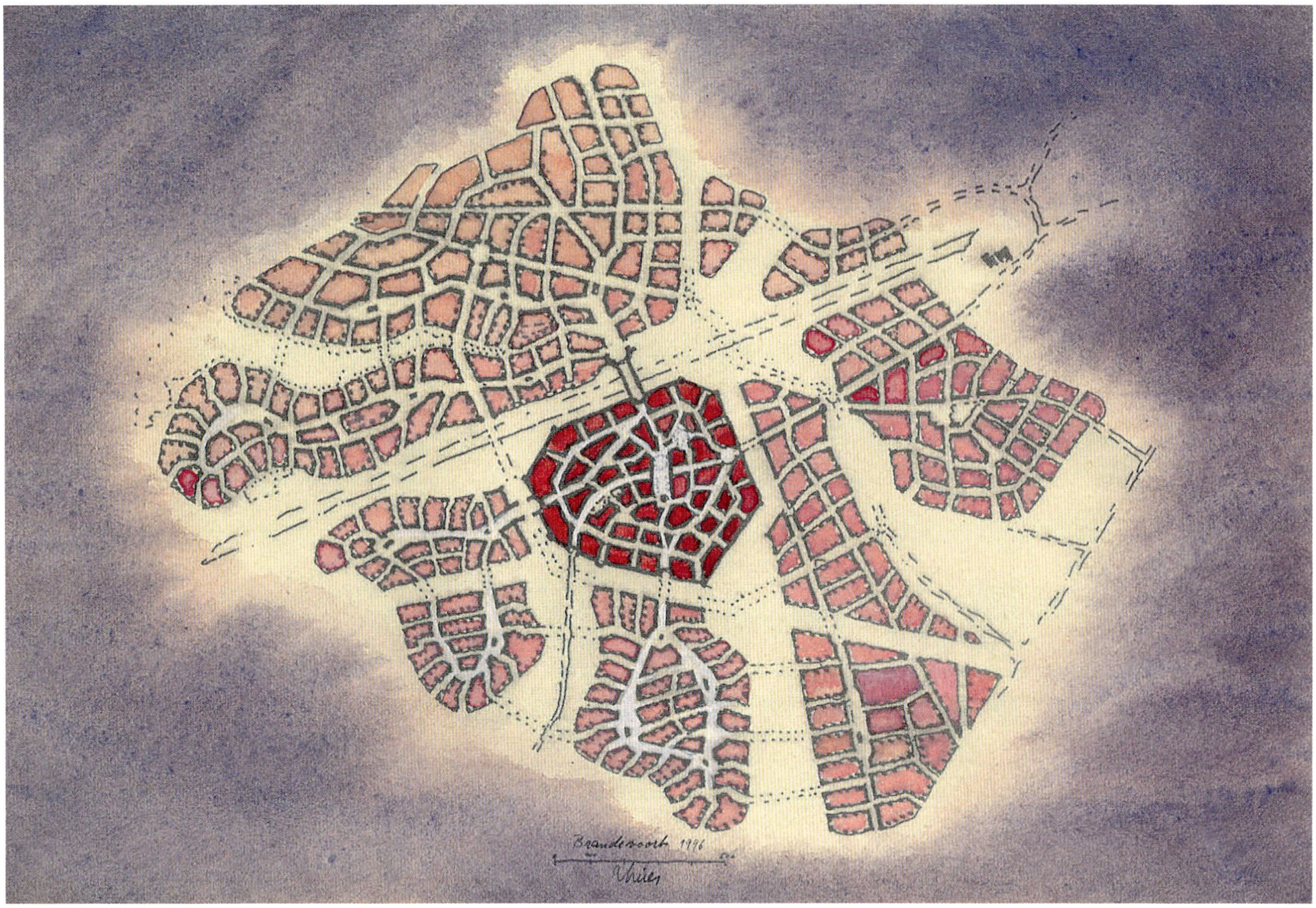

Site plan with centre and suburbs, Brandevoort, Helmond
Indian ink and pastels
Planimetric projection
84 × 59 cm
1996

Main pedestrian and cycle paths, Brandevoort, Helmond
Indian ink and pastels
Planimetric projection
30 × 21 cm
1996

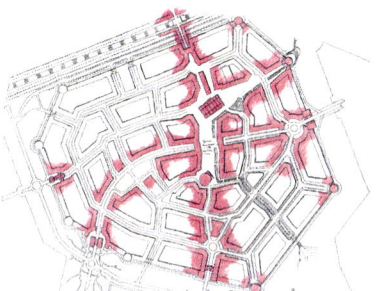

Cardo-Decumanus-System, Brandevoort, Helmond
Indian ink and crayon
Planimetric projection
30 × 21 cm
1996

Rob Krier
Born Luxembourg, 1938. Studied architecture in Munich and worked with O.M. Ungers and Frei Otto. Professor at the Vienna University of Technology from 1976 to 1998 and visiting professor at Yale University, New Haven in 1986. Established an office in Vienna in 1976 and relocated to Berlin in 1993 after the planning design for the Kirchsteigfeld project in Potsdam was awarded to his firm, since then he has operated in partnership with Christoph Kohl. Krier's main theoretical works include *Stadtraum in Theorie und Praxis*, a 1975 book dealing with the reconstruction of destroyed urban fabric and the return of traditional spatial composition to post-war urban planning. He also works as a sculptor, producing pieces mainly for public places.

Kirchsteigfeld, Potstam
Pastel on card
Bird's-eye view
21 × 21 cm
1992

Kirchsteigfeld, Potsdam
Kirchplatz, Kirchsteigfeld, Potsdam
Oil on canvas
Perspective (from top to bottom)
Kirchplatz,
Am Rondell
Torplatz
View towards the church
Hufeisenplatz
Hufeisenplatz mit Rondell
60 × 50 cm
1997

Wolf D. Prix

Photo: Duccio Malagamba

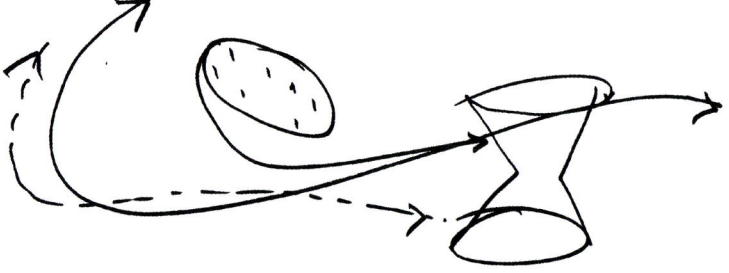

BMW Welt (BMW exhibition and event centre), Munich (2001–2007)
a. The BMW ensemble
b. The urban concept:
> the double cone as focal point, the incision in the roof
> visual connection between BMW headquarters and BMW Welt
c. The double cone – the eye of the hurricane
d. The building as passage, the bridge as connection
e. Horizontal layering

BMW Welt, Munich
Design sketch
2001

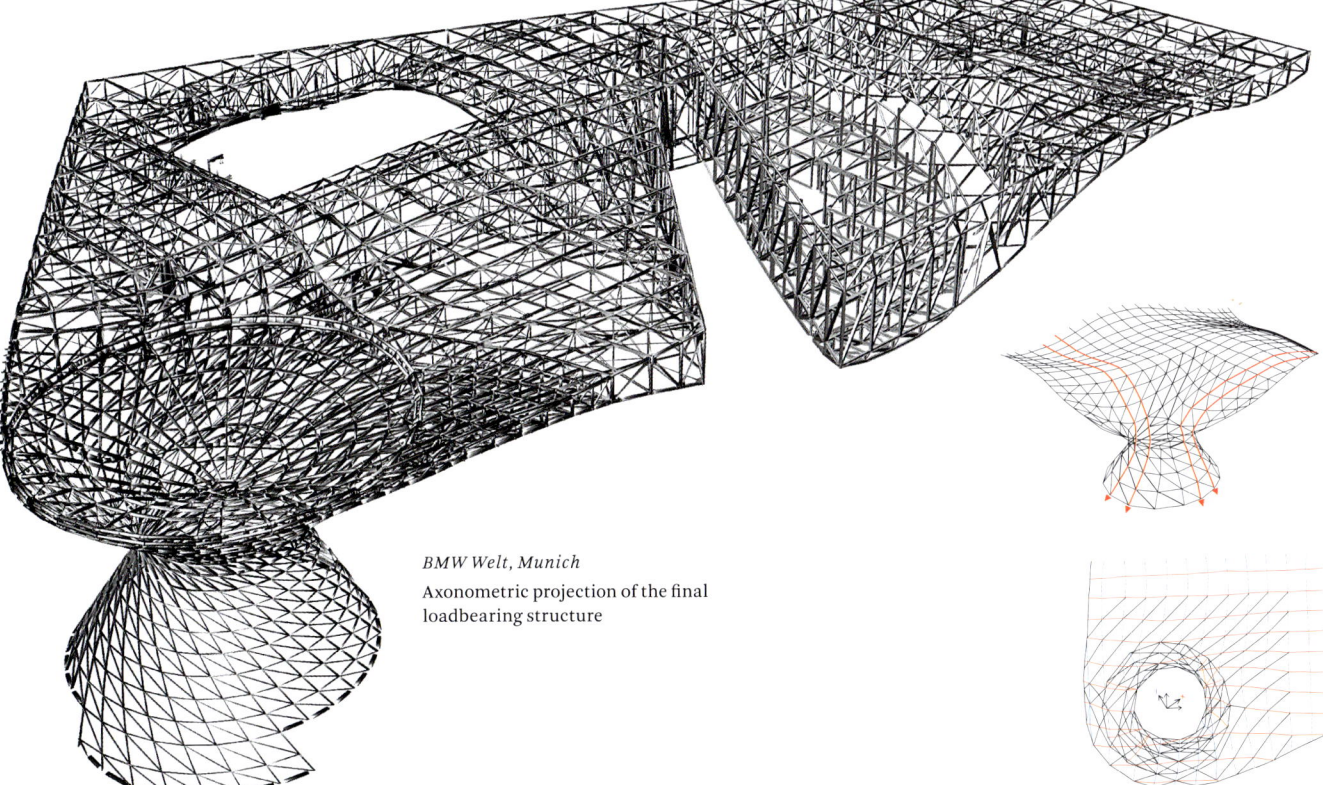

BMW Welt, Munich
Axonometric projection of the final loadbearing structure

The flow of forces from the roof into the double cone
Roof load transfer around the double cone. The cone is a loadbearing element which also provides horizontal rigidity.

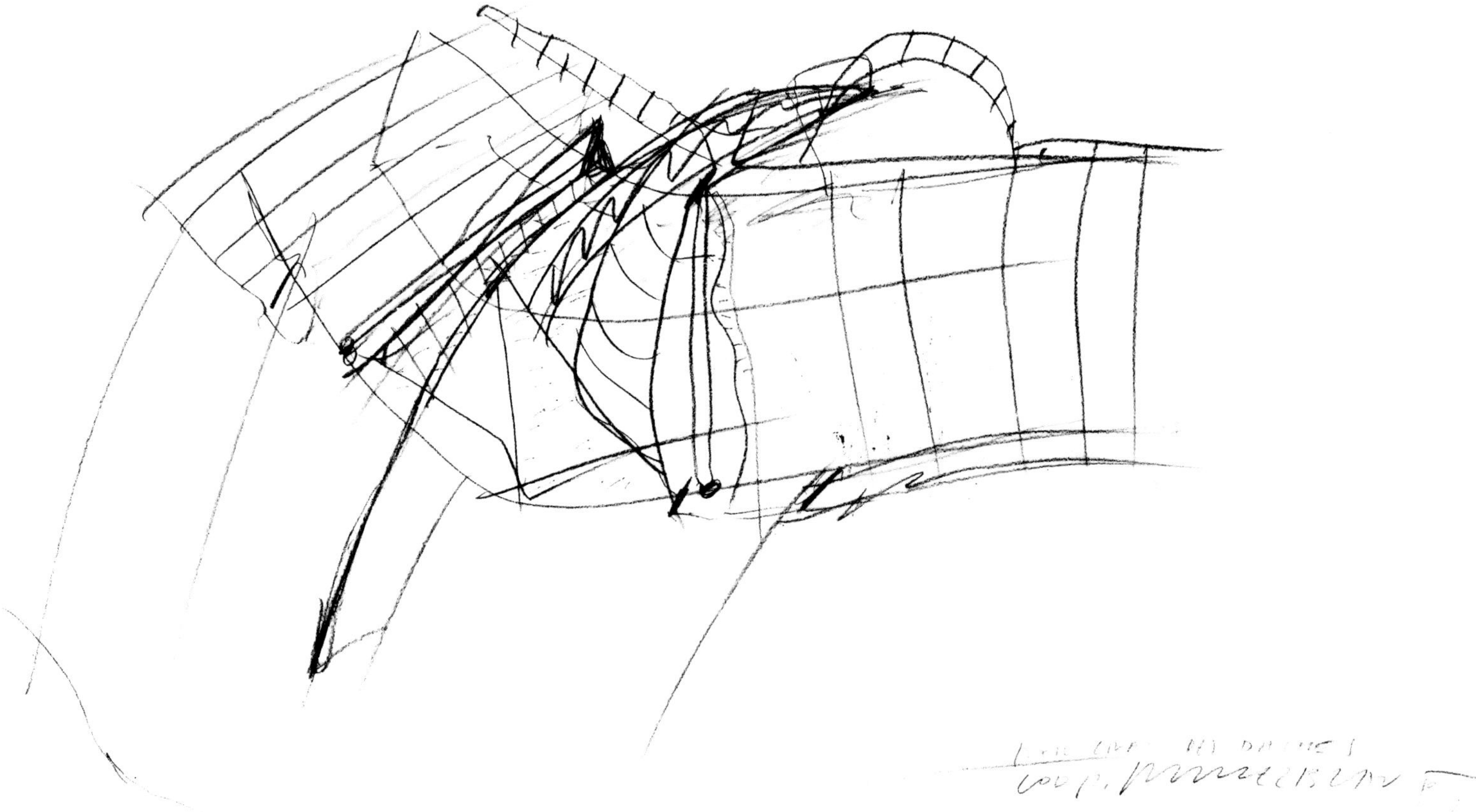

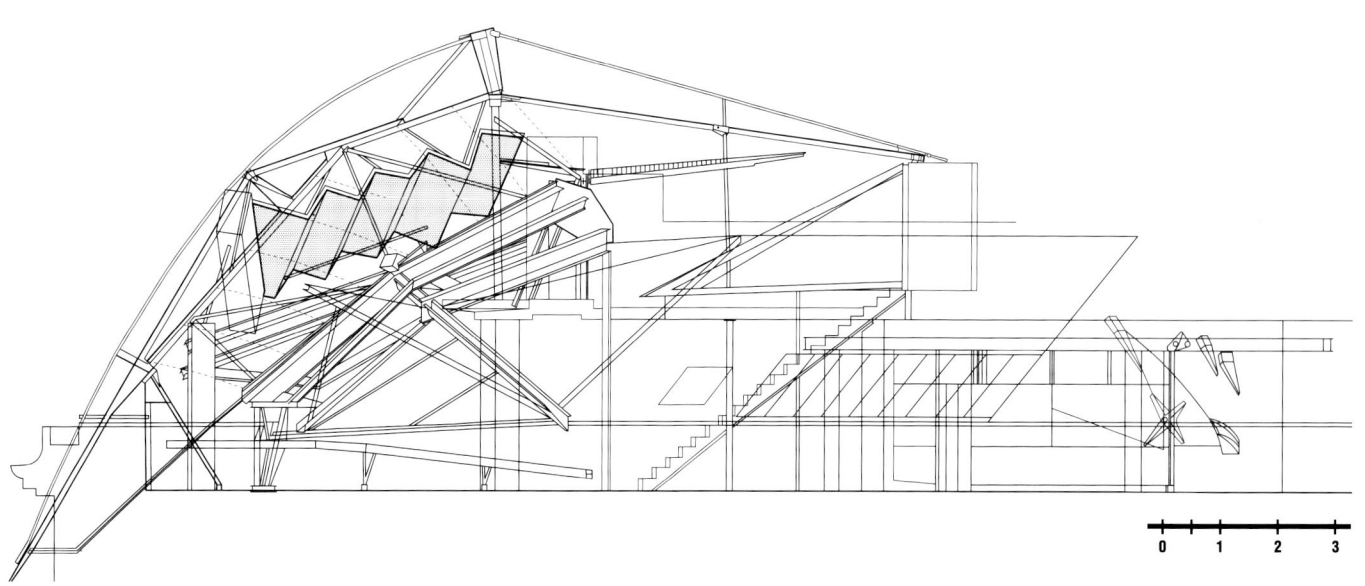

Design sketch and section

Superimposed model photo and design sketch

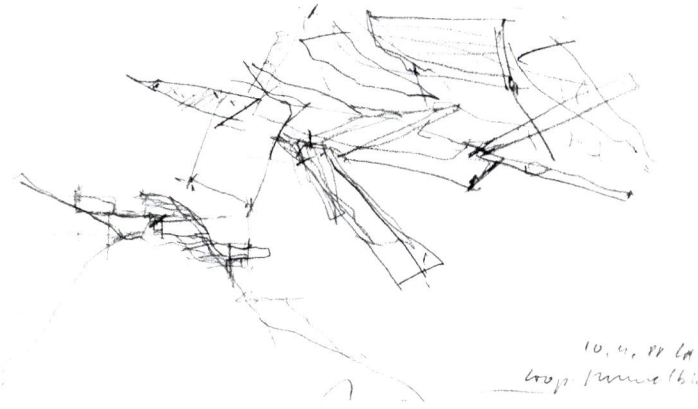

Design sketch
1988

Wolf D. Prix
Born Vienna, 1942. Studied architecture at the Architectural Association School of Architecture in London, the Vienna University of Technology and the Southern California Institute of Architecture in Los Angeles, CA. Co-founder of COOP HIMMELB(L)AU. Appointed Professor of Architectural Design at the University of Applied Arts in Vienna, 1993. Director of the Institute of Architecture, head of Studio Prix and vicerector of the University of Applied Arts since 2003. Has won numerous awards, including the City of Vienna Architecture Prize in 1998, the German Architecture Prize in 1999, and the Austrian Medal of Honour for Science and Art in 2009, in recognition of his creative achievements.

Alexander Radoske

Above: Ambassador's residence, Sofia
Watercolour on paper
Perspective of the competition phase
25 × 18 cm
2005

Right: Airrail Centre, Frankfurt
Copics on paper
Perspective of competition phase, atrium design
27 × 12 cm
2005

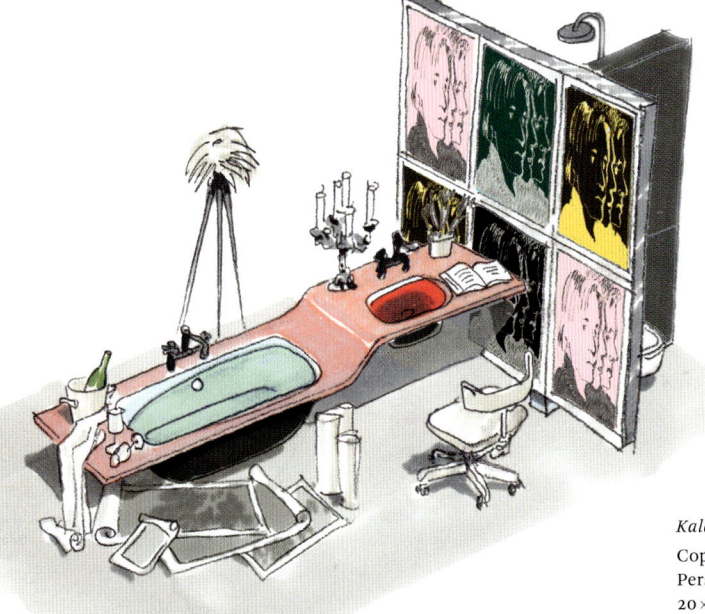

Kaldewei style icons
Copics on paper
Perspective of competition phase
20 × 17 cm
2010

Lufthansa HON Circle Lounge
Watercolour on paper
Perspective
26 × 17 cm
2003

Lufthansa First Class Terminal, Frankfurt
Watercolour on paper
Perspective of competition phase
30 × 13 cm
2003

Lufthansa First Class Terminal, Frankfurt
Watercolour on paper
Perspective of competition phase
20 × 17 cm
2003

Alexander Radoske
Born in Karaganda, Kazakhstan, 1966. Admitted to study architecture at the St. Petersburg Academy of Art, but interrupted his studies to undertake military service from 1984 to 1986. Emigrated to Germany with his family in 1989. In 1990, began additional studies at the architectural faculty of the Technical University of Darmstadt. Graduated in 1994, and worked on various projects in Germany and Russia. In 1997, he and Bernd Hollin set up a practice in Frankfurt am Main, Hollin + Radoske, specialising in structural engineering projects in Germany and international interior design. Today, it is one of the city's best-known interior design firms.

Christoph Sattler

Residential and business building, Leipziger Platz 8, Berlin
Pencil on paper
Perspective
2000

Leipziger Platz Karree, Berlin
Pencil on paper
Perspective and detail
2002

Ritz-Carlton, Berlin
Pencil on paper
Perspective
2000

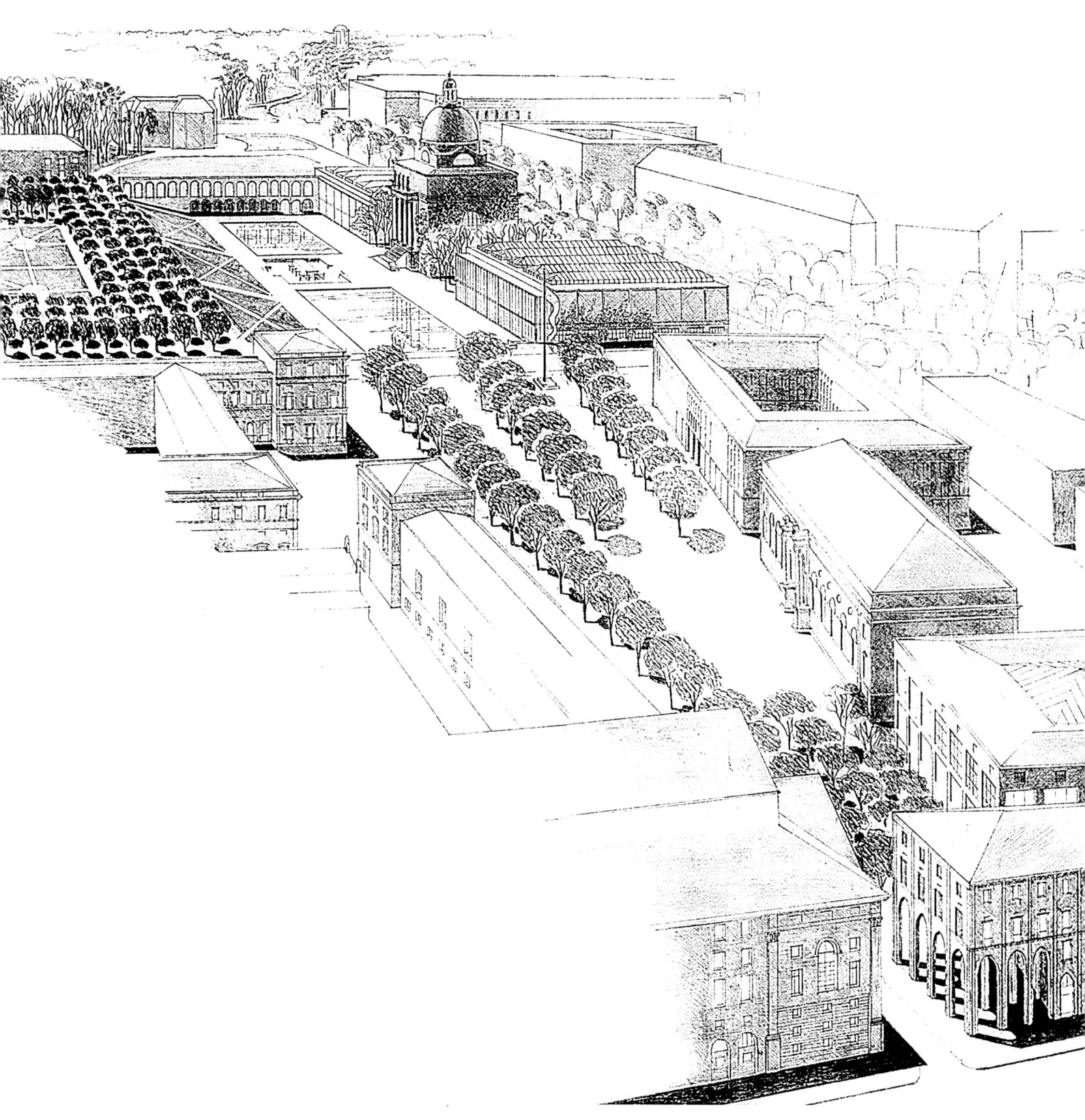

Hofgartenareal, Munich
Pencil on paper
Marstallplatz looking towards the Hofgarten
1986

Reconstruction of the Kulturforum, Berlin
Felt tip with oil pastels
2009

Christoph Sattler
Born Munich, 1938. Studied first at the Technical University of Munich from 1957 to 1963, and then at the Illinois Institute of Technology in Chicago, where he gained a Masters in science. His teachers included Myron Goldsmith and Ludwig Hilberseimer. In 1964, he worked for the Chicago firm of Ludwig Mies van der Rohe. In 1968, Sattler founded the firm of Hilmer & Sattler with his fellow student and friend Heinz Hilmer. Two other partners have since joined: Thomas Albrecht in 1994, and Rita Ahlers in 2010. The firm's most important architectural projects have included a house for the philosopher Jürgen Habermas, the restoration of the old town in Karlsruhe, the Gemäldegalerie in Berlin, the masterplan for Potsdamer Platz and Leipziger Platz in Berlin, and the Lenbach Gärten in Munich.

Sergei Tchoban

Left: CityQuartier DomAquarée, Berlin
Felt tip on tracing paper
Perspective
33 × 45 cm
2000

Right: CityQuartier DomAquarée, Berlin
Felt tip and crayon on tracing paper
Perspective
21 × 30 cm
2000

Below: CityQuartier DomAquarée, Berlin
Felt tip and crayon on tracing paper
Perspective
29 × 21 cm
2000

Far right: World Trade Center, Dresden
Crayon on paper
36 × 48 cm
1992

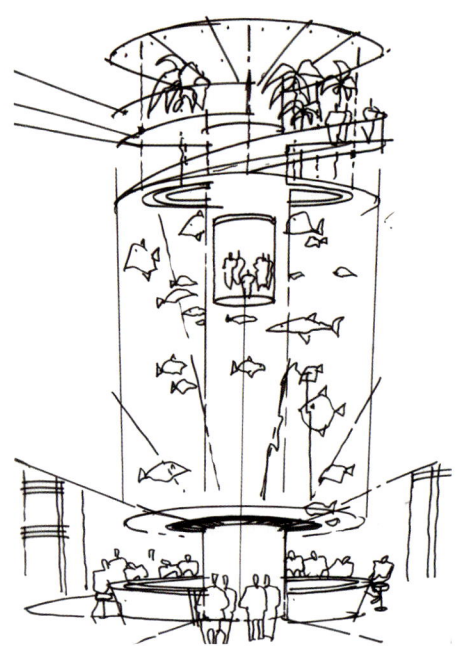

Top: Building on the Spree 1, Berlin
Charcoal on paper
42 × 30 cm
2003

Bottom: Building on the Spree 2, Berlin
Charcoal on paper
43 × 31 cm
2003

Right: Evolution of the Form 2
Charcoal on paper
Perspective
40 × 60 cm
2010

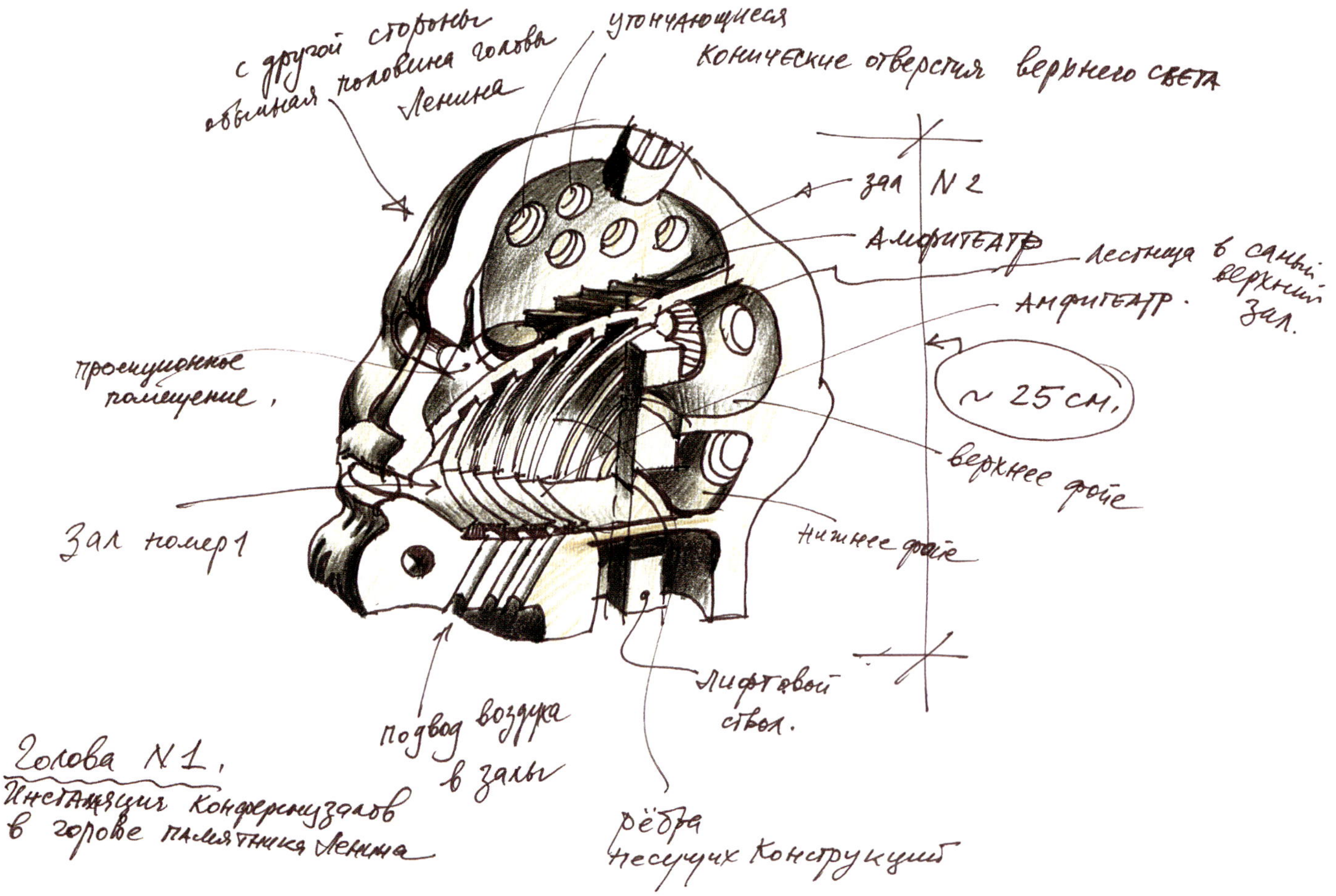

Expansion of conference halls in the head of a statue of Lenin
Felt tip and crayon on paper
Idea sketch
29 × 21 cm
2003

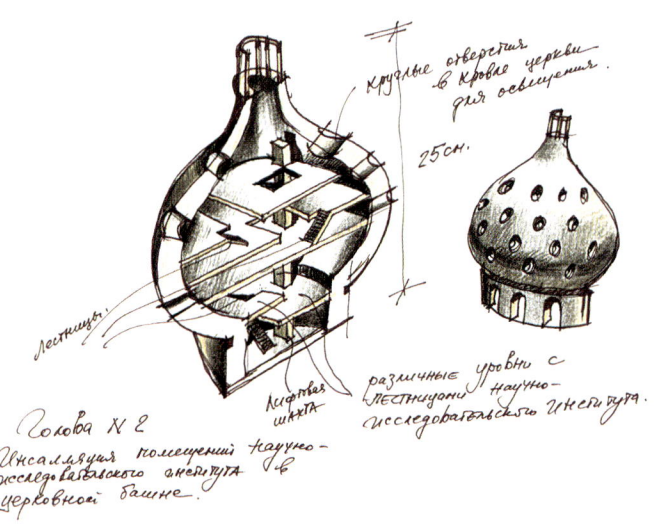

Construction of a research institute in a church tower
Felt tip and crayon on paper
Idea sketch
29 × 21 cm
2003

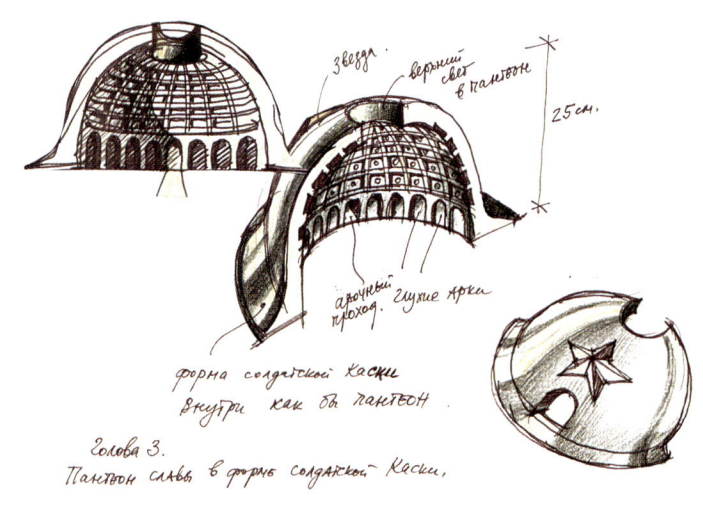

Memorial in the form of a soldier's helmet
Felt tip and crayon on paper
Idea sketch
29 × 21 cm
2003

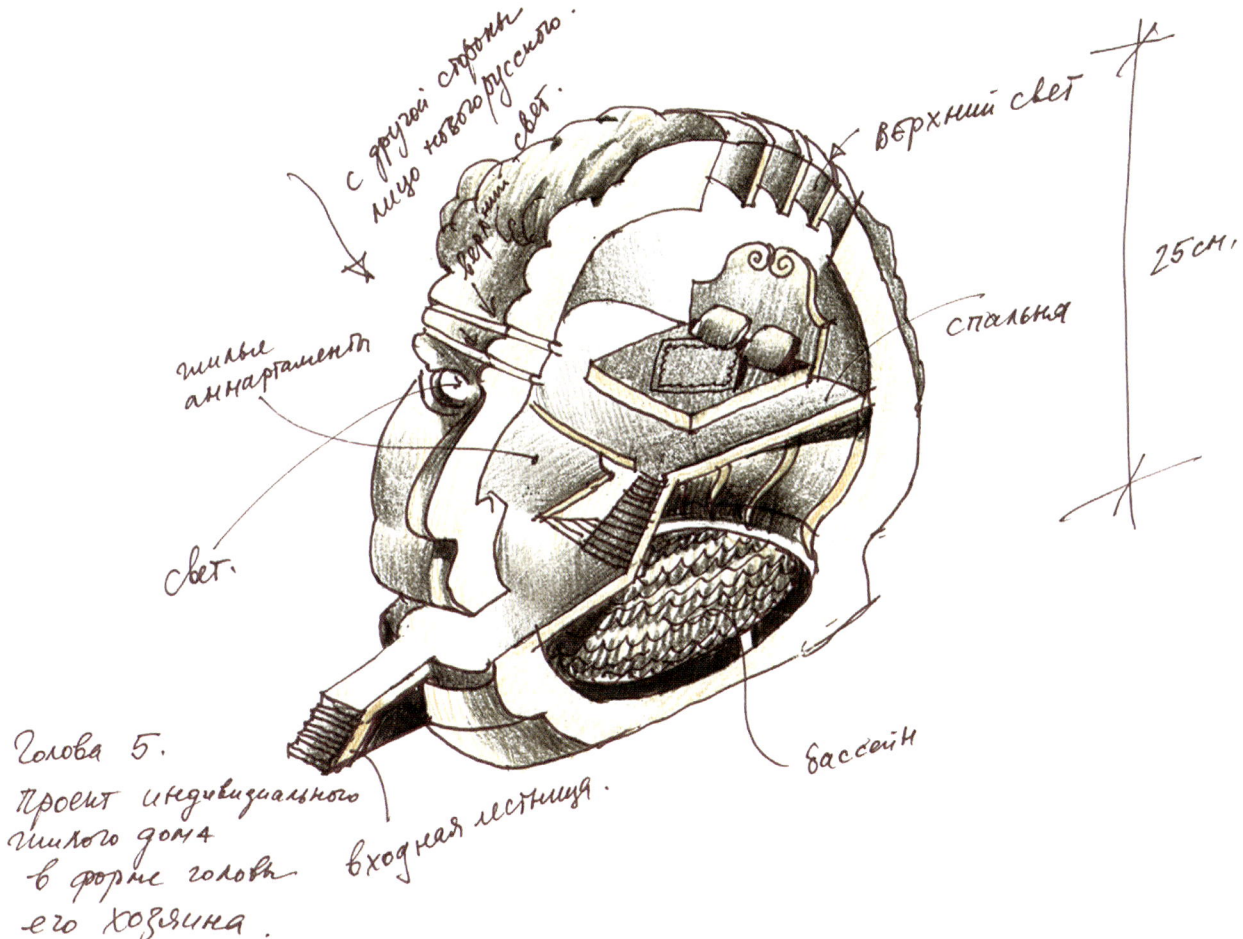

New Russian – Client's head villa
Indian ink and crayon on paper
Idea sketch
29 × 21 cm
2003

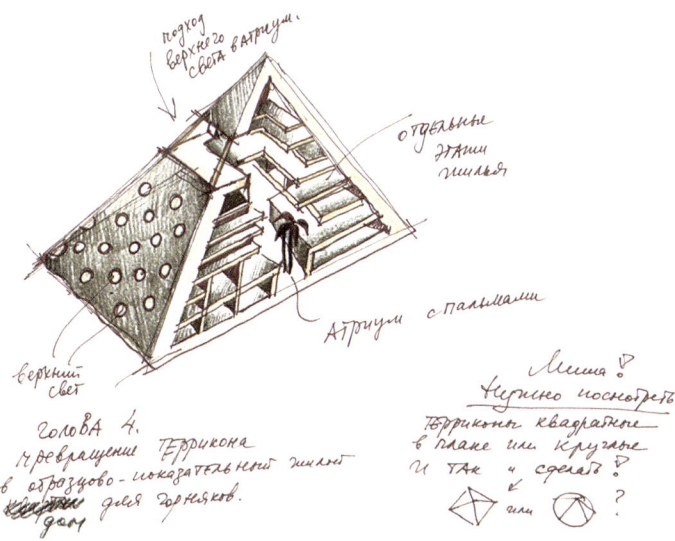

Conversion of a landfill site in an ideal house for miners
Felt tip and crayon on paper
Idea sketch
29 × 21 cm
2003

Sergei Tchoban

Born St Petersburg, 1962. Studied architecture at the St Petersburg Academy of Art. Worked as a freelance architect in Russia from 1989 onwards, and settled in Hamburg after taking part in an exhibition in 1992. Here, he joined nps Architekten, where he became managing partner in 1995. Tchoban has headed the Berlin office of nps tchoban voss since 1996, and in 2004 founded tchoban & partners in St Petersburg and SPeeCH Tchoban/Kuznetsov in Moscow. He has worked on a wide range of finished projects, including offices, shops, hotels, and residential and government buildings.

» **Architecture is a science arising out of many other sciences, and adorned with much and varied learning; by the help of which a judgment is formed of those works which are the result of other arts.«**

Marcus Vitruvius Pollio

Technical Drawing

119	**An Introduction to Technical Drawing**
	Natascha Meuser
121	**Working Tools**
122	Analogue Drawing Tools
129	Digital Drawing Tools
133	**Basics**
133	Standards
134	Paper and Drawing Sheets
135	Drawing Sheet Sizes and Sheet Folding
136	Headers
138	Drawing Sheets
140	Drawing Scales
142	Line Types and Line Widths
144	Dimensions of Architectural Drawings
146	Labelling Architectural Drawings
148	Shading
150	Stairs
152	Doors and Windows
154	Recesses
156	Roofs
158	Symbols
160	**Architectural Drawings in Practice**
160	Types of Architectural Drawings

GDR engineers at drawing boards
Source: German Federal Archives (image 183-70282-0001)

An Introduction to Technical Drawing
Natascha Meuser

Construction projects undergo different levels of planning and phases of work in their development and implementation. Depending on the status of the project, various methods of presentation are called for. Construction projects occupy the middle ground between art and construction. In the planning and construction process, various skills are required to put an idea down on paper, discuss the idea with others involved in the construction about the idea and ultimately give it concrete form. This therefore involves nothing less than communication and a balancing act between utopia and reality. Only exceptional persons can master the art of combining these requirements. The first and only German Pritzker prizewinner so far, Gottfried Böhm, combines these skills being both a gifted illustrator and innovative engineer. His artistic work is repeatedly included in many exhibitions and his buildings are – albeit sometimes controversial – masterpieces of modern architecture. Hans M. Schmidt once defined Gottfried Böhm's design process as follows: 'Before architecture is built, it usually undergoes various aggregate states of intellectual and methodical thinking, visual projection, and aesthetic and mathematical realisation on paper. It is often a very complex and tedious process of an idea being spontaneously jotted down, the scale blueprint intended for the construction and the construction plan.' However, it is possible to make generalisations about what applies to Gottfried Böhm's drawings since this equally applies to the rough sketch, artistic perspective and concrete final planning. While sketches and layout drawings are aimed at visualising an idea, technical drawing tends to implement a structure. Therefore, it is no less creative but uses a standard of representation that explains its contents, crossing linguistic and cultural borders simultaneously.

Thus, by means of the drawing, the architect masters an important medium of consistent and unambiguous communication with others involved in the construction. Precise knowledge about the current rules or technical drawings (construction drawings) is also necessary for both manual and computer-aided drawing. These drawing standards issued by the Deutschen Institut für Normung (DIN – German Institute for Standardisation) include the standards and recommendations of the international standards organisation ISO.

However, despite technical evolution, the rules and fundamental knowledge for creating a legible drawing have remained unchanged. For architects, different requirements are placed on the image outlined in the various phases of a project. Drawing types can be distinguished according to the cost of production, standards set, accuracy of representations and their intended use. In the following chapters, rules and minimum requirements in individual project phases related to drawing are briefly compiled.

Working Tools

Together with language, the image evolved as a means of communication. In early cultural human history more than thirty thousand years ago, the first cave paintings portray representations of animal and hunting scenes. Later in ancient times and the Middle Ages, the first technical drawings developed with the emergence and further development of the craft – initially these were completely formless, but as the technique developed they became increasingly practical, right up to their present use as an essential tool for communication.

A technical drawing which is true to size and form plays a particularly significant role within the range of an architect's duties. It is an engaging means of expression and communication at all planning levels. The distinction between the free artistic drawing and the more restricted technical drawing is quite clearly understood. In addition to standards and rules, styles, formats, techniques and materials are also presented in this chapter. These are made available to the illustrator, allowing them to discover and use individual display options. For centuries, traditional drawing tools used for this purpose remained virtually unchanged: charcoal, chalk, pastel chalk, oil chalk, pencil, crayon, brush and ink etc. The aforementioned appliances are not used nowadays on *graphics tablets*, which almost authentically implement the digital visual experience and open up new, slick worlds of symbols to the architect. Despite analogous, digital drawing instruments, a good illustrator still needs in-depth knowledge and must be fully aware of display techniques as well as numerous rules and standards.

Wherewith, by what means and where to draw
Drawing tables should be able to be adjusted in height and inclination so that working in both a sitting and standing position is possible. In turn, the size of drawing boards is matched to the sheet format. T-squares are available as lockable plastic rails or T-rails. The guide rail (a) is used to draw parallel lines. In order to create lines at a specific angle, set squares (b) with different angles are employed. Set squares are available in two designs: triangles with 90°/60°/30° angles and triangles with 90°/45°/45° angles. All angles can be drawn at intervals of 15° using these set squares and their combinations.

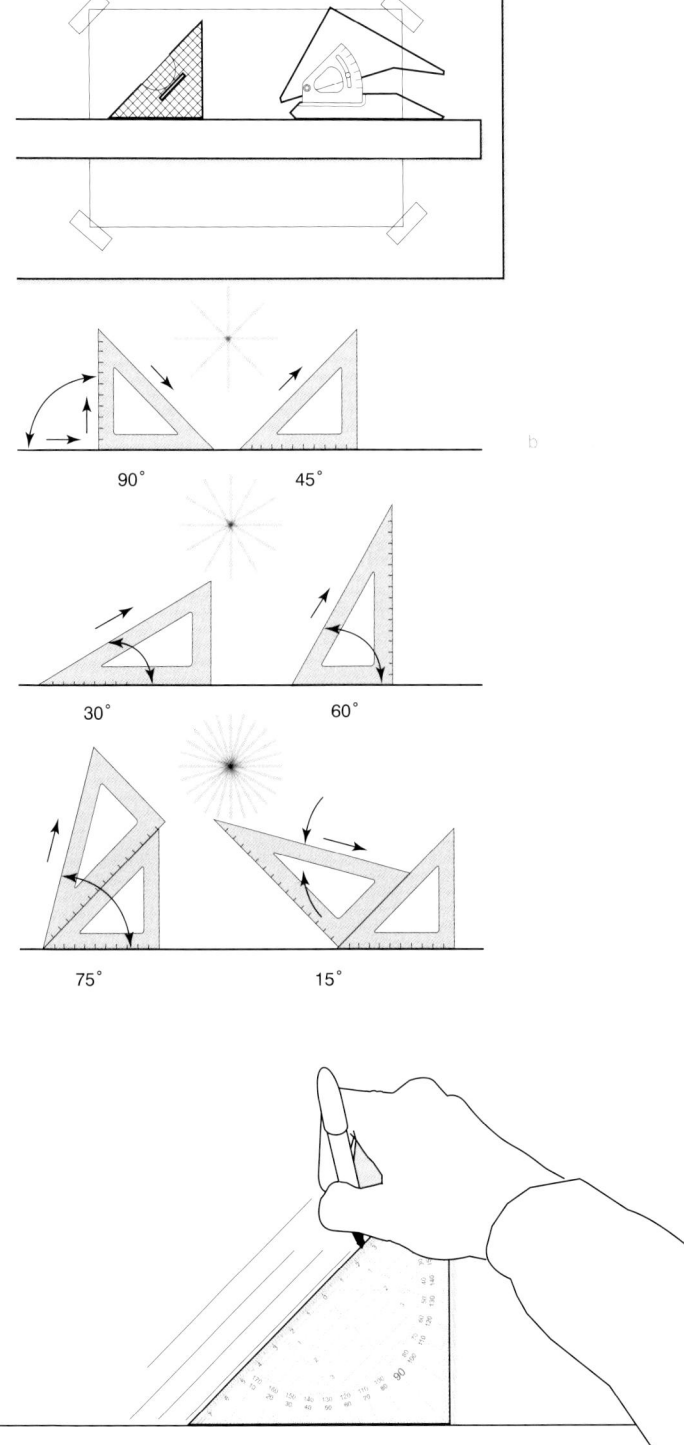

Analogue Drawing Tools

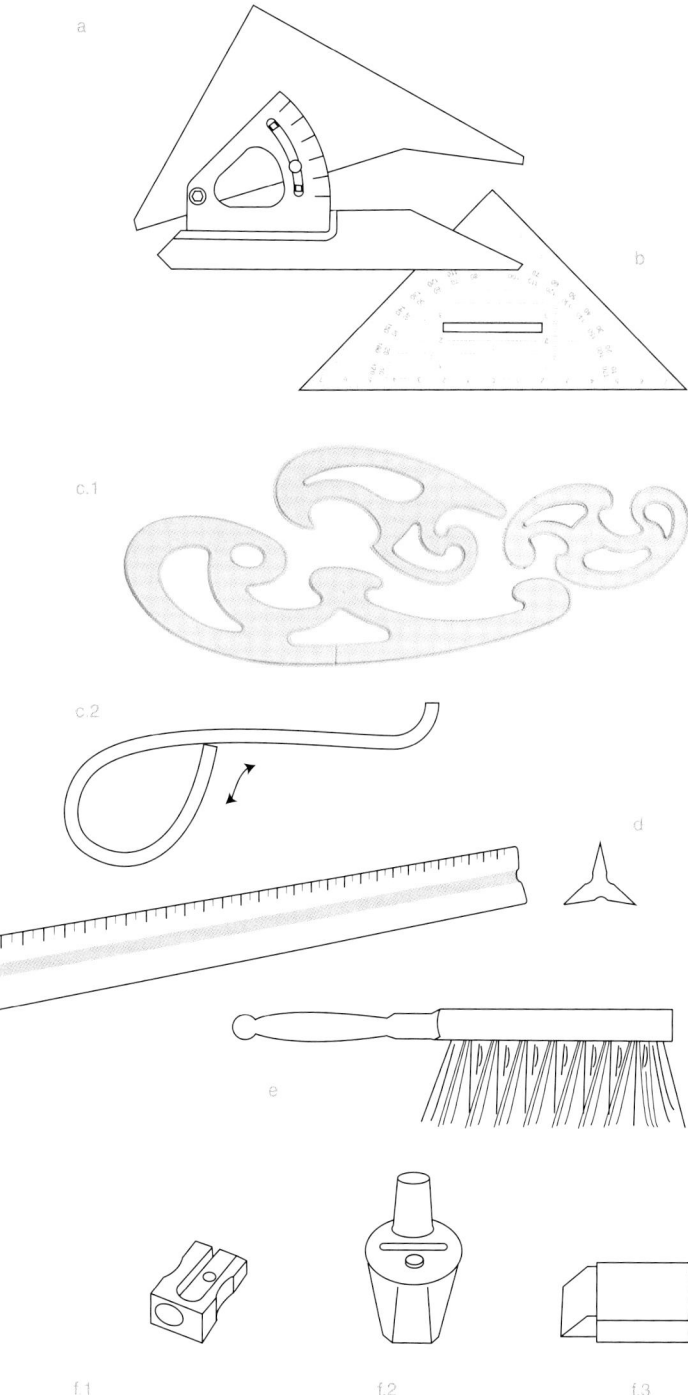

Speed square, adjustable
(a) Adjustable speed squares can be used on any drawing board or work surface. The high accuracy of the angle setting enables precise drawings at given angles.

Geometry set square
(b) The right-angled, isosceles geometry set square is available in a variety of sizes. The triangle is a combination of ruler and protractor.

French curve
(c) Bends, curvatures, ellipses, parabolas and hyperbolas can be drawn using these curve templates. A distinction is made between flexible and rigid curve rulers. For ink drawings these templates have special edges.
(c.1) Burmester templates
(c.2) Flexible curve ruler made of plastic or rubber

Triangular scale
(d) The triangular scale, three-edged wedge or prism scale is an approximately 30 cm long ruler with six different scales. Depending on its application, there are diverse measurement combinations and units of measurement. Usually, the architect uses the following measuring units:
Scale 1:20 / 25 / 50 / 75 / 100 / 125
Scale 1:100 / 200 / 250 / 300 / 400 / 500
Scale 1:75 / 125 / 150 / 200 / 250 / 500

Dusting brush
(e) The dusting brush is an indispensable device for creating technical drawings using pencil. The brush should have particularly fine and soft bristles to prevent lines smudging when sweeping.

Tools for sharpening and erasing
(f.1) Pencil sharpener
(f.2) Sharpener
(f.3) When drawing with lead a soft eraser is required. Hard rubbers or eraser pencils are used for ink drawings.

Working Tools
Basics and Standards
Types of Architectural Drawings

Erasing shield
(g) Technical drawings can be corrected in a precise and reliable manner using the erasing shield. The eraser is rubbed over the area of the drawing to be altered.

Compasses
(h) The dividers are used to adjust and plot recurring measurements, while circles and arcs can be drawn in lead, ink or colour using the compass.

Axonograph and circle template
(j) The circle template and axonograph (k) are both important auxiliary tools for drawing either diametric or isometric spatial representations.

Adhesive tape
(l) Beige, slightly crêped adhesive tape is used to affix paper and can be removed cleanly.

Sketchbook
Sketchbooks are available in a complete range of sizes and paper qualities. The sketchbook is a loyal companion when designing, travelling or simply for capturing thoughts and fleeting snapshots.

Sketching paper
(m) White and natural white sketching paper with matte or rough surface is available in all popular formats, as both blocks and sheets. When the weight of the paper is between 80 to 250 g/m² it provides an ideal canvas for different uses. Good light transmission makes tracing paper extremely versatile. The thin tracing paper roll (40 to 60 g/m²) is a patient repository of drawings and ideas, especially in the case of rapid designs and scribbles. The paper can be overlaid over and over again to allow for tracing. A further advantage of this stable but light material is that it can be used as a protective sheet for artwork and photographs. The paper lends itself to working with charcoal, graphite or coloured pencils, ink and watercolours.

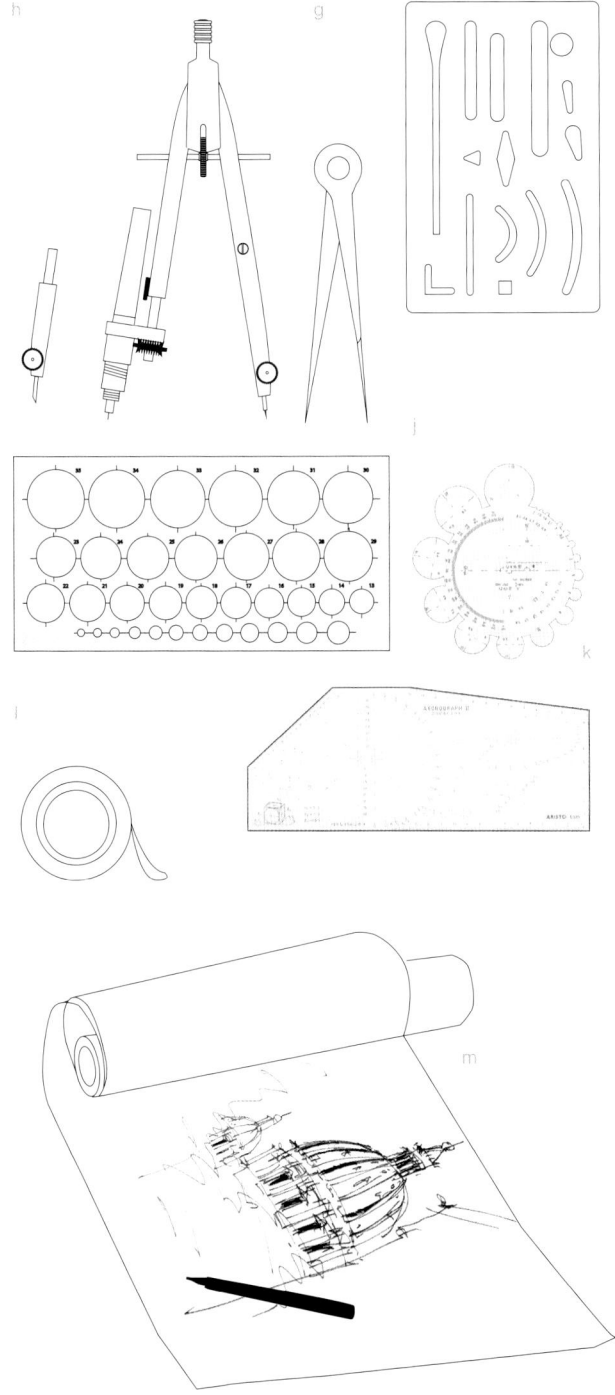

Analogue Drawing Tools

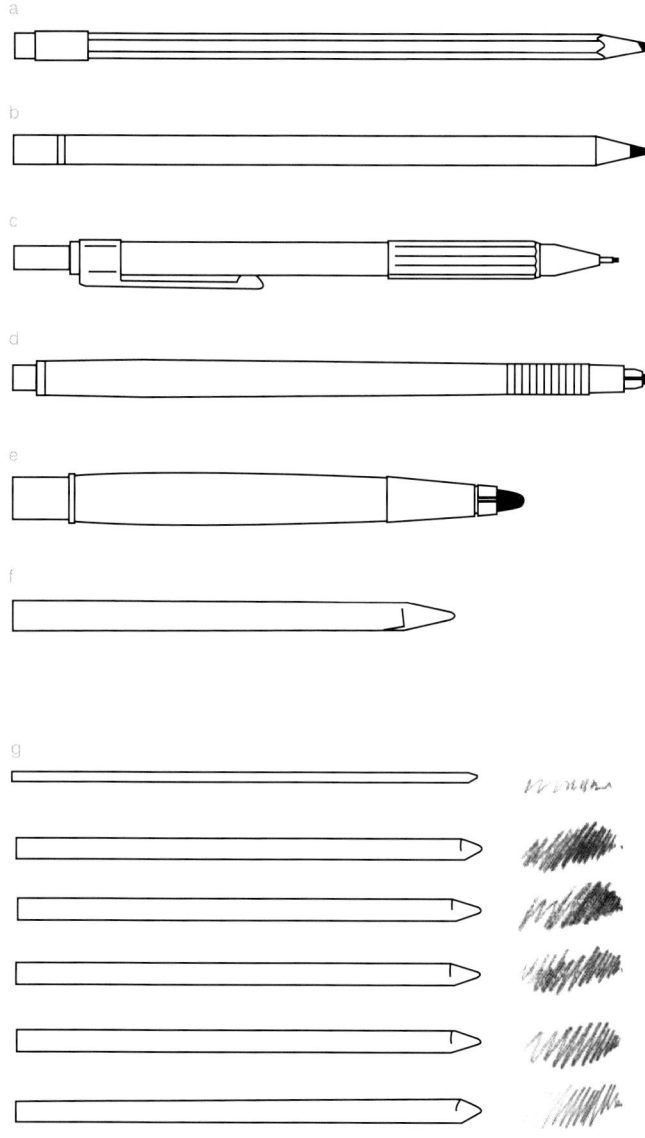

Wooden drawing pencils
Wooden drawing pencils are mostly hexagonal, sit well in the hand and do not roll away. A good pencil is one that can be sharpened correctly, draws an even line that can be rubbed out and whose lead is highly resistant to snapping. Harder lead pencils are suited for sketching and rough paper. However, softer pencil leads are selected for smoother paper and tracing.

Leads are produced in various degrees of hardness and are distinguished by the letters B, F or H. The degree of hardness is specified in accordance with English denominations – from soft to hard – by the abbreviations B (black), HB (hard-black), F (firm) and H (hard), with B and H additionally classified by the numbers 2 to 9 (the higher the number, the softer or harder the lead).

Mechanical pencils
Mechanical pencils are retractable pencils that contain a bundle of leads which are available in the most common thicknesses between 0.2 mm and 1.18 mm. The lead is held in place by a small clamp with prongs. Pencils with harder leads (2H and H) are predominantly used for sketching and shading, whereas softer leads (F, HB and B) are mainly used for tracing.

Clutch pencils
In contrast to mechanical pencils, clutch pencils use normal lead which is also held in place by a small clamp with prongs. The clutch pencil is available as a leadholder for interchangeable leads with a thickness between 2 mm to 5.6 mm. The hardness of the lead should be selected individually depending on the various kinds of lines and quality of the paper.

Full lead graphite pencils
The term *full lead pencil* is used to describe graphite crayon in the shape of a pencil. This is a full lead pencil without the wood casing. The pencil has a varnished surface to protect hands from contamination. When drawing, pressing lightly or firmly can produce widely varying grey tones – ideal for high-contrast drawing, writing and sketching.

a   Wooden drawing pencil
b   Graphite or charcoal pencil
c   Retractable pencil/mechanical pencil
d   TK clutch pencil
e   Leadholder
f   Full lead graphite pencil
g   Leads in varying hardnesses

Working Tools
Basics and Standards
Types of Architectural Drawings

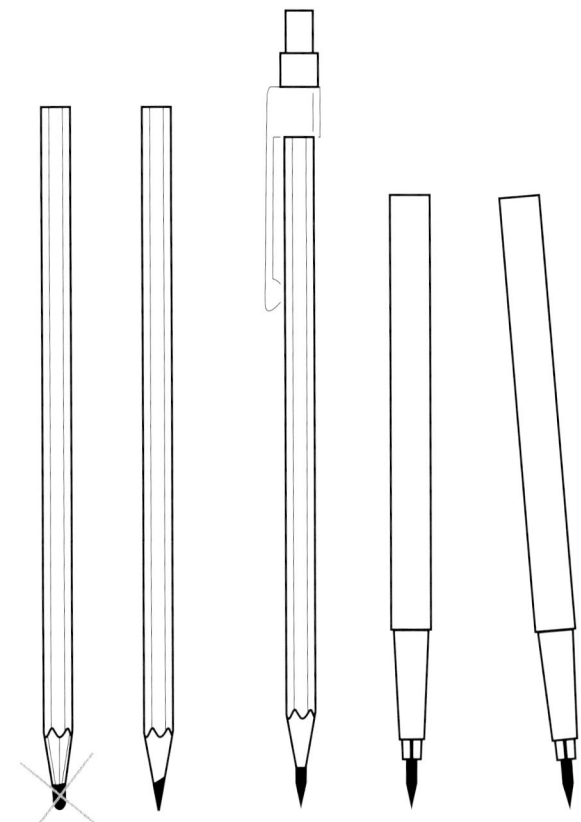

Handling drawing tools

In the case of rapid sketching, the pen (h) lies loosely between the thumb, index and middle figure and ends in the palm of the hand. The drawing tool is guided by the wrist until the whole arm – which is not propped up – is involved.

Drawing tools such as charcoal, pastel or red chalk (j) for coarser strokes and shadings are held between the thumb and four remaining fingers.

Similar to when writing, quills, fine pencils and brushes (k) are only held between the thumb, index and middle finger. 2H or 3H leads are suited for drawings on tracing paper, whereas H, F or HB leads are more suited for use on drawing paper or drawing boards.

Well-sharpened pencils are essential to drawing with pencil. The guidance of the pencil must also be taken into consideration.

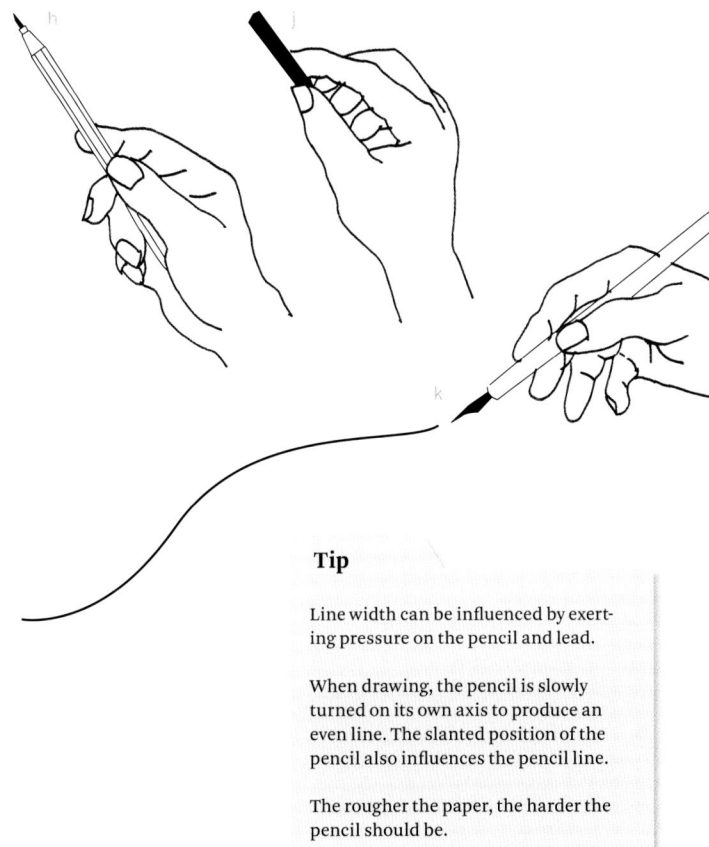

EU	USA	RUS	Pencil Grades	Use
9H	–	–	adamantine	
8H	–	–	steel-hard	
7H	–	–	rock-hard	for specific purposes
6H	–	–	rugged	
5H	–	–	extremely hard	
4H	–	–	particularly hard	
3H	–	–	very hard	for technical drawings and details
2H	#4	2T	harder	
H	#3	T	hard	
F	#2.5	–	medium soft	for technical drawings
HB	#2	TM	medium soft + black	
B	#1	M	soft + black	for writing and drawing
2B	–	–	soft + very black	
3B	–	–	very soft + very black	for freehand drawing and writing (limited)
4B	–	–	very soft + black	
5B	–	–	particularly soft + black	
6B	–	–	extraordinarily soft + black	
7B	–	–	exceptionally soft + deep black	for artistic sketch-like drawings and designs
8B	–	–	velvety + deep black	
	–	–	extremely soft + deep black	

Tip

Line width can be influenced by exerting pressure on the pencil and lead.

When drawing, the pencil is slowly turned on its own axis to produce an even line. The slanted position of the pencil also influences the pencil line.

The rougher the paper, the harder the pencil should be.

Analogue Drawing Tools

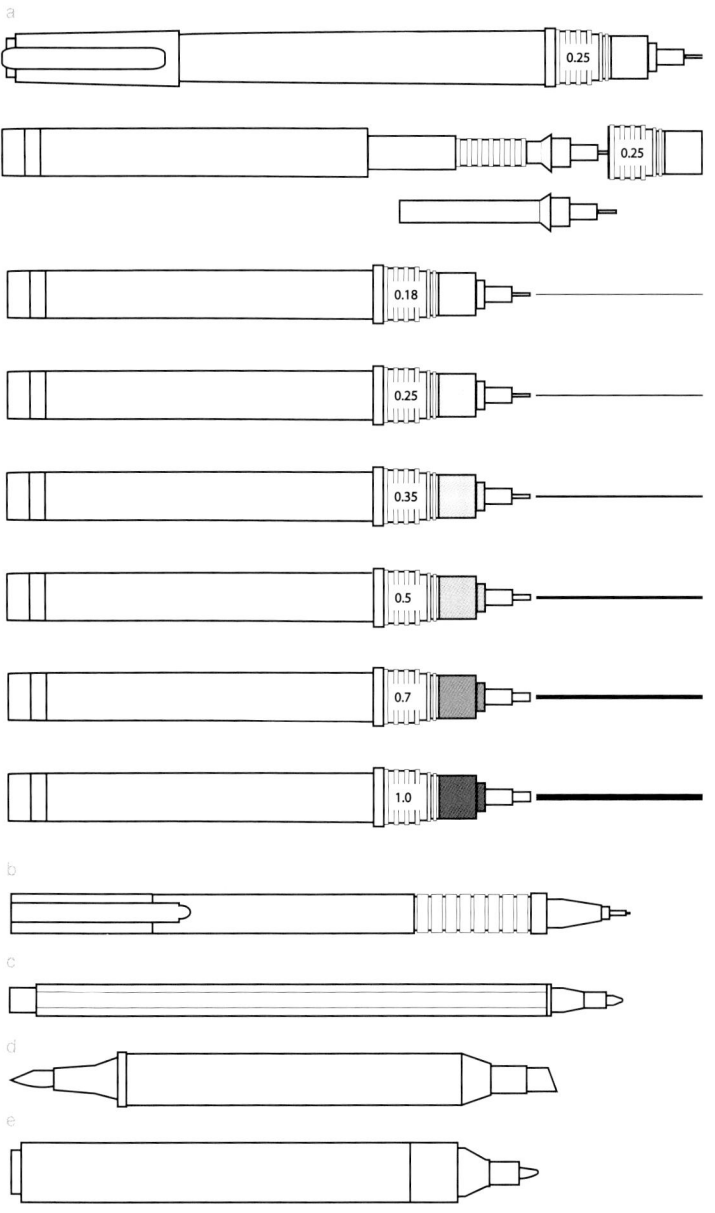

Following the rapid growth of digital drawing tools in recent years – with the result that, in the case of renderings, it is difficult to distinguish between reality and design – a combination of digital and analogue presentation drawings is increasingly asserting itself. This also meets the architect's demands to assert their individuality. The pens and markers described below are not erasable tools but guarantee a clean and well-protected drawing over an extended period of time.

Similar to pencil drawings, strokes also determine the style of the drawing when using a felt-tip. This can easily be coloured later on. If the drawing is scanned, the lines and areas can be filled out and coloured digitally (post-production).

Ballpoint and felt-tips
Ballpoint pens are suited for rapid sketches and drawings since they do not dry up and easily fit into any pocket without leaking. With felt-tips it should always be checked whether they bleed through paper or spread on it. Felt-tips also have softer tips and a shorter life span.

Ink and pigment pens
In order to protect preparatory drawings from fading and smudging, the lines are drawn in ink. The drawing can be reproduced as often as desired. This is achieved by *radiograph* pens which are filled with ink. These are particularly well suited for regular shading, are refillable and available in many different line thicknesses.

Markers
Shading and effects can be achieved through *rendering tools* such as markers. Layout markers are suited for free-hand drawings or the graphic elaboration of drawings. The markers are available in many variations, colours and degrees of transparency. Depending on the application and type of drawing, the pens can be used in many different ways. At the same time, a superposition of layers of colours and tonal values can be achieved.

a   Ink pen that creates lines of varying thickness
b   Pigment pen
c   Felt-tip
d   Marker with two tips
e   Permanent marker

Natascha Meuser: *Machträume* (Dreams of Power)
Illustrations for the political magazine *Cicero*
Felt-tip, digitally coloured
2004–2005

Computer workstation: modern today, outdated in a few years

Digital Drawing Tools

Digital drawings are increasingly revolutionising traditional drawing professions and are an integral part of the working world, especially in creative professions. CAD application systems for computer-assisted development, design and construction technologies play a major role here. The term *Computer Aided Design* (CAD) is understood to mean all systems, processes and technologies for computer-based development and construction. Thus, the artist no longer creates the drawing on paper in the ordinary sense, but on the screen of a special computer workstation.

Depending on the industry and use, there are plenty of CAD Programmes for the creation of technical drawings that today facilitate the creation of 2D, 3D or even 4D models of a room. A range of databases of standardised design features has been distributed mainly free of charge on the internet by companies and developers. CAD programmes allow design layouts to be created and edited. At the same time, they calculate objects, areas and volumes using a range of display options. Drawings are created, altered or documented accurately by entry. 3D models (renderings) can be displayed as wire frame models, surface models or volume models. Photo textures facilitate a realistic representation of the model. The fast and simple exchange with other planning partners simplifies the planning process.

Computer workstations
A computer workstation has both ergonomic demands on the user (see computer workstation checklist) and technical demands in the form of the customised design of the workstation. Both demands are geared towards the needs of the user. The most common tools are briefly described below. In most instances, graphical input devices such as the keyboard, mouse, digital pens, graphics tablets, 2D and 3D scanners now assume the function of the pen. Output equipment such as the screen, printer and plotter replace the function of the drawing board or drawing table. Digital drawings are presented on paper or in the form of moving images or films.

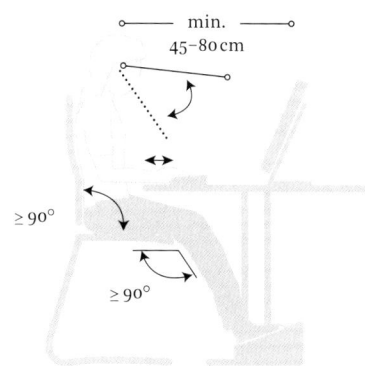

Computer workstation

Ideal lighting conditions for computer usage are obtained on the window facade facing north.

It is necessary to ensure sufficient circulation areas and areas set aside for the storage of equipment such as printers, scanners etc.

Workspaces should be naturally illuminated and ventilated.

Ideal shade and protection from glare and reflection are provided in the form of jalousies, lamellae or filter roller blinds.

Tripping hazards in the form of cable entries must be avoided. Cabling should be via wall and floor ducts.

Furniture should be flexibly height-adjustable in order to accommodate different heights.

Tables should be at least 80 cm thick and allow unrestricted legroom.

Chairs in specialist rooms with computer facilities should be adjustable in seat height between 31 cm and 51 cm.

The screen surface should be at a right angle with the window front.

The distance between individual rows of seats should be at least 100 cm – better 120 cm – so that individual workstations are well accessible between rows.

Digital Drawing Tools

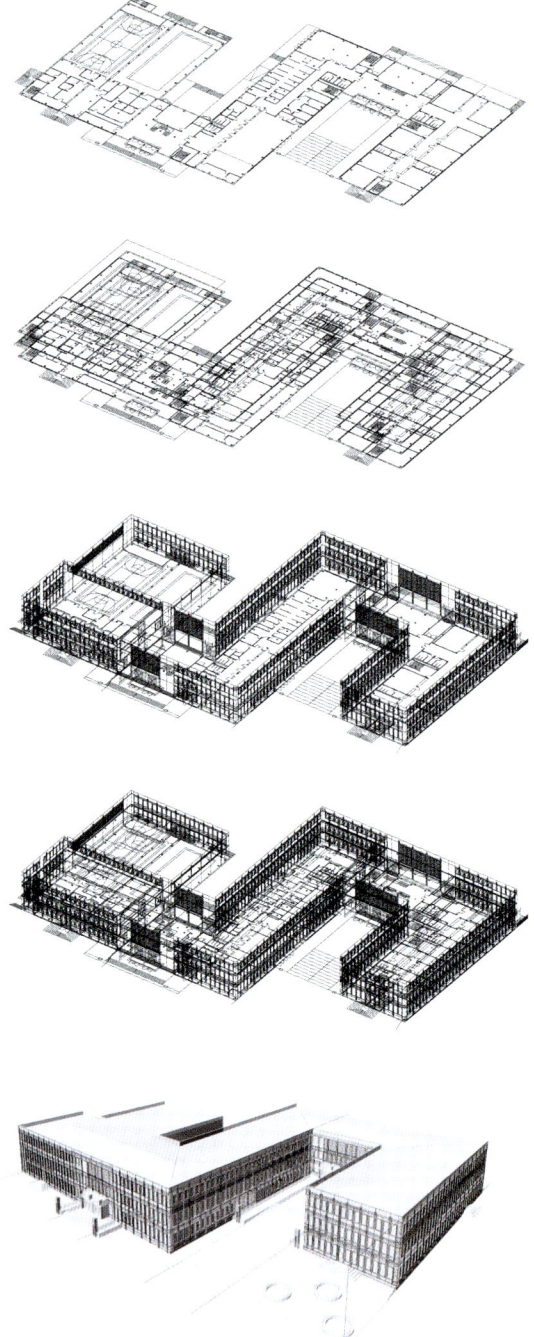

Digital drawings
A digital drawing does not significantly differ in its creation from an analogue drawing. However, its use demands different levels of technical skills and changes can be implemented more easily. Of course, digital drawings do not consist of matter but of abstract bits and bytes. Before it is printed or copied, the drawing must be stored on a hard disk. It is possible to draw with a simple mouse or on a graphics tablet. Battery-operated digital pens are no longer reliant upon electronic documents and can produce images with familiar handling in which every dot, stroke and line can be immediately saved digitally. Unrestricted usage opens up a world of new display options to the designer, which once more requires a good command of basic knowledge pertaining to portion, form and colour.

User interfaces
The graphic user interface is displayed on the screen. The digital drawing canvas is the central workspace and is bordered by various menu bars, toolbars and information pallets at both the top and lateral edge of the screen. The taskbar and start menu can be individually set and adjusted in a user-friendly manner.

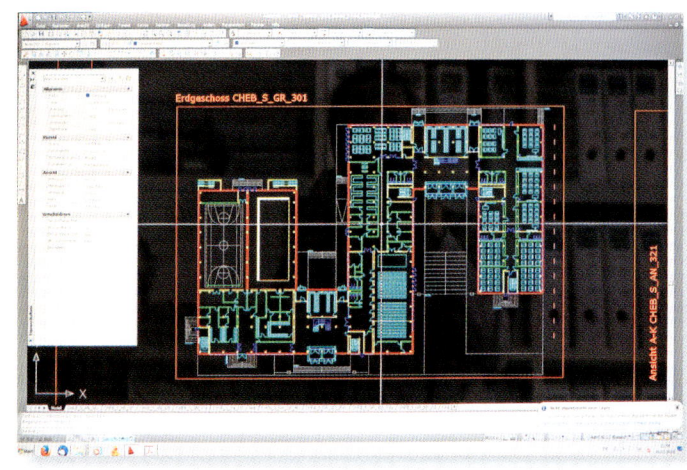

Working Tools
Basics and Standards
Types of Architectural Drawings

Drawing with a graphics tablet
Graphics tablets and digital pens offer a range of new drawing features owing to the latest graphics programmes. For example, drawing tools, surfaces and colours can be selected directly by computer. Furthermore, it is possible to experiment with numerous drawing techniques, surfaces, lines and line widths on various surfaces without having the necessary tools and drawing surfaces available. The tool has emancipated itself from its medium or pulse receiver. The drawing experiment takes place on the screen and the outcome is later presented in the printout. Plans and photos can be loaded to the programme and further graphically edited later. This provides further scope for detail and simplification depending on the size of the screen and by zooming in and out.

Yet what is the difference between drawing with a graphics tablet rather than a pen and paper? The fact is that a printout is only produced when the designer is satisfied with the result. Crumpled-up balls of sketching paper no longer end up in the wastepaper basket but are virtually destroyed with the click of a button. The vision and feeling embodied when drawing remains unchanged – only the technology and application have been modernised. A good freehand designer is also adept at using a graphics tablet and in some cases even constitutes a good architect. In this form of representation, virtuosity can only be achieved after long practice and once a basic understanding of architecture and related disciplines has been honed.

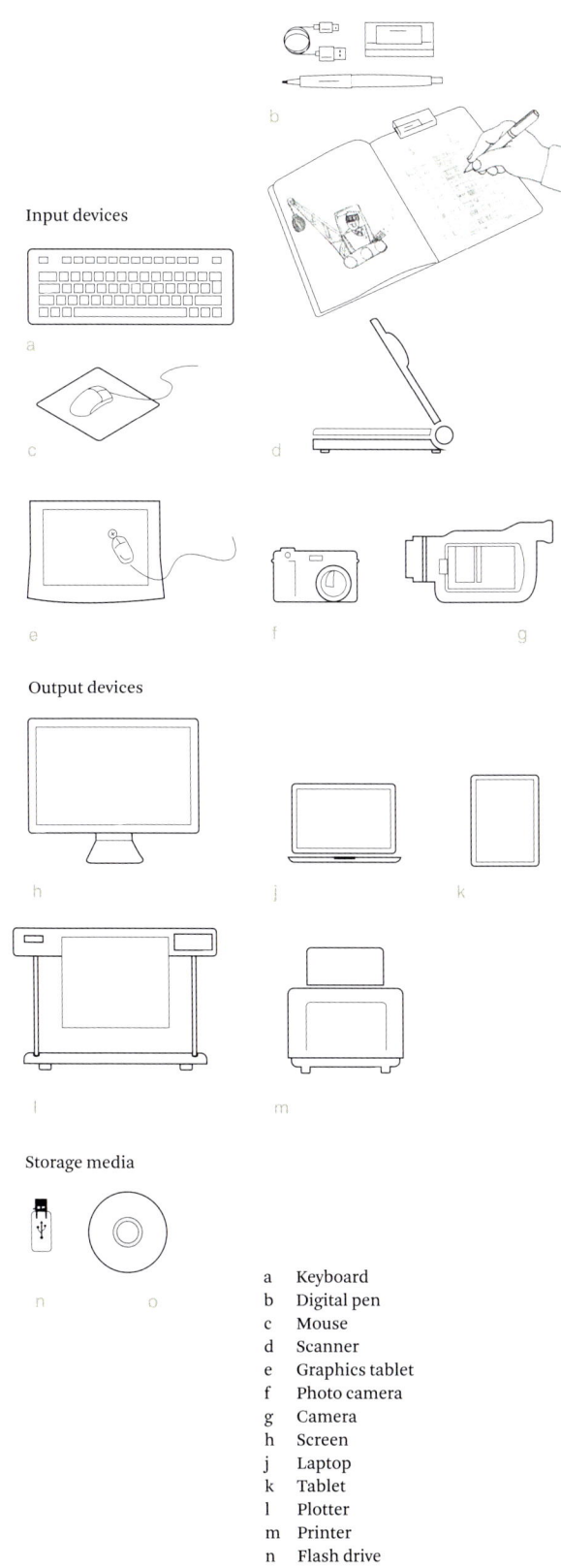

a   Keyboard
b   Digital pen
c   Mouse
d   Scanner
e   Graphics tablet
f   Photo camera
g   Camera
h   Screen
j   Laptop
k   Tablet
l   Plotter
m   Printer
n   Flash drive
o   CD-Rom

3D rendering of a church interior,
Design: Natascha Meuser (2010)

Basics

Construction terms

In light of the fact that this book was translated from German into English, images included in the text have in places been retained in their original form. For this reason, the following abbreviations and construction terms are explained below for the benefit of the reader:

B	Breite (width)
BD	Bodendurchbruch (floor opening)
BK	Bodenkanal (floor channel)
BRH	Brüstungshöhe (parapet height)
DD	Deckendurchbruch (ceiling opening)
DG	Dachgeschoss (attic)
EG	Erdgeschoss (ground floor)
FF	Fertigfußboden (finished floor)
FFB	Fertigfußboden (finished floor)
GL	Grundleitung (ground pipe)
KG	Kellergeschoss (basement)
OG	Obergeschoss (upper floor)
OK	Oberkante (upper edge)
OKBr	Oberkante Brüstung (upper edge of parapet)
OKFB	Oberkante Fußboden (finished floor level)
OKFF	Oberkante Fertigfußboden (finished floor level)
OKRD	Oberkante Rohdecke (unfinished floor level)
OKRF	Oberkante Rohfußboden (unfinished floor level)
RD	Rohdecke (unfinished floor)
RFB	Rohfußboden (unfinished floor)
RH	Rohrhülse (tubular sleeve)
Stg.	Steigungsverhältnis (rise-to-run ratio)
SW	Schmutzwasser (dirty water sewer)
T	Tiefe (depth)
UK	Unterkante (lower edge)
UKD	Unterkante Decke (lower edge of ceiling)
UKRD	Unterkante Rohdecke (lower edge of unfinished floor)
UKST	Unterkante Sturz (lower edge of lintel)
Wd	Wanddicke (wall thickness)
WD	Wanddurchbruch (wall opening)

Fertigkonstruktion	Finished floor level
Rohkonstruktion	Unfinished floor level
Sturz	Lintel

Standards

EN, ISO, BS and DIN standards are an international means of communication according to the recognised rules of technology. They provide uniformity and and serve as recommendations, considered to produce a technical effect. As early as the beginning of the twentieth century, national standards were valid. In 1926, the European Committee for Standardisation (CEN) and the International Organisation for Standardisation (ISO) were established, whose worldwide members adopt collectively developed standards largely as national standards. There is no obligation to adopt.

ANSI Standards	American National Standards Institute
BS Standards	British Standards Institute
DIN Standards	German Institute for Standardisation
GOST Standards	Euro-Asian Council for Standardisation, Metrology and Certification (EASC)
EN Standards	European standards
ISO Standards	International standards

 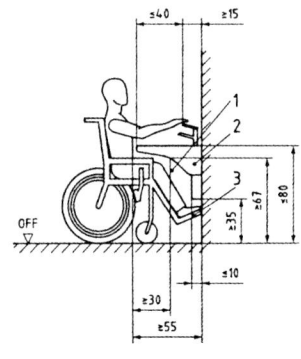

Paper and Sizes

Size	Trimmed (mm)	Untrimmed (mm)	Drawing Area
A0	841 × 1189	880 × 1230	831 × 1179
A1	594 × 841	625 × 880	584 × 831
A2	420 × 594	450 × 625	410 × 584
A3	297 × 420	330 × 450	287 × 410
A4	210 × 297	240 × 330	200 × 287
A5	148 × 210	165 × 240	138 × 200
A6	105 × 148	120 × 165	95 × 138

Standard paper sizes

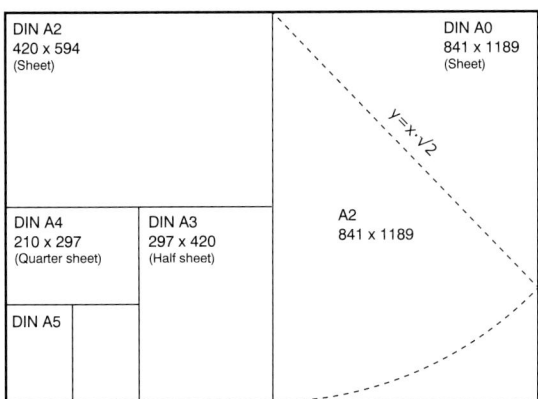

The A series sizes as defined by the ISO 216 standard

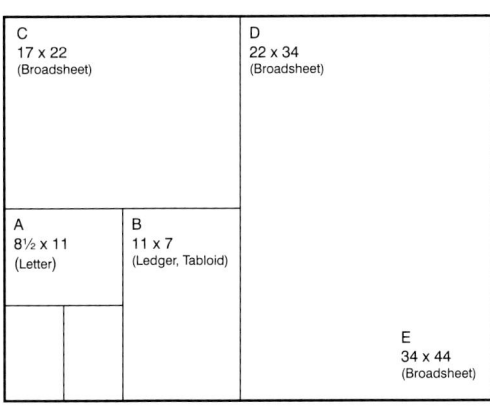

Common North American paper sizes of the ANSI series

Paper and drawing sheets
Lightweight sketching paper that can be overlaid over and over again is suited for the drawn depiction of an idea, a first overview or a design. Tracing paper rolls or sheets are used for the final drawing. Architectural drawings are usually created on clear paper (tracing paper) or drawing cardboard. When choosing a type of paper, strength and surface quality must be taken into consideration. Roughened surfaces are more suited for pencil drawings whereas smooth surfaces lend themselves to ink drawings. Fine quality drawing cardboard should be white, smooth and, above all, eraser-proof. The dimensions of untrimmed and trimmed sheets (trimmed size) are specified in both DIN EN ISO 5457 and DIN EN ISO 216.

Sketching paper
Available in rolls or sheets
Paper weight: 20 to 40 g/m²

Drawing paper
Made of cellulose in rolls or sheets in paper sizes A4/A3/A2/A1/A0; paper weight: 60 to 110 g/m²

Card stock
A type of cardboard with a weight of between 120 and 170 g/m²; A4/A3/A2/A1/A0

Card
A basis weight between paper and paperboard (single or multi-layer); A4/A3/A2/A1/A0; paper weight more than 150 m²

Graph paper
Paper with a rectangular grid with a mesh size of 1 mm in paper sizes A4/A3

Isometric pad
Isometric grid of evenly spaced lines at 30° for dimensional, parallel perspective representations; sizes: A4/A3

Tracing paper
Translucent paper in rolls or sheets that is suited for tracing.
Paper weight: 40, 80, 115 g/m²

Drawing sheet sizes and sheet folding

When referring to sheet sizes, it is possible to distinguish between an untrimmed sheet, a trimmed drawing sheet and the drawing area. A border measured outwards from the trimmed size is included to limit the drawing area. The distance between the title block and the border of the drawing is:
- In paper sizes A0 to A3: 10 mm
- In paper sizes A4 to A6: 5 mm

Reproductions of original drawings are folded to A4 format and stored for construction plans or archiving. Drawings stored in a folder should be able to be easily folded and unfolded.
- The first fold (incl. the margin) must be 21 cm wide
- The title block is always located on the cover page
- The margin for hole-punching is 20 mm
- A distance of at least 50 mm must be left clear between the left border and any illustrations and labelling
- Fold marks facilitate easier folding

Title blocks

The title block is always situated as the eye travels on the cover page at the bottom edge of the folded drawing. Title blocks can be customised to meet individual requirements. The width should be 185 mm, whereas the height, layout, column width and the number of lines are arbitrary.

Required fields are:
- Title (e.g. Ground Floor Layout)
- Document type (e.g. planning approval, detailed plan)
- Planner (architect, engineer)
- Draughtsman
- Authorised people (e.g. architect)
- Code number
- Segment/sheet number
- Issue date

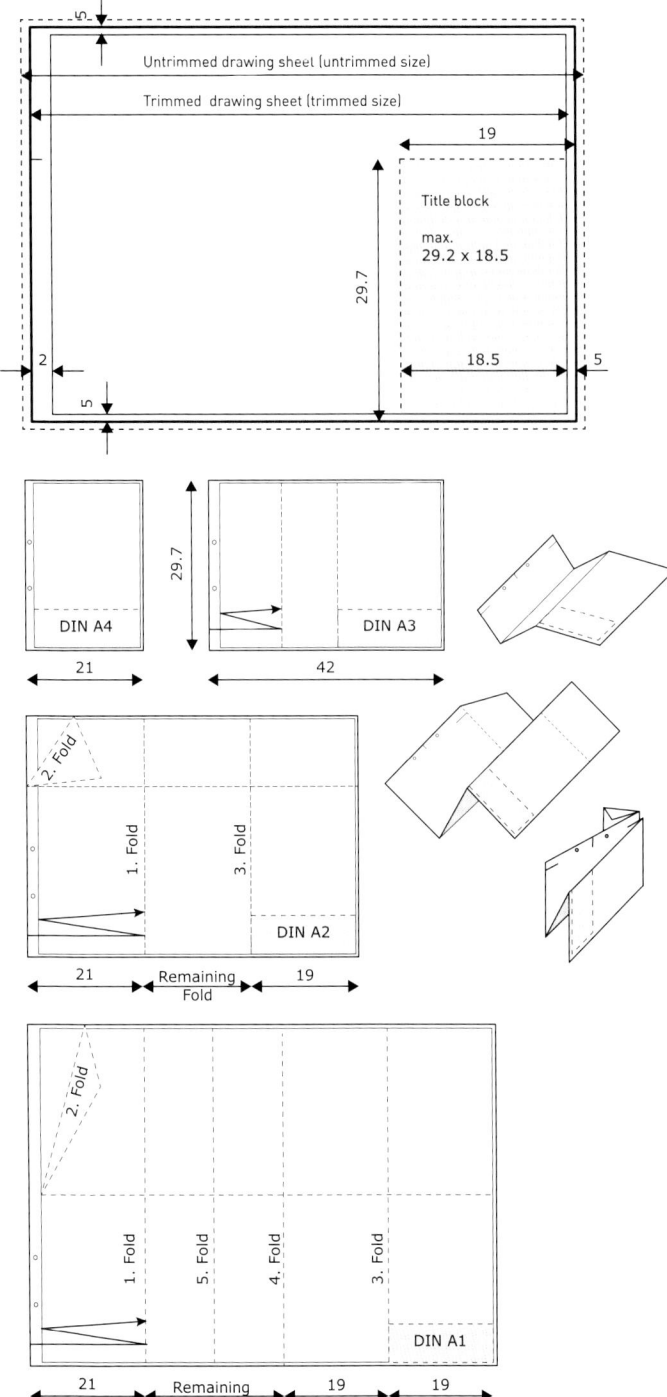

Folding to filing format A4 for binders

Headers

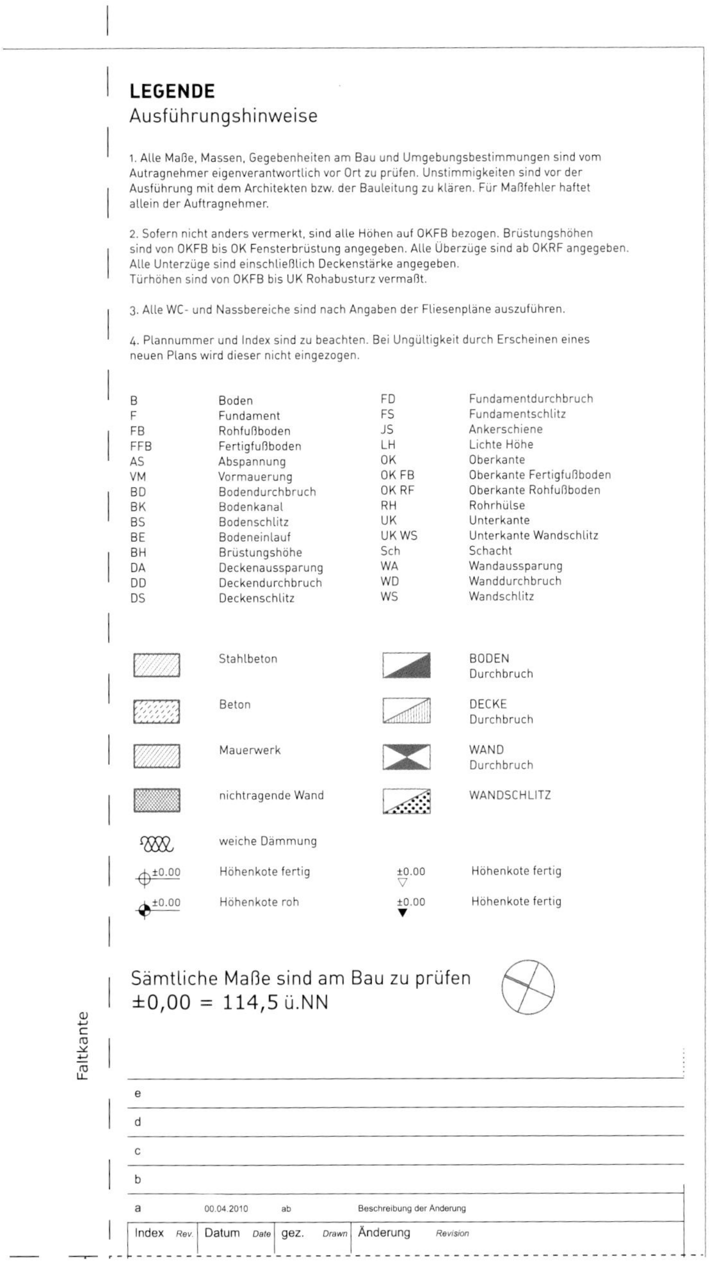

German example of a legend

Depending on the type of drawing, additional supporting details can be provided in the header as well as the required fields:

Change index
Changes to technical drawings are labelled with a revision number that identifies the different versions of a document. The annotation scheme is designated by numbers or letters.

Number of sheets
If there are multiple sheets of paper that belong together, the total number of sheets must be indicated in order to certify that the plans are complete.

Language characters
Abbreviations for the language used must be applied for international projects.

Additional titles
The subheading provides additional information that is of importance to the project.

Classification/key words
Key words or identifiers in written form facilitate a retrieval of the drawing.

Document status
Specific terms such as *preliminary*, *in process*, *approved* or *withdrawn* denote the status of the drawing.

Paper sizes
In order to facilitate printouts, enlargements or reductions, the paper size standard convention should be provided on the plan.

Modifications to drawings
If a drawing is already in circulation – that is to say the plan has already been passed on to planning partners or the authorities – any drawing that bears the annotation *withdrawn* can be replaced by a new one. Small modifications are marked at the corresponding position in the drawing and noted in the index.

Working Tools
Basics and Standards
Types of Architectural Drawings

Index
- Indication of date of amendment
- Description of modifications
- Numbering of modifications
- Author of modifications
- Release memo issued by specialist engineers

Contact details of the client ....

Address of the construction project ....

Description of the construction project ....

Document type (e.g. building application etc.) ....

Plan number/segment number/sheet number ....
scale/planned magnitude/issue date/draughtsman ....

Contact details of the architect ....

Contact details of the technical planner ....

German example of a header

Drawing Sheets

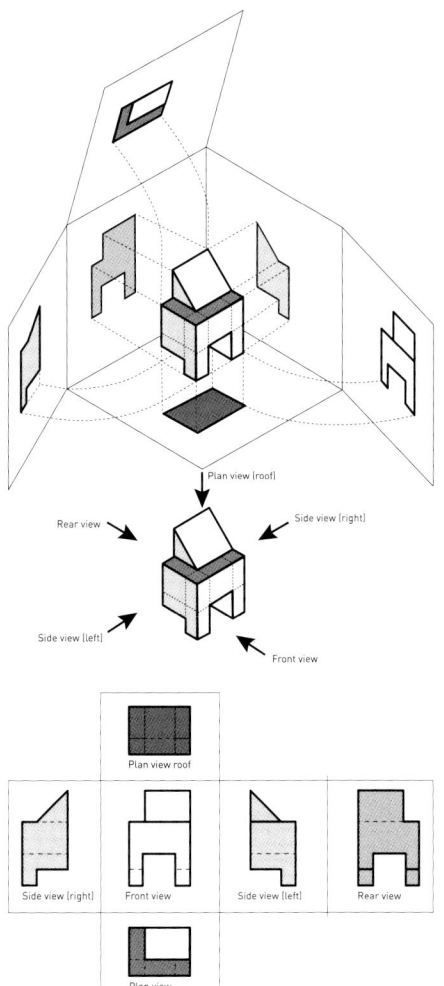

The assembly of construction components in an architectural drawing is governed by the international DIN ISO 128-30 standard. Based on the front view, the other views can be arranged as follows:

The plan view is below.
The view from the left side is placed on the right side.
The soffit is above.
The rear view may be placed to the left or right-hand side.
The view from the right side is placed on the left side.

Right:
Sample of a clearly-structured German competition entry, design: Natascha Meuser (2011)

Layout on drawing sheets
Plans, sections and elevations are the most common architectural drawings since an orthogonal representation enables a full-scale, unabridged and undistorted illustration in terms of form, size and proportion. The aim is to display references and forms in a clear and understandable manner in the drawing. When preparing a drawing, it must first be taken into consideration which information is to be provided at which scale, in addition to where and by what means. The paper size is also to be determined by the designer. Should this involve different illustrations on the same sheet, certain rules must be observed for the layout, presentation and labelling. It is particularly important that the illustrations are equally aligned and set in relation to each other. The left edge of the drawing sheet should always be free of illustrations and labelling so that the sheet can be stapled. The aforementioned parameters fundamentally determine the layout of information in a digital drawing. In contrast to the analogue drawing, considerations of this kind relating to the creation of a technical drawing using a CAD system have no significance since adjustments can at any time be amended and rearranged with minimal effort.

Presentation drawings
Presentation drawings mainly serve as a communication tool for architects. The aim is to present a planning concept in a clear and structured manner so that it is described in legible and understandable terms for the client and general public. The layout and selection of text and images are just as important in this context as the actual contents of the drawing or the design. Depending on the scale of the presentation, care should be taken to ensure that labelling, drawings and images are clearly legible on a smaller scale and from a distance.

Presentations
In addition to a presentation drawing, aims, methods and tools for planning can be clarified in an oral presentation. Adequate preparation and practice of the presentation is recommended.

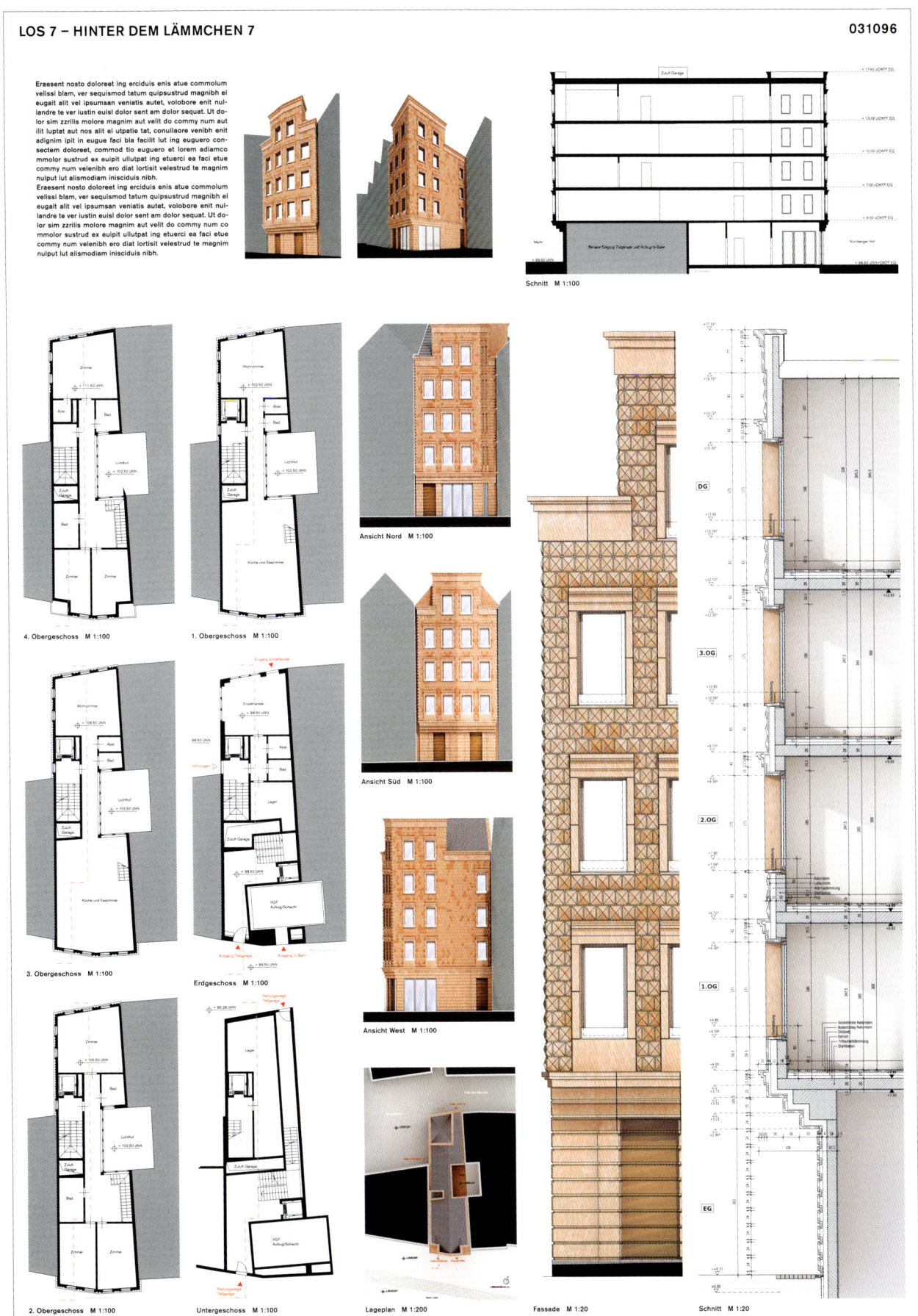

Drawing Scales

a Overview of scales

Field of Application	Scales
Site plans	1:1000, 1:500
Preliminary designs	1:500, 1:200
Designs	1:100
Planning applications	1:100
As-built drawings	1:50
Detail drawings	1:25, 1:20, 1:10, 1:5, 1:2

b Examples of scale calculations

True length cm	1:10 mm	1:5 mm	1:20 mm	1:100 mm	1:50 mm	1:200 mm	1:25 mm
				Drawing Dimensions with a Scale			
10	10	20	5	1	2	0.5	4
15	15	30	7.5	1.5	3	0.75	6
50	50	100	25	5	10	2.5	20
100	100	200	…				
125	125	…					
150	150	…					

c **Example**

Example: Actual length: 1.67 m, scale 1:20

Solution: Length in the drawing = $\frac{1670\ mm}{20\ mm} = 83.5\ mm$

Example: Length in the drawing: 2.5 cm, scale 1:50
Solution: Actual length = 2.5 cm × 50 = 125 cm

Example: Actual length: 4.00 m,
Length in the drawing: 20 mm

Solution: Ratio is taken as $\frac{4000\ mm}{20\ mm} = 200 >$ scale 1:200

Drawing scales

In order to depict elements and modules with different dimensions, different drawing scales are necessary. These give the ratio of the drawn objects to their true size. Example: a plan at a scale of 1:50 represents reality fifty times smaller. For other sample calculations see Fig. (b) and (c). Usually, architectural drawings are produced on a reduction ratio.

Natural size 1:1
Reductions 1:2, 1:5, 1:10, 1:20, 1:50
Enlargements 2:1, 5:1, 10:1, 20:1, 50:1

The principle scale of the drawing is given in the title block and all other scales in close proximity to the detail drawings. The scale chosen specifies the size of the representation which in turn determines the size of the drawing sheet.
Scales according to the most common standards are:
1:500, 1:200, 1:100, 1:50, 1:20 (1:25), 1:10, 1:5, 1:1

Scales for plans (selection)

from 1:25.000	Topographical maps, Official map series
1:50.000	Regional land use plans
1:10.000	Plans of land utilisation
1:5.000	Zoning plans
1:2.000	Infrastructure or transport plans
1:1.000	Urban development plans, development plans
1:500	Cadastral maps, land register maps
1:200	Competition plans, preliminary designs, designs
1:100	Building requests, preliminary designs, designs
1:50	Execution planning
1:20	Facade cross section, details
1:10/5/1	Detailed plans
Exclusive of	Sketches, organisational charts

Working Tools
Basics and Standards
Types of Architectural Drawings

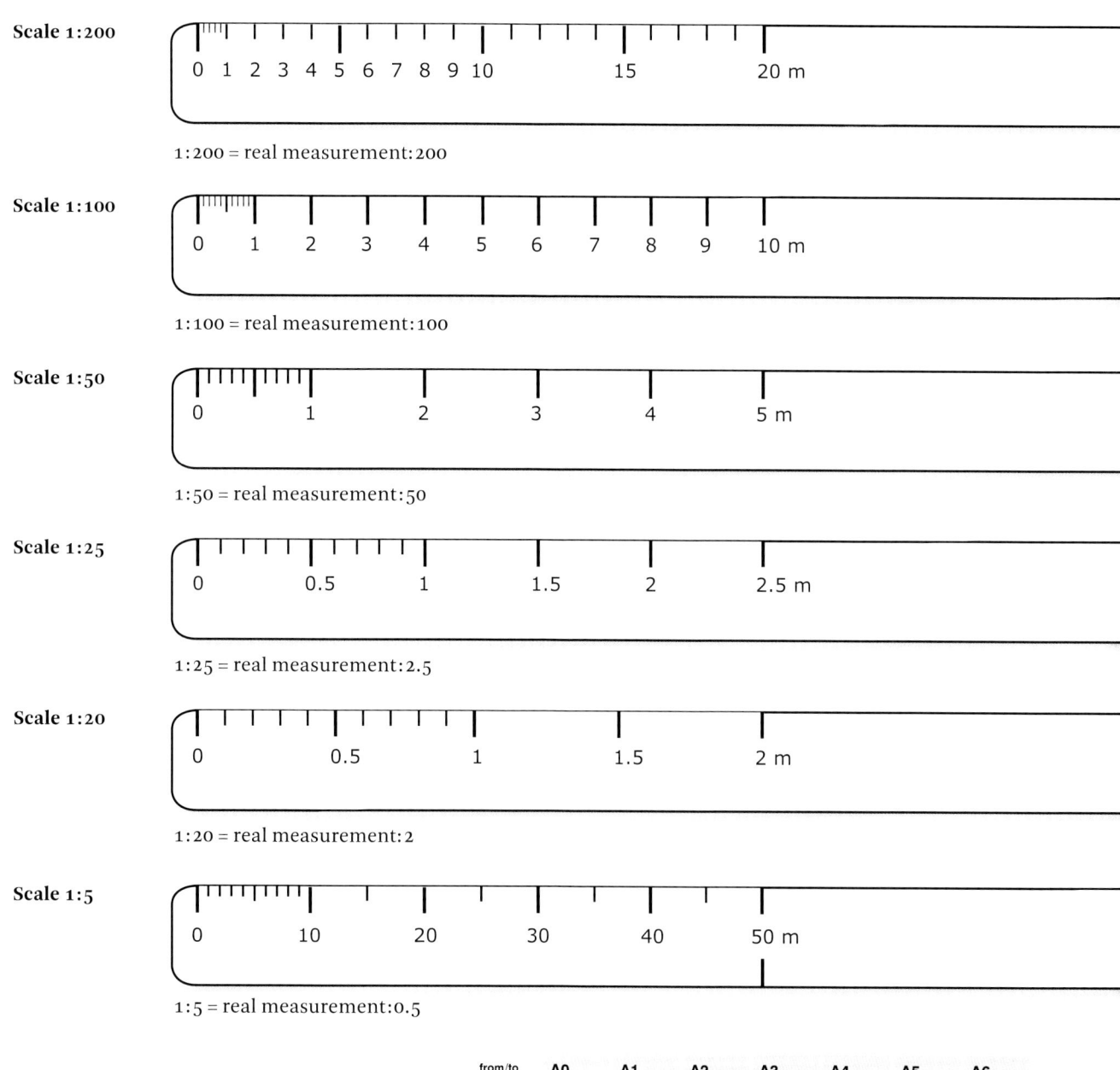

Scale 1:200

1:200 = real measurement:200

Scale 1:100

1:100 = real measurement:100

Scale 1:50

1:50 = real measurement:50

Scale 1:25

1:25 = real measurement:2.5

Scale 1:20

1:20 = real measurement:2

Scale 1:5

1:5 = real measurement:0.5

Drawings on a scale must be often be scaled accordingly for dispatching or for storing on a copier. In this context, a conversion table for A series sizes is helpful. The respective scaling factor should always be indicated in the drawing.

from/to	A0	A1	A2	A3	A4	A5	A6
A0	100%	71%	50%	35%	25%	18%	12.5%
A1	141%	100%	71%	50%	35%	25%	18%
A2	200%	141%	100%	71%	50%	35%	25%
A3	283%	200%	141%	100%	71%	50%	35%
A4	400%	283%	200%	141%	100%	71%	50%

Line Types and Line Widths

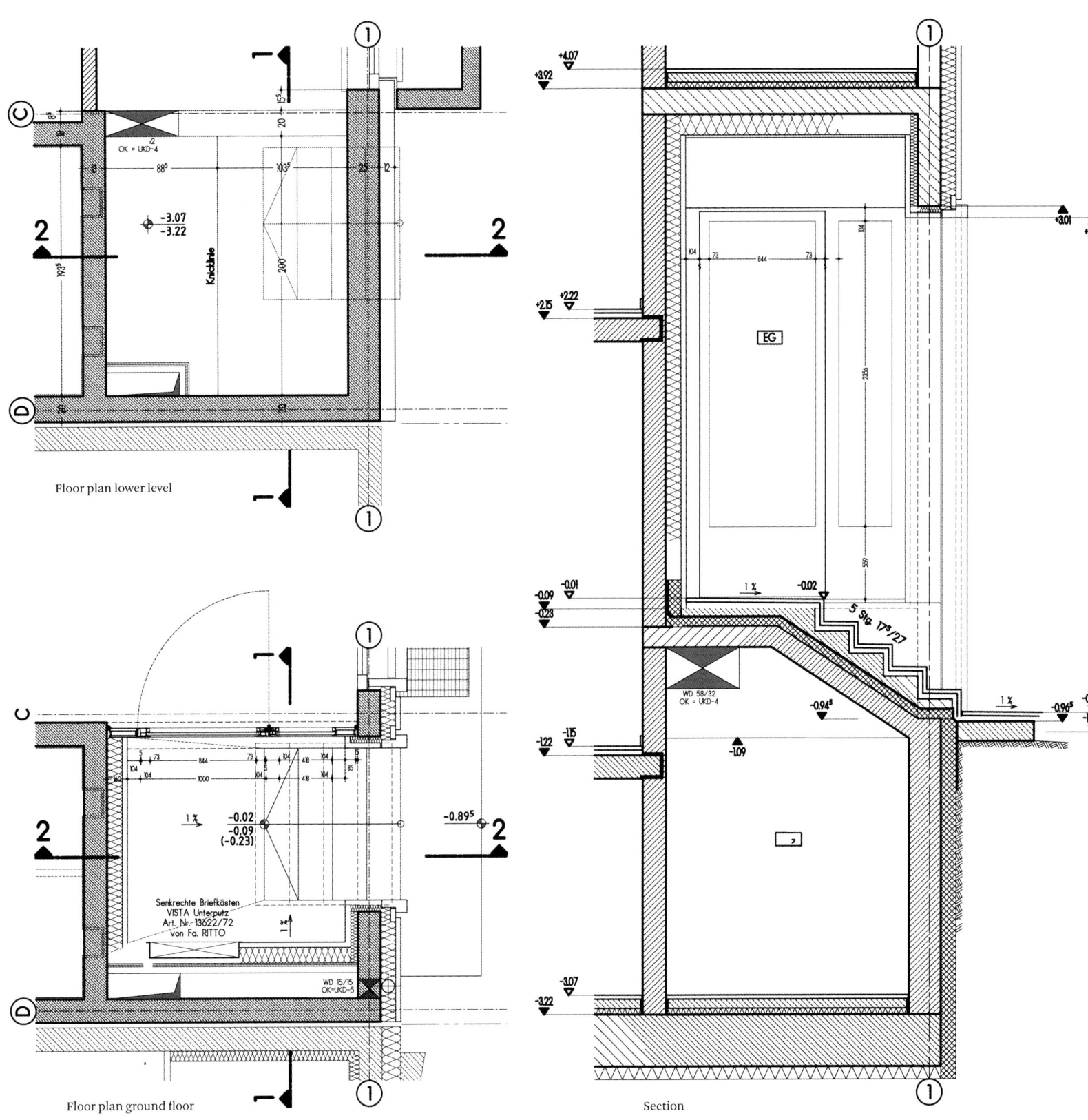

Floor plan lower level

Floor plan ground floor

Section

Detailed design example, scale 1:20 (reduced by 50%)
Legible line widths must also be provided for on a reduced scale

Line types and line widths

In order to create a drawing that is convincing and easy to read, different types of lines and line widths are used. In terms of lines, a distinction is made between continuous lines, dashed lines, dot-and-dashed lines, dotted lines and freehand lines. Line widths apply to the creation of ink drawings and are used in CAD drawings accordingly. These should be roughly observed for pencil drawings. Generally, everything that is visible and important is drawn out heavily compared to that which is concealed or whose position is to only be implied. Heavy continuous lines are used for visible edges and outlines.

These are finely drawn out for reference and dimension lines. Evenly dashed lines are used for invisible edges whereas dot-and-dashed lines are used for centre lines, axes and to indicate section planes. Freehand lines that are slightly wavy and curved are used for broken edges, as well as to indicate cross sections. In the case of other lines, these are used to complement the aforementioned lines or to indicate different denotations.

Identification of Line Types		Illustration	Use	Line Width Scale ≥ 1:100	Scale ≥ 1:50
Continuous line	broad		To define areas and intersected components	0.50	1.00
	broad		Visible edges of components, to define narrow or small surfaces of intersected components	0.35	0.5
	narrow		Dimension lines, extension lines, leader lines, walking lines, simplified representations, shading	0.25	0.35
Dashed line	medium		Hidden outlines, contours of components	0.35	0.50
	narrow		Hidden outlines, contours of components	0.25	0.30
Dot-and-dashed line	broad		To mark the position of section planes	0.50	1.00
	medium		To mark changes in the section line	0.35	0.50
	narrow		Centre lines, symmetrical lines, axes, grid lines	0.25	0.35
Dotted line	narrow		Components in front or above the section plane	0.35	0.5
Freehand line			To shade sectional areas of wood	0.18	0.25
Measured values			Character height	0.35	0.5

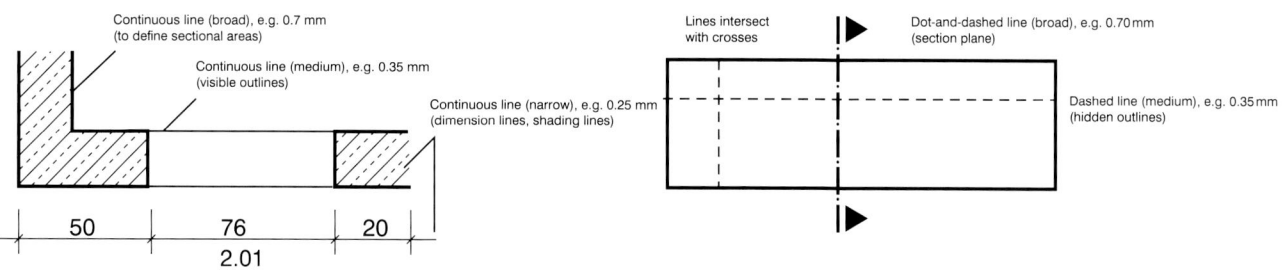

Dimensioning

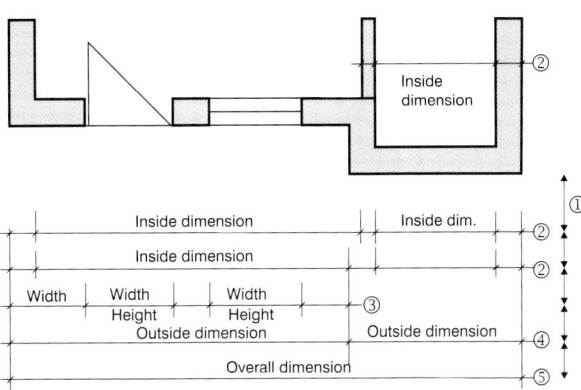

Chain dimensioning layout

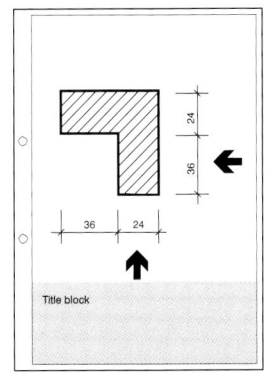 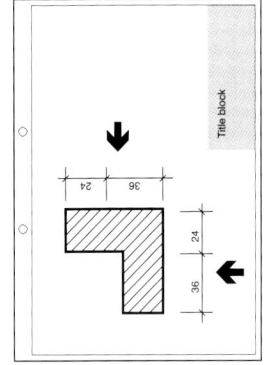

Labelling and reading orientation of measured values

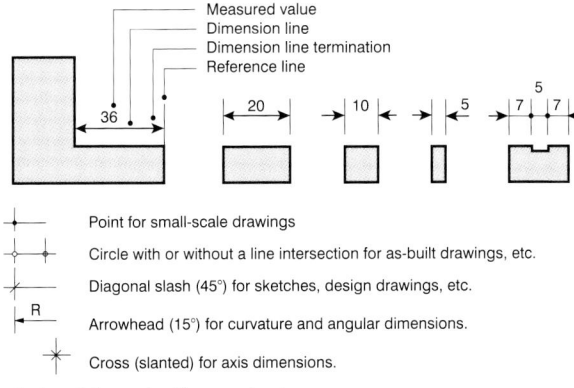

- ─┼─ Point for small-scale drawings
- ─⊕─ Circle with or without a line intersection for as-built drawings, etc.
- ─╱─ Diagonal slash (45°) for sketches, design drawings, etc.
- ─►─ Arrowhead (15°) for curvature and angular dimensions.
- ─✱─ Cross (slanted) for axis dimensions.

Display of dimension line terminations

Unit of measure	cm	m, cm	mm
Under 1 m	80	80	800
	36.5	36^5	365
Above 1 m	236.5	2.36^5	2365

Dimensioning guidelines
The most important requirements for dimensions and labelling are clear legibility and uniformity. Depending on the type of drawing, the range of dimensioning varies. For instance, in the case of building applications, dimensions are widely used in order to calculate areas. With as-built drawings, a high quantity of dimensions are indicated accordingly. This is in order to construct the building without calculating additional dimensions.

Dimension lines and extension lines
The dimension line is a continuous line that is drawn parallel to the edge of the object at a distance of 10 mm. The extension line is drawn out longer towards the component so that the reference edges can be clearly indicated. The order of the dimension lines in architectural drawings is as follows:
Inside dimension(s) (if applicable, in the drawing of the building)
Aperture dimension(s)
Overall dimension(s), outside dimension(s)
The first dimension line is drawn at a greater distance to the component. Further distances between the dimension lines are smaller and spaced at regular intervals.

Dimension line termination and dimensioning
- The dimension line termination represents the mark of the points of intersection of dimension lines and extension lines, which can take different forms.
- Diagonal slashes (45°) or circles and arrows are used in architectural drawings when dimensioning both radii and diameters.
- Dimensions under 1 metre are given in cm. For dimensions above 1 metre this is in m. Millimetres are added to the dimension and, if necessary, are rounded to the nearest 5 mm.
- Measured values are displayed on the dimension line with a distance of roughly 1/3 of the height of the measured value.
- In the case of openings, the measured value is written above the dimension line. The height dimension is written below it.
- Where space is limited, the measured values are shifted to the left or right or positioned staggered in height.
- Reading the measured values takes place as the eye travels from *bottom* and *right* toward the angle of dimensioning.
- Dimensions in unfinished state are usually indicated in architectural drawings.

Dimensioning of oblique projections

For isometric drawings, the extension lines are in continuation of the edges of the object. The dimension line termination is usually represented by a circle.

Leader lines, reference lines

In case there is not enough space in the drawing or for special notes, information can be *extracted* from the drawing. This is achieved by reference lines arranged at right angles. The leader lines end e.g. within an area or at an edge.

Height dimensions

Height dimensions (e.g. for floor heights, clear room heights, window, door and lintel heights) can also be represented without dimension lines by height indicators. Height dimensions mostly refer to the finished floor level on the ground floor ±0,00.
▽   Blank triangles measure finished heights.
▼   Filled in triangles measure the shell construction.
The dimensions above are written as a positive measurement and the dimensions below as a negative one. The dimensional reference may be explained by additional information such as lower edge of lintel, upper edge of parapet etc. The numbers are displayed in sectional views above or below the triangle, in the ground floor right of the triangle.

Angular dimensions

For angular dimensions, extension lines are drawn as an extension of the angle leg. The angle is given in degrees and is shown above the circular dimension line. Alternatively, the radian or chordal dimension may also be provided.

Cross section dimensions

Rectangular cross sections can either be shown using dimension lines or in the dimensions width/height.

- Rectangular cross sections   15/20
- Square cross sections   15/15 or 15□
- Circular cross sections   Ø 30

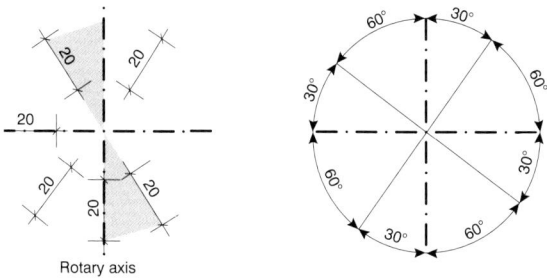

Reading orientation in oblique dimensioning

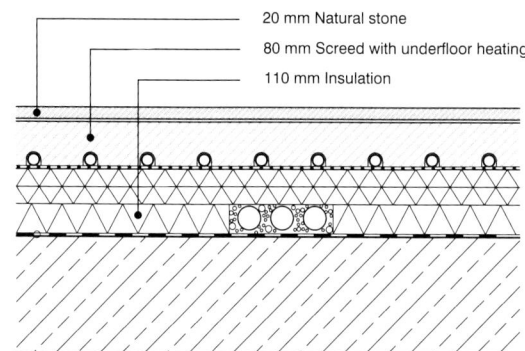

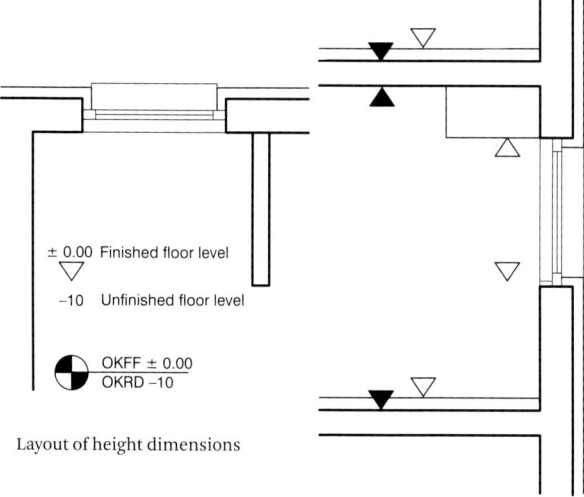

Layout of height dimensions

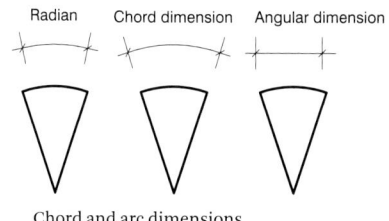

Chord and arc dimensions

Labelling and Sectional Areas

Character Size		Line Width	Minimum Difference Between			
For Uppercase Letters Nominal Size h	For Lowercase Letters		Baselines for Letters Without Descenders	With Ascenders	Characters	Words
10/10 h	7/10 h	1/10 h	14/10 h	16/10 h	2/10 h	6/10 h
2.5	–	0.25	3.5	4	0.5	1.5
3.5	2.5	0.35	5	5.7	0.7	2.1
5	3.5	0.5	7	8	1	3
7	5	0.7	10	11.4	1.4	4.2
10	7	1	14	16	2	6
14	10	1.4	20	22.8	2.8	8.4
20	14	2	28	32	4	12

Standard lettering (dimensions in mm)

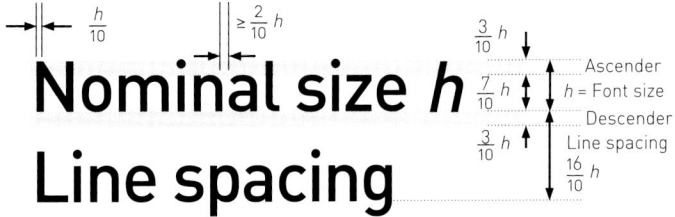

ABCDEFGHIJKLMNOPQRSTUVWXYZÄÖÜ
abcdefghijklmnopqrstuvwxyzäöüß
[(!?:;"-=+×-√$&»«±]]
123456789 ½

Standard lettering written vertically

ABCDEFGHIJKLMNOPQRSTUVWXYZÄÖÜ
abcdefghijklmnopqrstuvwxyzäöüß
[(!?:;"-=+×-√$&»«±]]
123456789 ½

Standard lettering written in italics

Labelling
Standard lettering is a standard font which serves to unify labelling and dimensioning in technical drawings. Standard lettering can be used both horizontally and vertically in various written forms and variants. The following design principles should be observed:

- Use as few different fonts as possible.
- Use uniform typeface designs (corporate typeface).
- Labelling, reference notes and leader lines are to be arranged in block form.
- Everything on top of the structure must also be arranged on top in the labelling.
- Abbreviations must be explained by the legend.
- The size of the font is dependent upon the drawing format.

Font size
Three font sizes are provided in order to label drawings:
Small font: 0.25 mm for indices and exponents
Medium font: 0.33 mm for dimensions and verbal notes
Large font: 0.5 mm for measuring and labelling sections

Font sizes are geared to the line group used (see table) and are marked with the letter h (height). With the application of CAD, the manual drawing of fonts in technical drawings has become relatively insignificant. The aforementioned font size rules are taken into account within CAD drawings.

Dimensions for standard lettering lines:
- Line thickness 0.25: font size h 2.5 mm;
  Height of lowercase letters 7/10 h (1.75 mm)
- Line thickness 0.5: font size h 5 mm;
  Height of lowercase letters 7/10 h (3.5 mm)
- Line thickness 0.7: font size h 5 mm;
  Height of lowercase letters 7/10 h (4.9 mm)
- Line thickness 1.0: font size h 10 mm;
  Height of lowercase letters 7/10 h (7 mm)

The distance between two baselines is generally 22/14 h.

Working Tools
Basics and Standards
Types of Architectural Drawings

Labelling sectional areas

The legibility of a drawing is emphasised by labelling the construction materials used in the form of sectional areas and shading, which are produced manually or by computer. Construction materials can range from reinforced concrete to natural stone, timber and bricks. Areas are clearly denoted by labelling them in the legend. The distance between the shading lines is adapted to the height of both the sectional area and scale. Dimensions and labelling within shaded areas must be legible to ensure that they are clearly recognisable.

Sectional areas need to be highlighted:

- by broadly outlining the sectional area
- by applying a grey dot grid to the area
- by shading (reading orientation: 45°)
- by blackening (particularly narrow sectional areas)

When planning renovations, the corresponding components are denoted with colours.

New building	maroon
New concrete/reinforced concrete	pale green
Demolition	yellow
Existing	black/grey

Material/Component		Illustration Black/White	Colour
Soil	fill		sepia
	natural		sepia
Concrete	unreinforced		olive green
	reinforced		blue green RAL 6000
Precast concrete units			violet
Stonework	artificial stone		maroon RAL 3016
	natural stone		blue grey
Mortar and plaster			white
Wood	end grain (solid wood)		brown
	long grain (solid wood)		brown
Steel			black
Barrier material	against moisture		black/white
Insulating material	thermal/acoustic insulation		blue grey
Old components	in the section		black
New components	in the section		acc. to material
	in the elevation		varnished yellow
Components to be demolished	in the section		yellow RAL 1016
	in the elevation		
Soil to be removed			

Typical shading for components used by most technical standards

Shading

Selection of shading with varying scaling from AUTOCAD 2012

Working Tools
Basics and Standards
Types of Architectural Drawings

Below is a selection of the most important guidelines for the shading of drawings.

The intersected components can also be drawn without shading or as a coloured area. However, shading is always in the direction that the eye travels across the architectural drawing.

Shading should be executed, as far as possible, with a finer line width than that of the component outline.

Only components that represent wood are drawn by freehand by shading (reading orientation: 45°).

Shading should either be aligned to the outline or symmetry axis of the component.

Corresponding components should be shaded in the same direction to achieve cohesiveness.

Abutting sectional areas are to be shaded in a different direction.

Dimension line terminations are to be in drawn in the opposite direction to the shading pattern. Shading is interrupted for dimensioning.

Shading with dashed lines or dot-and-dashed lines should be done at a distance from the area boundary lines.

It is only possible with relatively large sectioanl areas to draw the patterned areas at the edge.

Shading is displayed and indicated in the legend.

Section line
The section line is represented by a dot-and-dashed line with a broad line width and must only be drawn in the outer area of the building. The line of sight leading to the section plane is represented by a right-angled triangle. These are labelled by the same letters (e.g. A–A/B–B).

Material	Illustration	Material	Illustration
Stone fibre insulation		Sealing in general	
Glass fibre insulation		Primer	
Wood fibre insulation		Spackling paste	
Peat fibre insulation		Naked cardboard	
Foam plastic		Sealing strip	
Cork		Sealing strip (with metal foil)	
Wood wool panels		Sealing strip (with plastic foil)	
Gypsum boards		Plastic film	

Shading for waterproofing and insulation in compliance with flat roof guidelines

Annotation of Sections in the Floor Plan	Universal Symbols
Direction	
Height of surface – Finished floor level – Unfinished floor level	
Height of lower surface – Finished floor level – Unfinished floor level	
Indication of section orientation in viewing direction	
Indication of horizontal section orientation for floor plan type B	
Radius	

Stairs

Direction of rise of stairs and ramps in the floor plan

Description	Representation
Single-flight staircase	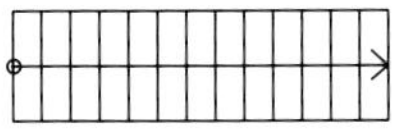
Double staircase	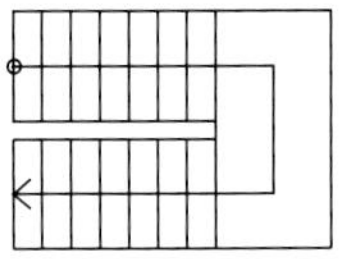
Newel stair	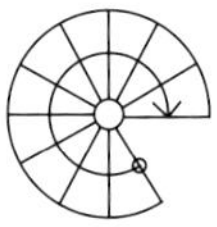
Flight of stairs cut horizontally with the flight below	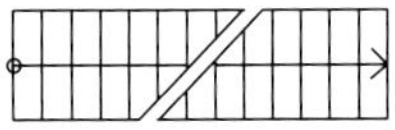
Flight of stairs cut horizontally with the flight above	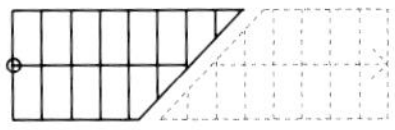
The representation of stairs corresponds to that of ramps	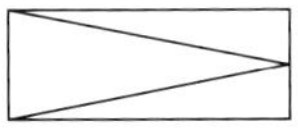

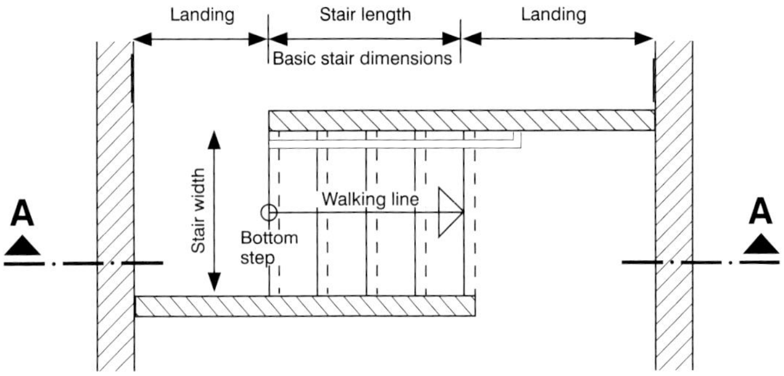

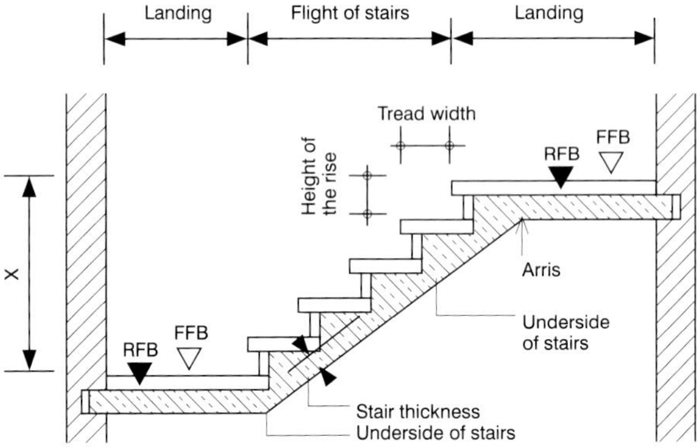

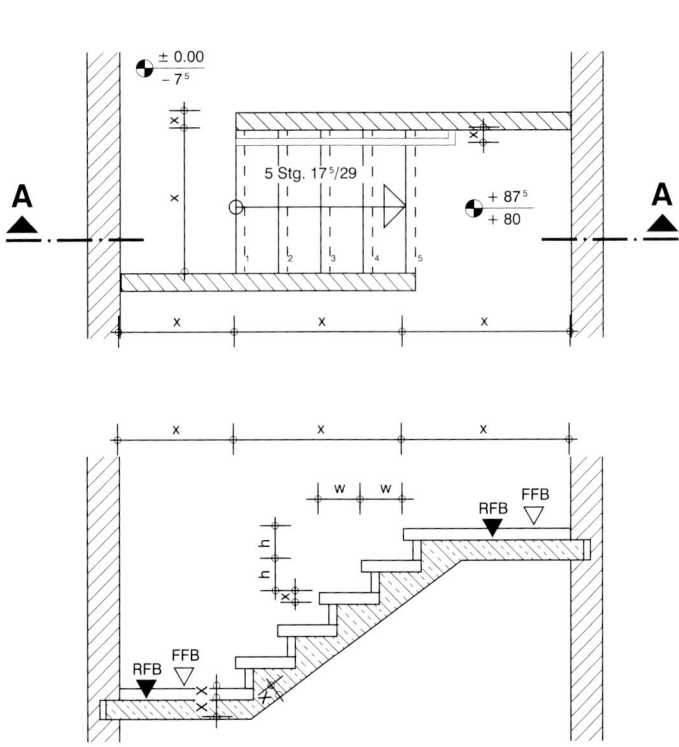

Special conditions can apply to structures of a particular nature (such as hospitals or meeting rooms). In general, stairs are represented in the floor plan and section. The direction in which a staircase ascends is illustrated with a walking line which is marked with a start tag and an arrow in running direction. In the case of overlapping stairs, the flight of stairs is trimmed in the floor plan and the subjacent staircase is drawn further. The overlying staircase is represented by a dotted line.

Included in the section are the following: the structure and building materials used, the bearing, the design of the stairs and the connection of stair treads. The stair dimensions contain: the number of risers, the height of the risers, the foothold, the stair length, the stair width, the height difference, the floor construction, the landing thickness and the staircase construction width.

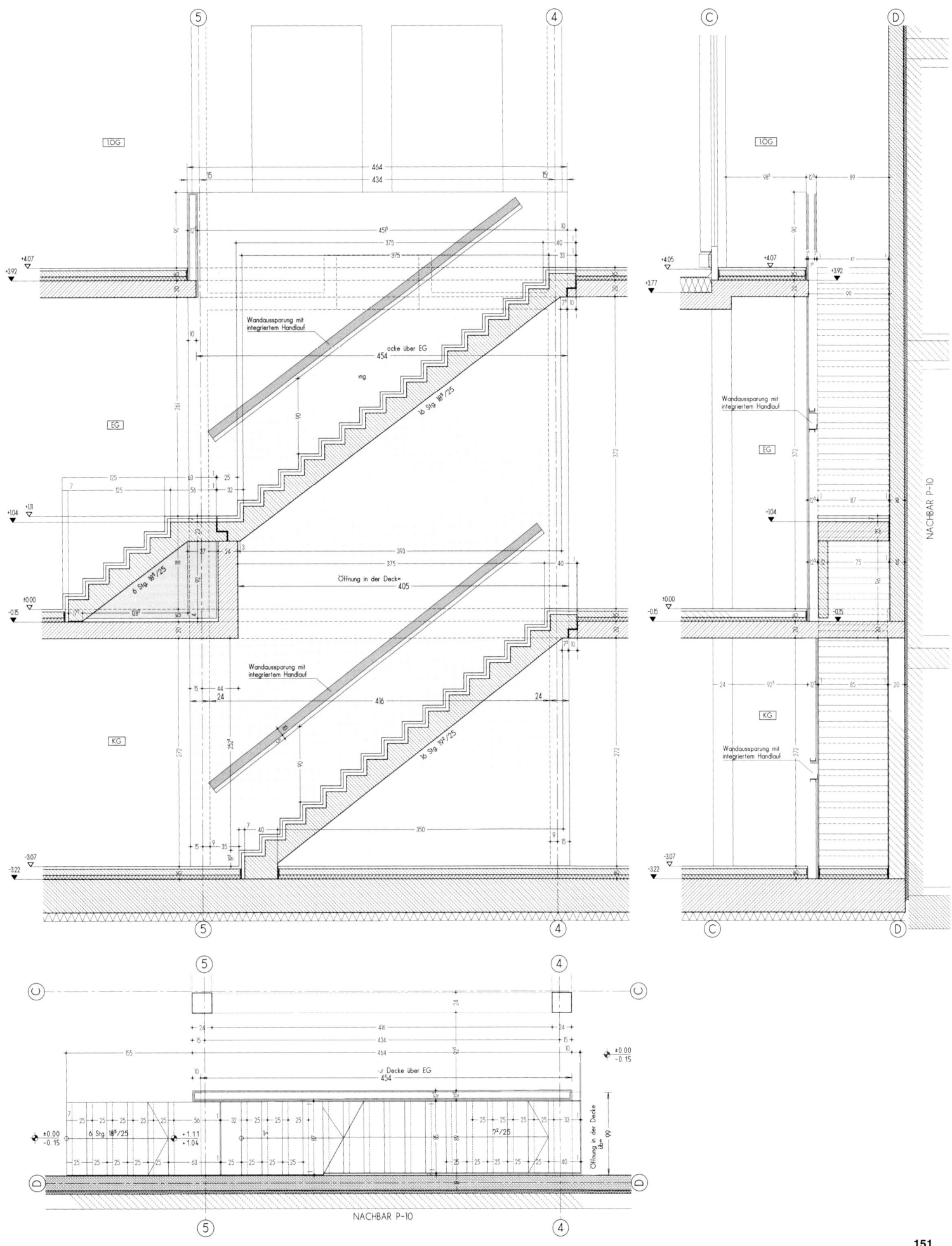

Doors and Windows

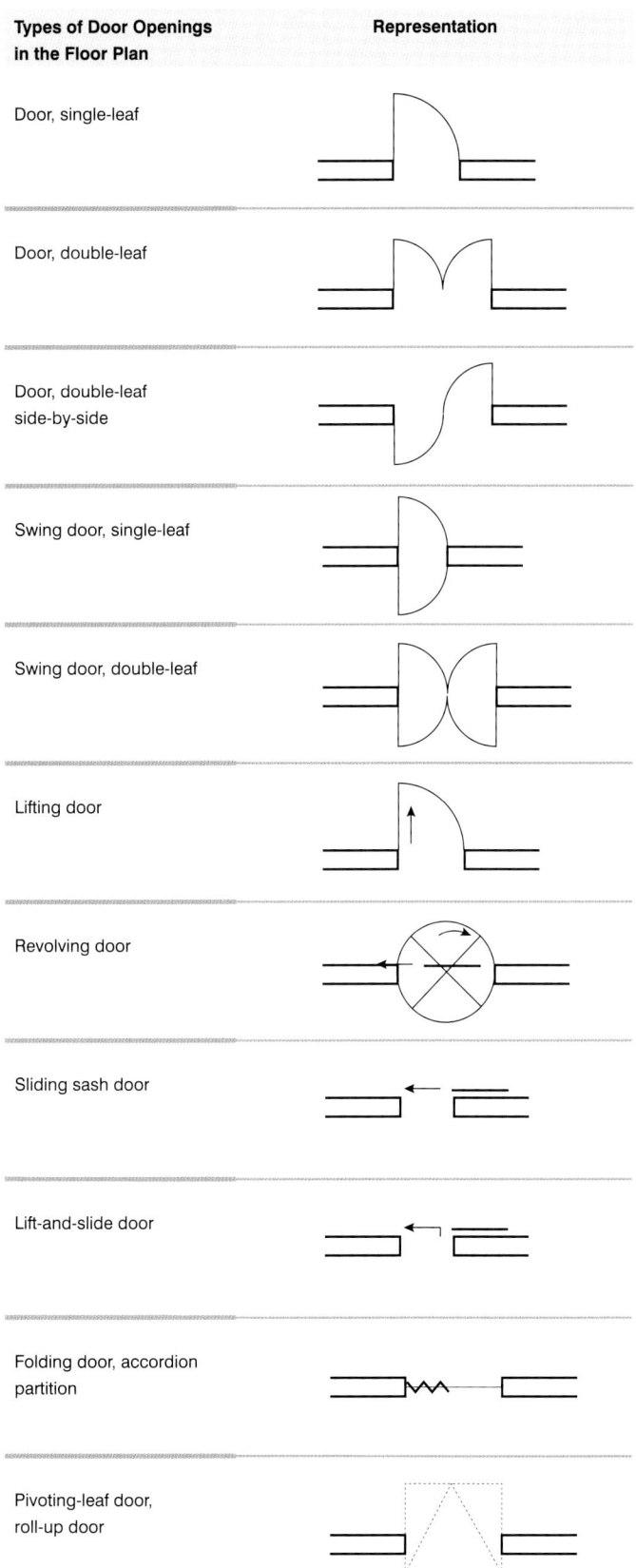

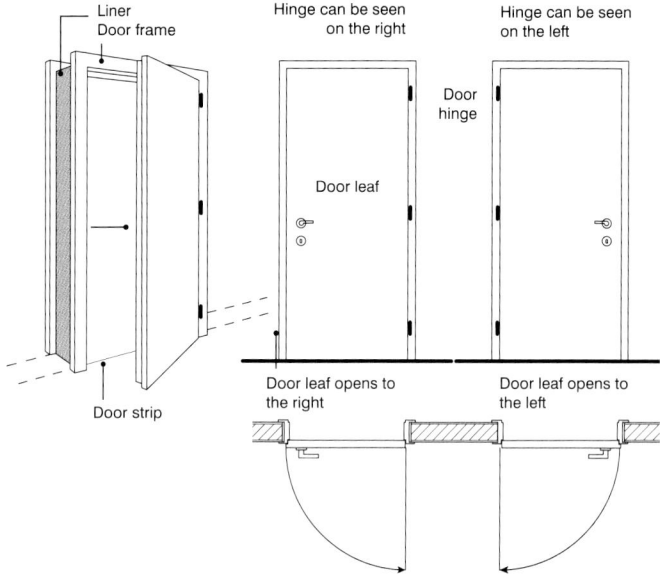

Doors and windows

In addition to the direction of rotation, other possible types of openings are listed with drawings based on standards such as: vertically pivoted windows, horizontally pivoted sash windows, vertical sliding windows, horizontal sliding windows, lift-tilt-slide windows/doors, lift-and-slide windows/doors, sliding-swivel windows, projected top-hung windows, horizontal pivot-hung windows, top-hung windows and louvred windows.

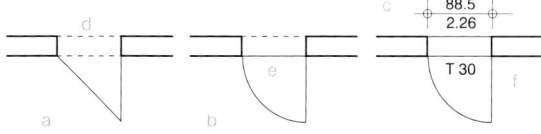

(a/b) The representation of the door is scale-dependent and is either drawn as a 45° line or as a circular arc section.
(c) The height of the openings in the wall from the finished floor level to the lower edge lintel is given in the floor plan under the width of the opening.
(d) In the case of doors that are not full-height, the lintel edge is shown with a dashed line.
(e) A door strip or screed replacement is shown with a solid line.
(f) Door specifications are correspondingly labelled, such as T 30 = fire-retardant door or SR = smoke resistant.

Construction Terms

Opening dimensions/door opening dimensions
Most technical standards define reference edges and differentiate between rebated and non-rebated door leaves. A distinction is made between opening dimensions (wall opening dimensions) and door leaf outer dimensions.

Door frame
The door frame or doorway is the side support of the door leaf and is located in the wall opening.

Door hinges
Door hinges, also referred to as door checks, connect the frame or the blind frame with the door.

RC Resistance Class
The European standards DIN V ENV 1627, 1628, 1629 and 1630 specify six resistance classes (RC 1 to RC 6) for certified burglary protection.

Fire protection closures for windows and doors
These are outlined in the respective State Building Regulations.

Parapet
The parapet is the area below the opening to the floor. It must be clearly indicated in the legend whether the height indication refers to the finished or unfinished floor, or the upper edge of the parapet.

Lintel
A lintel is normally a loadbearing element that lies across the opening. It is shown with a dotted line in the floor plan and is shown as a height in the section and elevation. Lintels are also found over portals and fireplaces.

Window height
The window height comprises the dimension of the upper edge of the parapet to the lower edge of the lintel. This is measured in the floor plan underneath the opening width of the closed chain dimensioning. The dimensions of the parapet height and window height are given in the section. This is in addition to the lintel on a larger scale.

Jamb
The jamb forms the side of an opening in the floor plan.

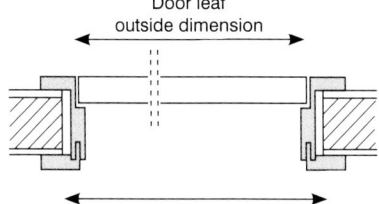

Wall opening dimension/rough opening dimensions

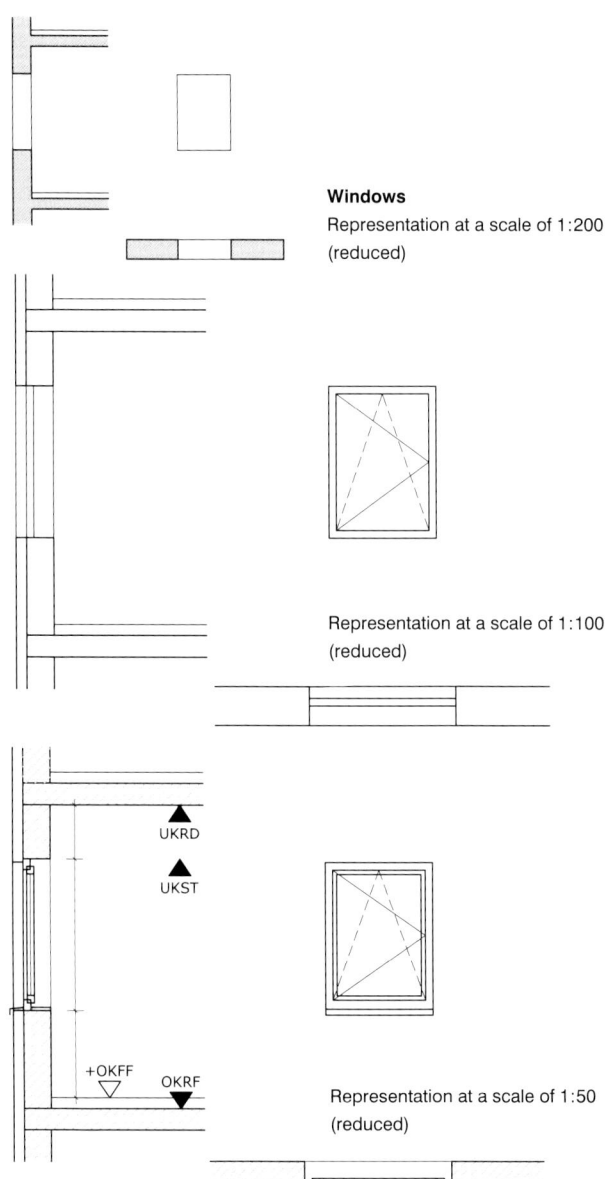

Windows in a scale-dependent representation (by way of example, without scale): In architectural drawings, the opening direction of the windows can be drawn from a scale of 1:100. This does not usually occur in presentation drawings. Window parts such as frames, casements, fittings and sunshades are also drawn from a scale of 1:100.

Recesses

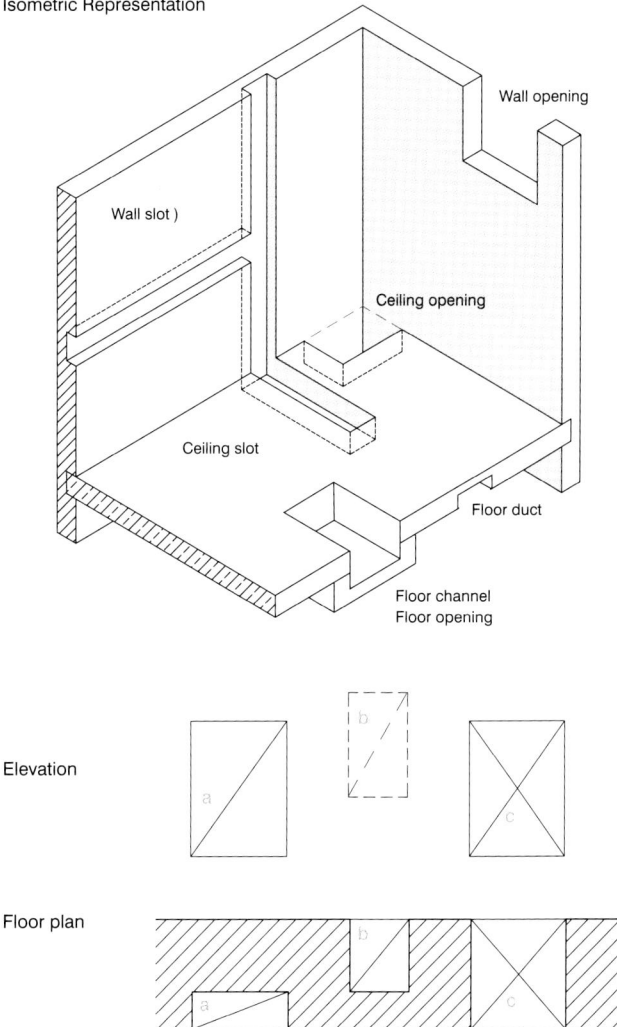

A typical example for displaying recesses in the floor plan and elevation

Recesses

Installations must normally lead through walls and ceilings. These are drawn in so-called installation or slot plans at a scale of 1:50.

Representation of recesses

(a) Recesses (niches) with a smaller depth than components are shown in the view with a diagonal line.

(b) Concealed views are displayed with dotted diagonal lines.

(c) In the case of recesses (openings), the depth is equal to the component thickness. Intersected lines are used for labelling the floor plan and view.

- Each recess in the wall of the floor depicted and the recesses in the ceiling above the floor depicted are displayed in the floor plan.
- Information on the intended use, the component, the type of recess and dimensioning, as well as the height above ±0,00 is used for labelling the recesses and openings.
- Reference dimensions must be indicated in the floor plan.
- So far as continuous slots are concerned, no information is required.
- The lower edge of wall slots beginning in the floor must be specified.
- The upper edge of wall slots ending in the floor must be specified.

Recommendation

Avoid positioning in bearing areas, underneath lintels and in the vicinity of openings.

Working Tools
Basics and Standards
Types of Architectural Drawings

Intended Use	Component	Type of Recess	Dimensioning cm
Sanitary	Floor	Opening	w × d × h
Electric	Ceiling	Slot	Height indication
Gas	Foundation	Channel	
Heating	Wall		
Ventilation			

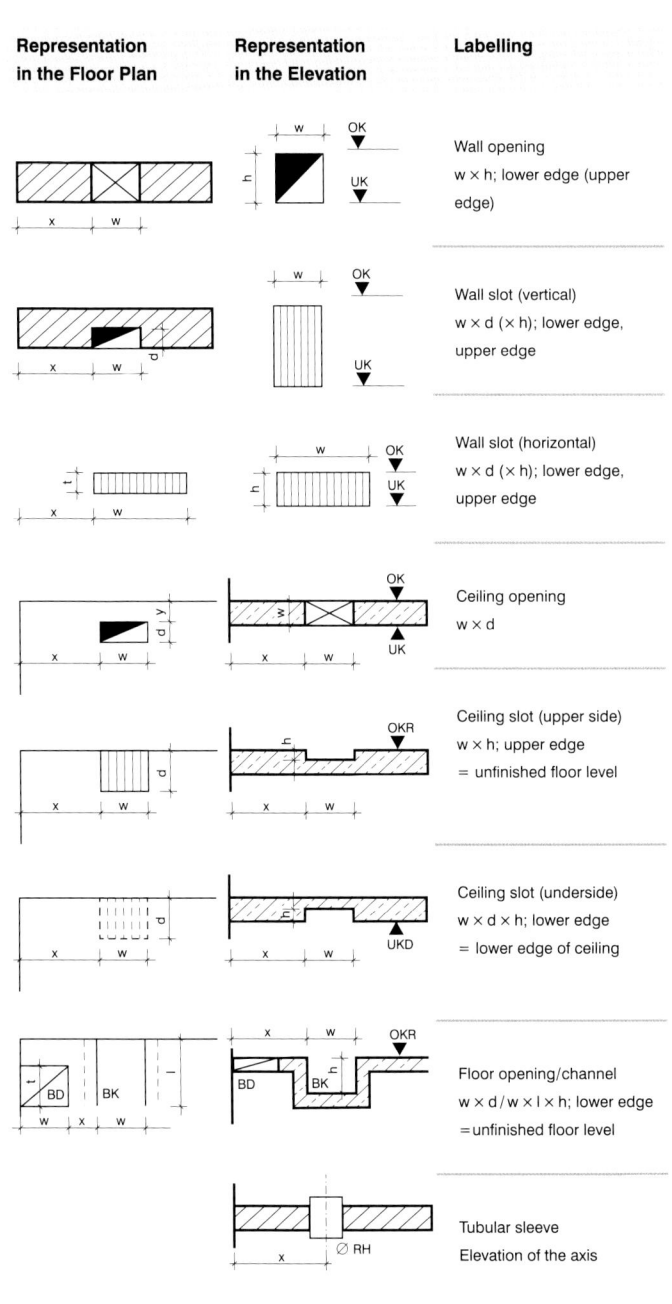

Representation in the Floor Plan	Representation in the Elevation	Labelling
		Wall opening w × h; lower edge (upper edge)
		Wall slot (vertical) w × d (× h); lower edge, upper edge
		Wall slot (horizontal) w × d (× h); lower edge, upper edge
		Ceiling opening w × d
		Ceiling slot (upper side) w × h; upper edge = unfinished floor level
		Ceiling slot (underside) w × d × h; lower edge = lower edge of ceiling
		Floor opening/channel w × d / w × l × h; lower edge = unfinished floor level
		Tubular sleeve Elevation of the axis

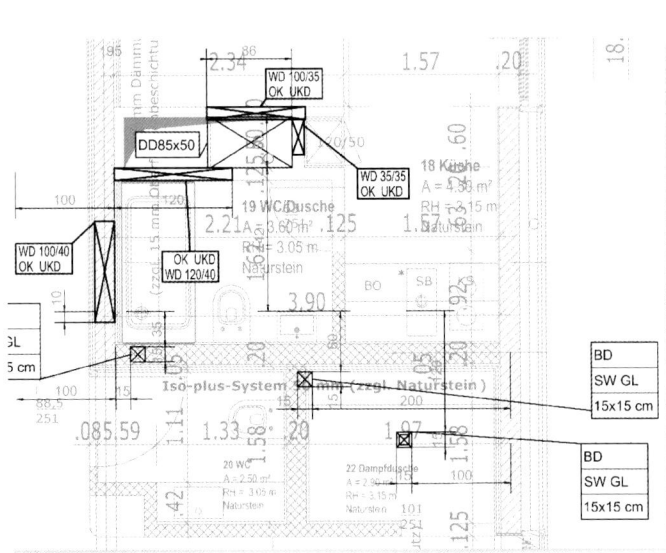

Opening drawing section at a scale of 1:50 (reduced)

Note:

With regards to smaller recesses, black triangles can be used to aid recognition for the benefit of the viewer.

Ceiling openings are shown in the ceiling above. Provided there is no floor situated below (e.g. basement), the openings are specified as floor openings.

Roofs

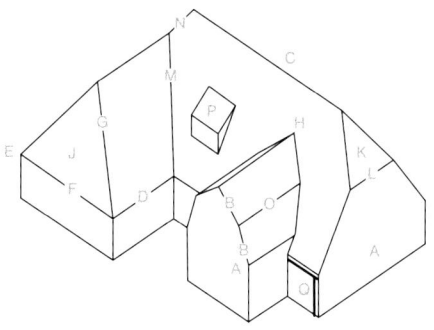

A	Gable	L	Partial hip eave
B	Verge	M	Valley (internal edge)
C	Ridge	N	Hip rafter (upper part of the ridge)
D	Main eave	O	Mansard line, curb roof
E	Eave corner	P	Dormer
F	Hip eave	Q	Downpipe
G	Arris	R	Emergency overflow
H	Apex	S	Outlet
J	Hip	T	Attic
K	Partial hip		

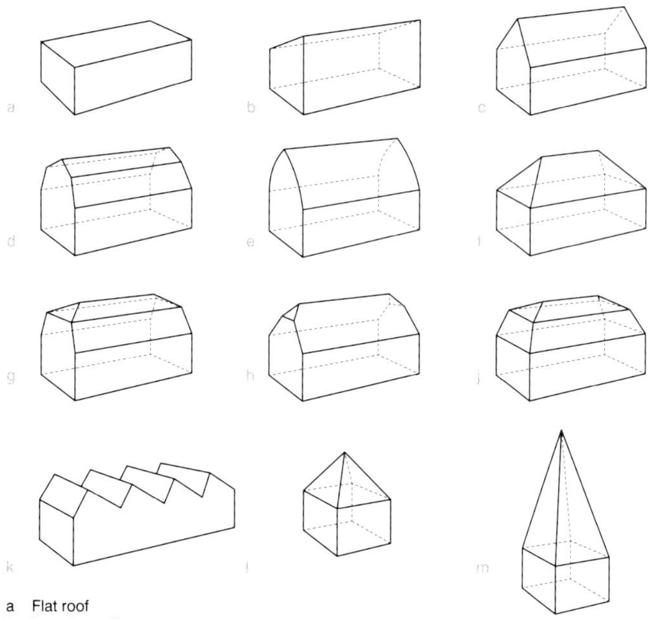

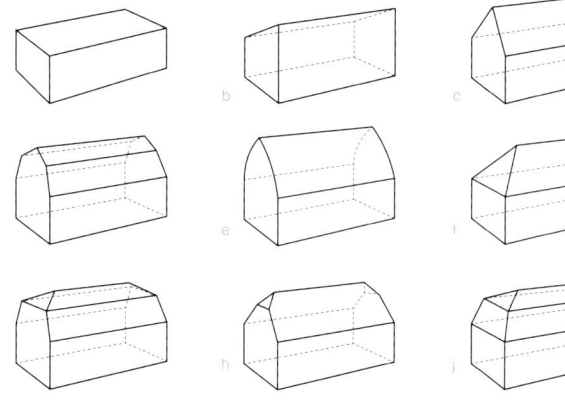

a Flat roof
b Lean-to roof
c Saddle roof
d Mansard roof
e Curved saddle roof
f Hip roof
g Masard partial hip roof
h Partial hip roof
j Mansard hip roof
k Tented roof
l Shed or saw-tooth roof
m Steeple roof

Basic styles of roof

Styles of roof

There exists a large variety of regional-typical and climate-induced roof variants, which have mostly created inclined roofs in wet/humid climatic zones and flat roofs in dry zones. In addition to the traditional styles of roof of European origin built by carpenters, styles have also developed in contemporary architecture whose typology, in its diversity, is still undergoing a definition process. Therefore, images (a) to (m) illustrate typical styles of roof in a simple geometry. When referring to roof areas or floor plans with different compositions, the representation becomes increasingly complex regarding the laws of descriptive geometry. The various roof pitches are typologised as follows:

- Flat roofs (up to 10°)
- Reasonably steep roofs (10 to 40°)
- Steep roofs (over 40°)

A building roof can be described by roof lines and roof areas. Examples of rooflines include: verge, ridge, main eave, eave corner, hip eave, arris, apex, partial hip eave, valley (internal edge), hip rafter (upper part of the ridge), mansard line, curb roof. Examples of roof areas include: main roof area, side roof area, gable, hip, partial hip.

The traditional forms of inclined roofs can be distinguished by their cross section in double pitch roofs, mansard roofs and monopitch roofs and their longitudinal section in gabled roofs, partial hip roofs, hipped roofs and tented roofs. This allocation can be extended and combined in a multitude of ways.

Roof design

If a roof is drawn in the floor plan, the roof lines can only be shown in abridged form in the two-dimensional representation. The term *roof design* is understood to mean geometrically determining the position of the roof edges with regard to the ridges, arrises and roof valleys – in their true size – that result from the combination of roof areas. The roof design is of major importance for the carpenter in order to calculate the beam dimensions for the hip and valley rafters. By using the roof design, it can also be determined at the planning stage where components which jut out from the roof (e.g. roof outlets, windows or chimneys) can be optimally positioned in the floor plan without intersecting too many unnecessary roof boundary lines.

When the roof slope is the same, all roof intersection lines either run in the angle bisector or in a parallel direction to each eave. Different eave heights and roof slopes require the calculation of contour lines. In the field of descriptive geometry, this is also known as *topographic projection*.

Example

Using an L-shaped floor plan with various wing widths, the methodology for the roof design is described below.

Step 1: First the centre of each part of the building is determined because the ridge always runs through the centre when the roof slope is the same. As building parts have different widths, these differ when the roof slope is the same (F1/F2).
Step 2: Valleys are drawn bisecting for re-entrant building corners.
Step 3: Arrises are drawn from the external building corners.
Step 4: If the roof only has one reentrant building corner, then it must have a hip that connects the end of the valley with the apex of the arris.
Step 5: Ridge lines are extended.
Step 6: In order to make the top view of the roof better legible, shading can also be used.

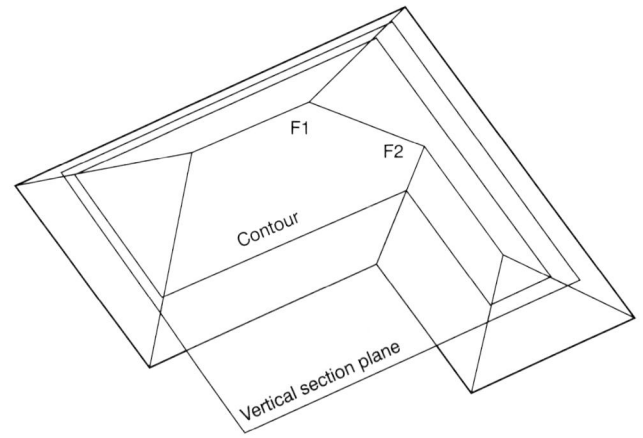

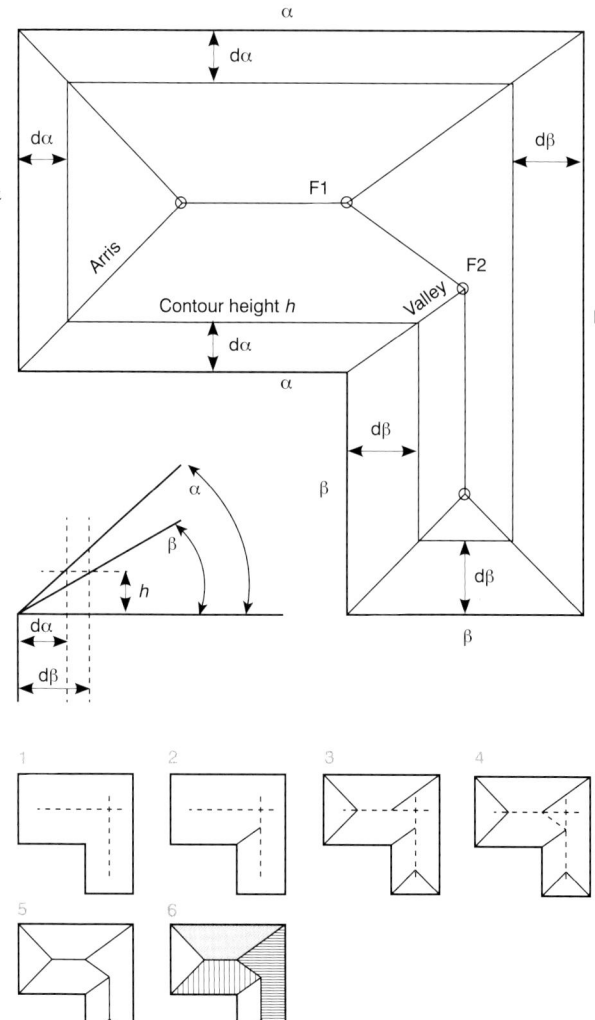

Symbols
Electric/Sanitation/Furniture (Selection)

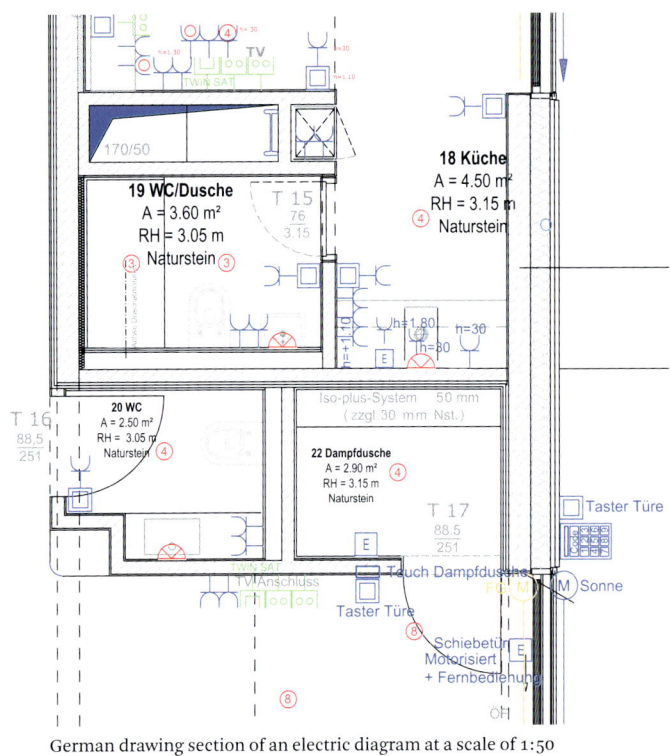

German drawing section of an electric diagram at a scale of 1:50 (reduced)

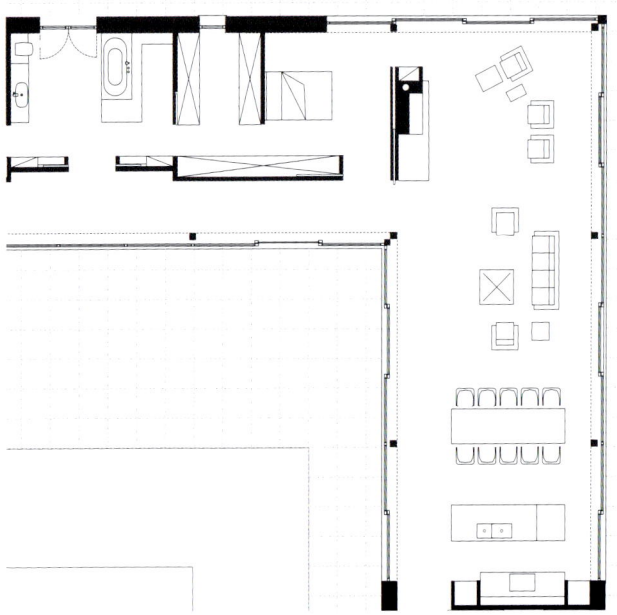

Drawing section of furniture (not to scale): It depends on the type of drawing whether furniture is represented in the floor plans. The location of furniture is primarily necessary for wet areas in order to position the corresponding recesses and cable routing.

Symbol	Description	Symbol	Description
	Light fixtures in general		Fluorescent lighting in general
	Lighting with a switch		Strip lighting fixture
	Portable lighting		Motion detector
	Electric cooker with oven	t	Timer
	Key switch		Socket
	Lighting key switch		Multiple socket
	Switch with pilot light		Ground contact socket
	Single/double/three-pole switch		Ground contact double-socket
	Switch 4/1 Gang switch, single-pole		Switched socket-outlet
	Switch 5/1 Series switch, single-pole		Vertical arrangement of sockets
	Switch 6/1 Toggle switch, single-pole	E	Electricity supply in general
	Toggle switch as a pull switch		Ventilation switch
	Switch 7/1 Intermediate switch, single-pole	RWA	Manual fire alarm
	Time switch		Fire alarm (Manual alarm)
	Dimmer	EDV	Data socket
	Proximity switch		Telephone socket
	Touch switch		Antenna socket

Working Tools
Basics and Standards
Types of Architectural Drawings

Furniture Living/sleeping	Description (w × d × h) cm	Furniture Cooking/bathing/home use	Description
	Table for 4 people 85 × 85 × 78		Base unit 30/50/60/80/100 × 60 cm
	Table for 6 people 130 × 80 × 78		Wall unit 30/50/60/80/100 × 40 cm
	Round table for 6 people d = 90		Sink/double bowl sink 100/150 × 60
	Chair/stool 45 × 50		Electric cooker
	Armchair 70 × 85		Gas stove
	Two seater sofa 175 × 80		Electric cooker with oven
	Couch 195 × 195		Dishwasher
	Wing 200 × 150		Fridge
	TV/flat screen		Freezer
	Cabinet module 60 × 120		Microwave oven
	Wardrobe 60 × 120		Air conditioner Range hood
	Desk 70 × 130 × 78		Washbasin/double washbasin
	Single bed 100 × 200		Sink
	Cot 70 × 140 to 170		Flush tank WC WC without a tank Bidet Urinal
	Double bed 180 × 200		Bath Shower

159

Types of Architectural Drawings

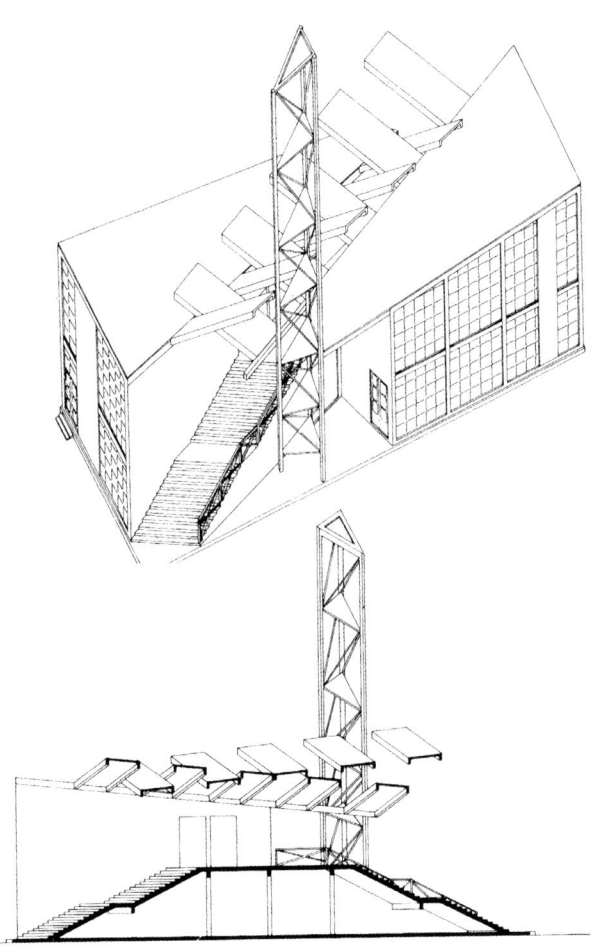

Konstantin Melnikov: Design for the Soviet Pavilion at the World Expo in Paris (1925)
Source: Chan-Magomedow, Selim: Konstantin Melnikov. Moscow 1990, p. 91

Sketches and freehand drawings
Sketching is both the search for and sampling of shapes and designs, as well as a form of expression for architects to convey ideas that are confined to the most essential features. Such ideas must not always be drawn to scale and can be drawn freehand. Sketches are thus an essential component of the architectural creative process and simultaneously provide a useful tool.

Diagram
Diagrams help to communicate and visualise complex ideas, systems and contexts across language and cultural barriers in a clear and comprehensive manner. Yet, in addition to serving this function they also act as small design objects created in the unmistakable style of their author. They have long formed a new inspiring art discipline.

Preliminary design drawings
The preliminary design drawing is the representation of the planning concept with the principal dimensions, design, function, position on the building site and integration in the surrounding area – if necessary with the participation of other planning services. It forms the basis for assessing the requirements for granting planning permission.

Measured drawings
Architectural drawings accurately convey the current state of construction. These are created to the extent and scale necessary.

Design drawings
Design drawings serve as the basis for required building documentation and present a planning concept by consolidating, for example, creative, functional, economic, site-specific or ecological requirements by involving other experts involved in planning. The process may also include requirements for the protection of both nature and species.

Building instruction drawings
Building instruction drawings are draft designs supplemented by information that is required by building guideline regulations of the respective country. These drawings form the basis of the application for a building permit and serve building authorities in the legal and technical evaluation of planned construction measures.

Working Tools
Basics and Standards
Types of Architectural Drawings

As-built drawings
As-built drawings contain illustrations required for the completion of the project, as well as information based on blueprints, approval planning and the contributions of other experts involved in planning. Particulars mentioned in working plans and detailed drawings serve as a basis for technical specifications and the completion of construction work.

Settlement drawings
All services performed in accordance with calculations can be clearly identified due to settlement drawings.

Working drawings
Working drawings contain all relevant information on a property or enclosure for the respective purpose.

Position plans
Created by the structural engineer, these are based on the conception design and are used to explain static calculations.

Formwork drawings
In addition to as-built drawings, formwork drawings also show the components to be encased in either concrete, reinforced concrete or prestressed concrete structures.

Carcass drawings
Carcass drawings are the basis for the assembly of the structure. They contain all forms relevant to the carcass and dimensions of recesses, openings etc.

Reinforcement drawings
The representation contains all information required for bending and laying the reinforcement in reinforced and prestressed concrete structures.

Prefab drawings
For the construction of prefabricated structures made of either concrete, reinforced concrete, prestressed concrete or brickwork in a factory, prefab drawings and lists of parts are produced.

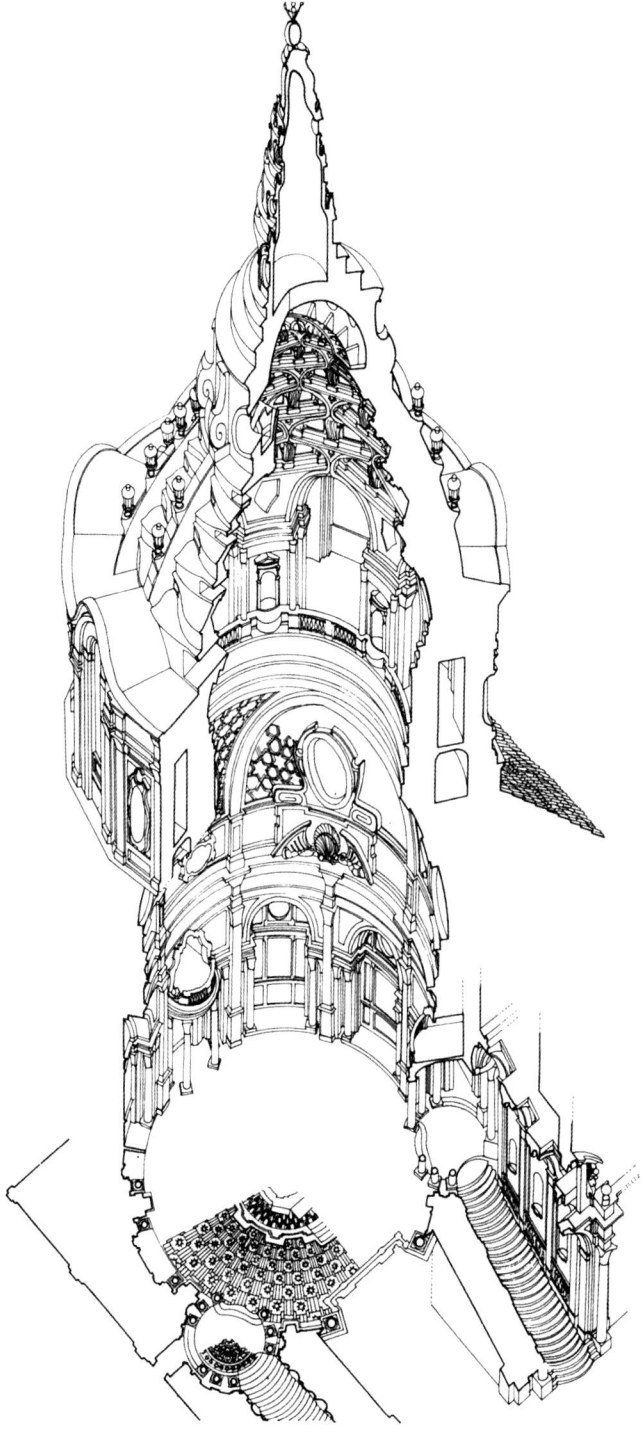

Guarino Guarini: Axonometry of SS. Sidone in Turin
Source: Hinse, Ton: The Morphology of the Times. European Cities and their Historical Growth. Berlin 2014, p. 122

Floor Plan Drawings

Of all the forms of representation, floor plan drawings are the most abstract and, at the same time, the most spatial. The floor plan drawing – the horizontal section through a structure – organises and imposes order on the design concept. However, not every space can be cut into sections when trying to achieve the geometric form. When a building is too complicated, the layout reaches its limits. Famous architects can also tell a thing or two about this. For instance, Hans Scharoun's Berlin Philharmonic concert hall already demonstrated this in the early sixties. The drawings of the master of organic architecture defied every standard of technical drawing. It was only through a multitude of models, sections and spatial studies that Scharoun was able to develop his interlaced space in the first place. The deconstructivists faced a similar challenge. However, technical presentation methods were already more evolved in the eighties than was the case with Scharoun. The first computer programmes supported the designer in his work. Increasingly complex building forms plot this trend, albeit with the effect that architects are increasingly reliant upon technical tools. What amounts to a reduced workload, essentially, must not result in the architect leaving designs and representations entirely to the computer. Drawing requires thinking and finding a form to begin with. Yet drawing also entails the observation of the grammar of language in order to make oneself clearly understood in the planning process by other parties involved in construction.

The floor plan (Greek: *ichnography*) is the horizontally cut building viewed from the top and is drawn for each individual floor. As a rule, the building is cut to a third of the storey height. This is in order to display essential components such as stairs, walls, openings and apertures. The cut parts are highlighted graphically by varying line thickness, brightness values, models or colours. Continuous lines show the visible boundaries and edges of the top surfaces of the components. Edges that are above the intersection line, such as beams and ceiling openings are shown, for example, by dashed lines. Functional areas such as transport zones can be denoted by different textures.

Working Tools
Basics and Standards
Types of Architectural Drawings

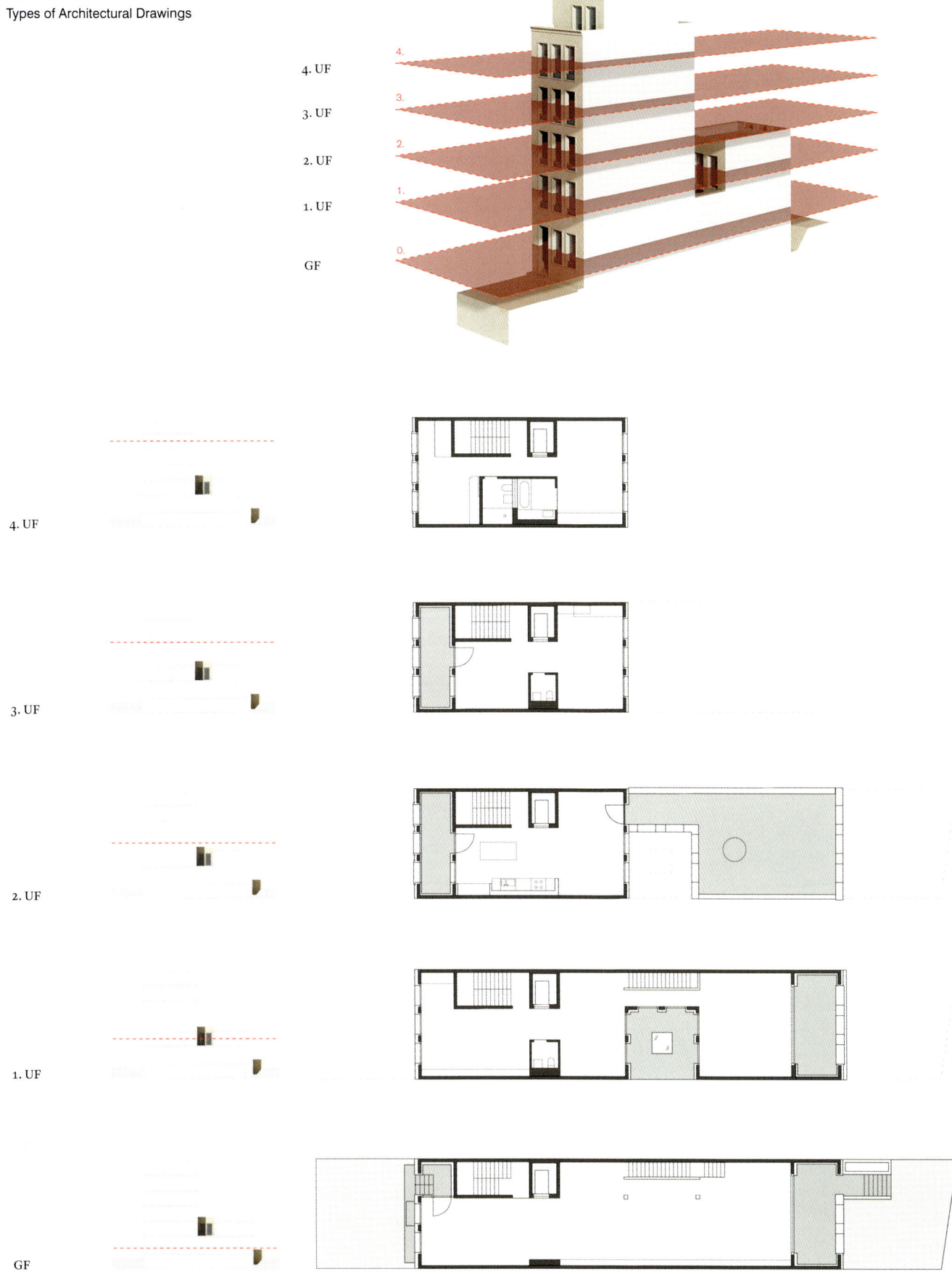

4. UF

3. UF

2. UF

1. UF

GF

Section Drawings

Section

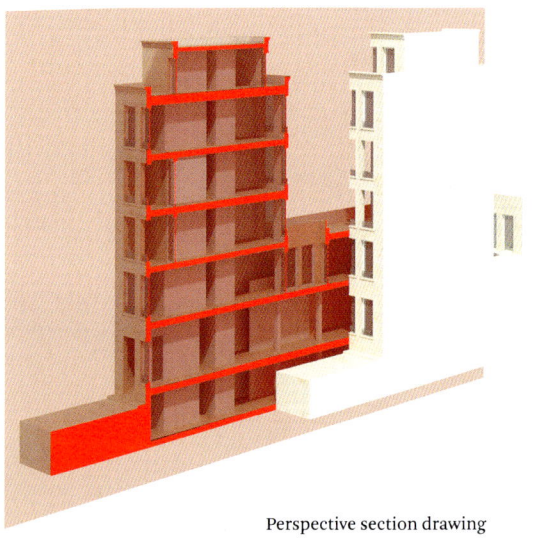
Perspective section drawing

In section drawings, the structure is divided into vertical segments. Thus, the gaze of the observer is always directed at the sectional area. Depending on the section plane, the drawing is either referred to as a longitudinal section or cross section. In the case of section drawings, the requirements declared for floor plan drawings shall apply correspondingly to technical drawings. Here, too, visible object edges are displayed with thicker line widths to facilitate legibility. The contours of the component which can be seen in the elevation, together with the dashed lines showing the invisible concealed edges and outlines of the solid structures, are drawn using thinner lines. In addition, sectional areas are usually flatly arranged or filled with shading. Shading that consists of lines, cross-lines, dashed lines or dots – with different line widths and spacing – is used to label these surfaces and areas. The section line is entered in the floor plan and the intersection line is labelled alphabetically (e.g. A–A).

Full section
For full sections, the structure of the outer edges is usually cut along the longitudinal axis or perpendicular to the longitudinal access. The location of the section is freely selectable.

Partial section
Only one part of the building is displayed in the partial section. The sectional area can be denoted by a boundary line (freehand line or zig-zag line).

Layered section
For layered sections, the important parts of the building are cut along an intersection line to be determined by the designer. In this regard, the intersection line can shift.

Perspective section drawing
A very clear and, most of all, spatial representation, the sectional view is of an object in axonometry or perspective.

Exploded-view drawing
For exploded section drawings, also known as *exploded-view drawings*, individual areas are shown offset to gain a better overview so that the components do not overlap.

Elevation Drawings

Factually speaking, the elevation (Latin: *facies* = face) is the parallel projection to the respective side of the building on the vertical image plane. However, elevation drawings are much more. They are indispensable for the two and three-dimensional presentation of designs. They bring together geometric accuracy and pictorial expression beyond that which is specified in rules and technical standards, as well as make the proportions and rhythmicity visible in their depth dimensions. Furthermore, they provide information on the type of construction, materiality and the plastic-spatial quality of the structure. In facade drawings, a visual effect can be achieved through the display of textures and materials, the brightness and thickness of lines, light and shadow, as well as attention to detail. The realistic representation of the facade permits an examination of the design at a greater distance from the building. Similar to the floor plan and section, the scale of the drawing regulates the drawing content. The content shown must be visually simplified for elevations on a smaller scale, while greater attention to detail, information content and a statement concerning the materiality are expected on drawings or drawing extracts on a larger scale.

- Elevations differ according to the direction from which they are viewed. West Elevation means the view of the West side. Elevation North-West means the building is oriented to the North and West.
- Elevations at the scales of 1:50 and 1:100 must display all significant sections in the structure.
- Identical components are drawn with an identical line width.
- In addition to the elevation, facade sections can be shown.
- Light and shadow can also be shown.
- The most emphasised component always dominates the view.
- The boundaries and outlines of the upper sides of the components that are visible from the front are represented as visible outline by continuous lines.
- The number of views is limited to the minimum amount necessary in order to determine the structure or component in a clear and comprehensible manner.

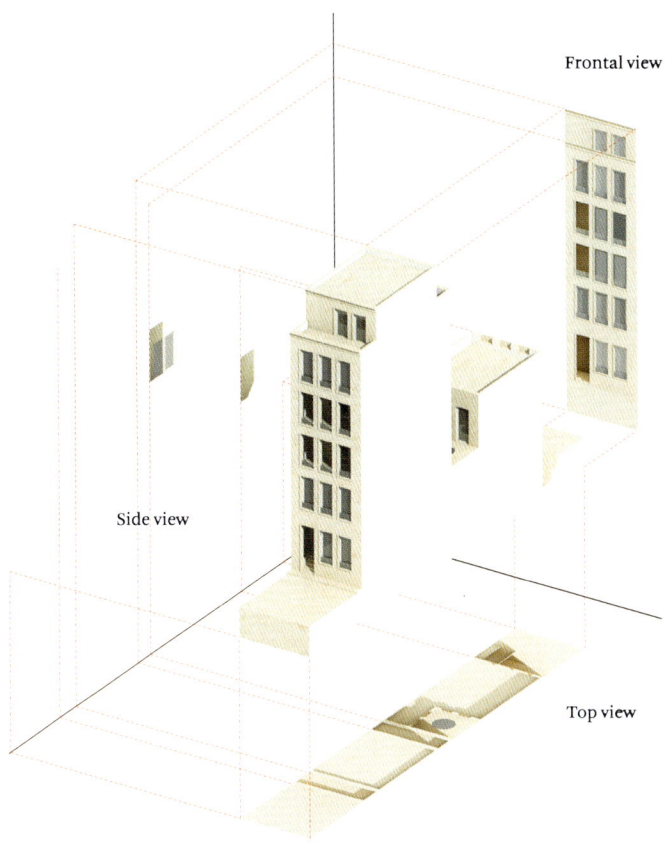

Orthogonal projection

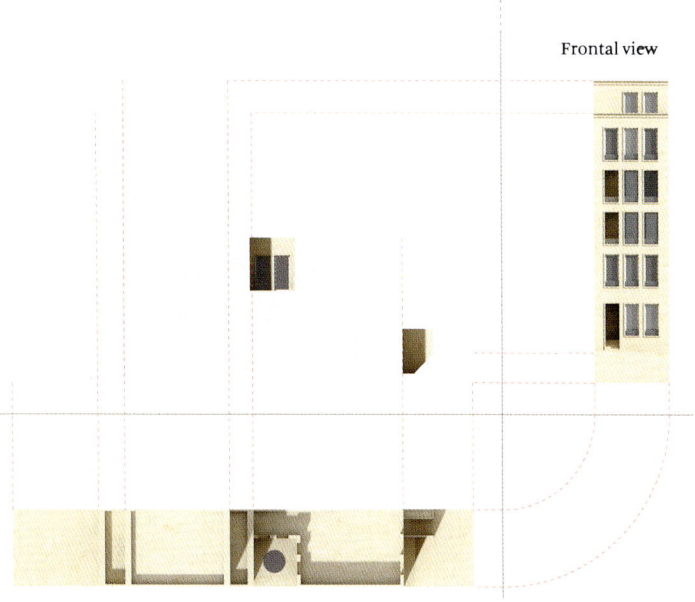

Site Plans

Scale 1:1.000/1:500

Cadastral site plan (plat)
The plat is the declaratory part of the Land Survey Register. It is available depending on state law regulations with regard to the competent registry agency, publicly appointed surveyors or surveying experts. The cadastral land register is the official body which determines how land is described in the land register. Land and buildings are described and represented graphically in the cadastral land register, including their design, size and location, as well as the type and delimitation of use. An excerpt of the plat is required for the site plan for the construction application. This is also used as evidence of site boundaries as well as for planning, land division and land transactions.

The site plan (according to BauvorlV)
The site plan is depicted at a scale of no more than 1:500 based on the plat and a local inventory. According to building guideline regulations, the site plan is part of the building application and consists of a written and graphic part. The plot of land is described in the written part, as well as further information being provided on the construction project. The graphic part shows the outline of the planned building, drawn to the correct scale. Here the land is viewed from above.

The site plan must present the following content in so far as this is necessary for evaluating a project:

- Scale and the north direction
- Parcel boundaries of the site and neighbouring properties
- The approval of a development plan on coverable property areas and the approval of an open space plan for the respective parcel of land
- Adjacent public traffic areas with an indication of both the elevation and latitude
- The proposed structure including external dimensions, the style of roof and elevation of the ground floor slab that faces the street
- Areas proposed for compensatory and replacement measures
- Land affected by easement
- Clearance areas
- The elevation of the natural or the fixed ground surface and the corners of the proposed structure in relation to the respective height reference system
- Use and division of unbuilt surfaces
- Existing structures on the site and neighbouring properties
- Existing buildings or land
- Public traffic areas that are to be used for the completion of construction projects
- et al.

Other representations must be explained.

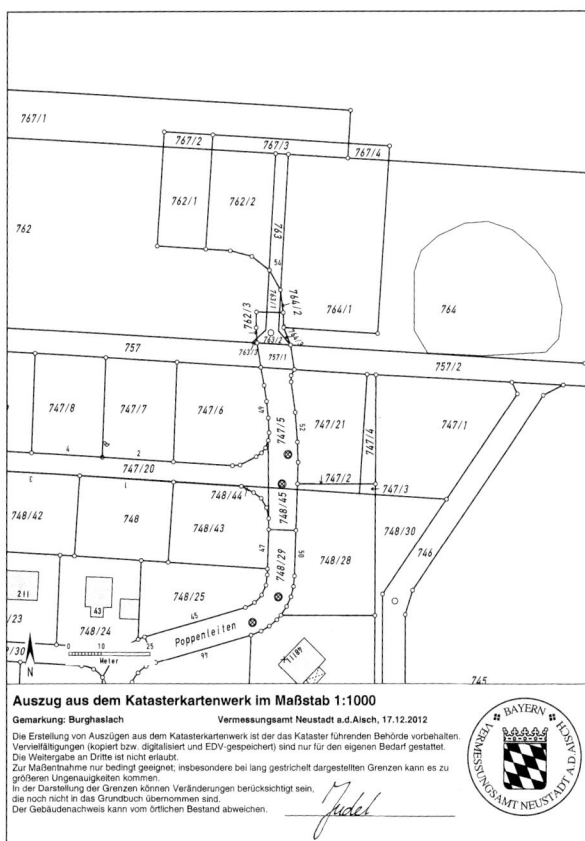

A German cadastral site plan (plat)
Source: Vermessungsamt Neustadt a.d. Aisch

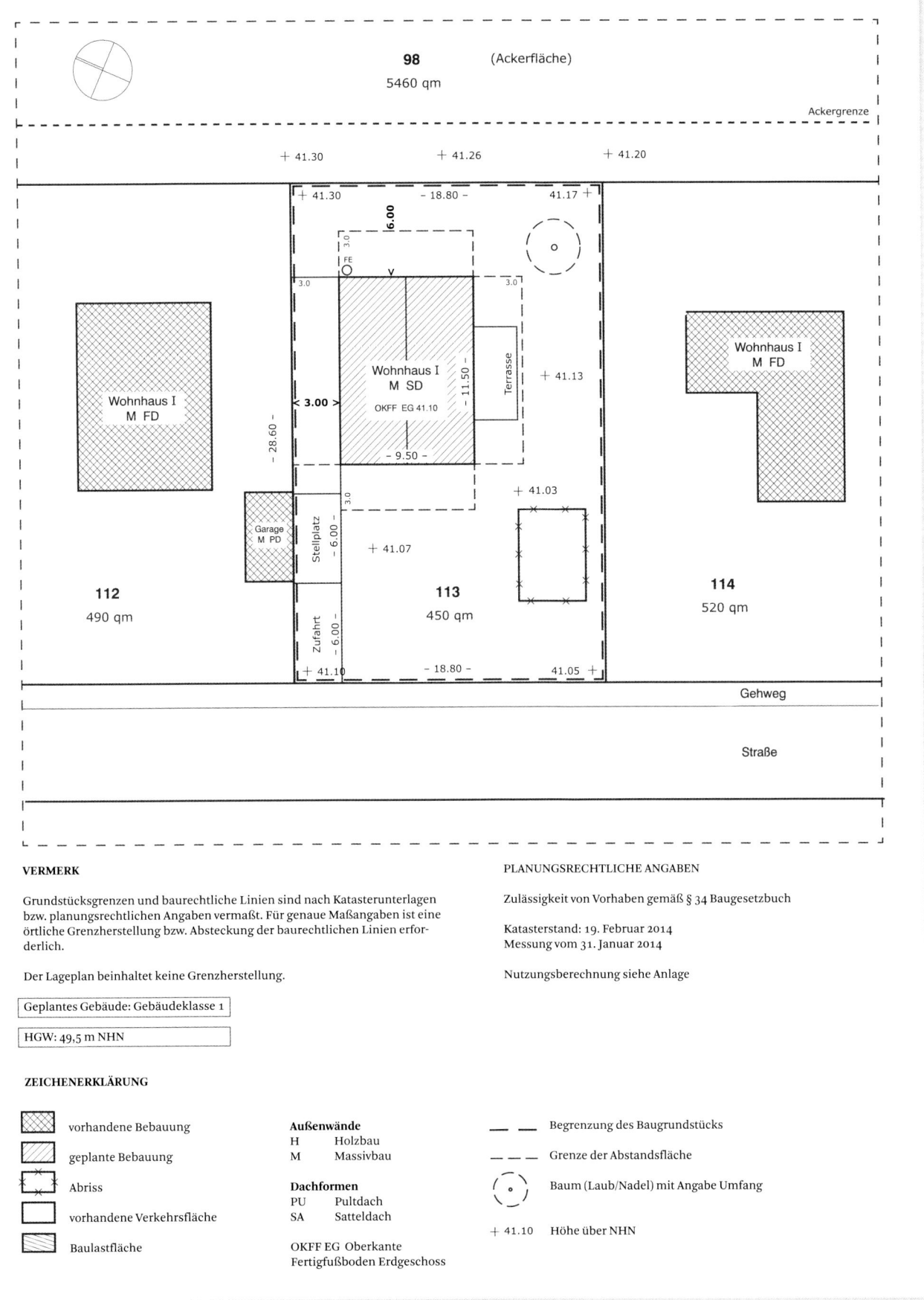

VERMERK

Grundstücksgrenzen und baurechtliche Linien sind nach Katasterunterlagen bzw. planungsrechtlichen Angaben vermaßt. Für genaue Maßangaben ist eine örtliche Grenzherstellung bzw. Absteckung der baurechtlichen Linien erforderlich.

Der Lageplan beinhaltet keine Grenzherstellung.

Geplantes Gebäude: Gebäudeklasse 1

HGW: 49,5 m NHN

ZEICHENERKLÄRUNG

	vorhandene Bebauung
	geplante Bebauung
	Abriss
	vorhandene Verkehrsfläche
	Baulastfläche

Außenwände
H Holzbau
M Massivbau

Dachformen
PU Pultdach
SA Satteldach

OKFF EG Oberkante Fertigfußboden Erdgeschoss

PLANUNGSRECHTLICHE ANGABEN

Zulässigkeit von Vorhaben gemäß § 34 Baugesetzbuch

Katasterstand: 19. Februar 2014
Messung vom 31. Januar 2014

Nutzungsberechnung siehe Anlage

— — Begrenzung des Baugrundstücks
- - - Grenze der Abstandsfläche
Baum (Laub/Nadel) mit Angabe Umfang
+ 41.10 Höhe über NHN

Preliminary Design Drawings

As a general rule 1:500/1:100

Preliminary design drawings in the form of sketch-like drawings, diagrams etc. are used to explain a planning concept in so far as this is necessary, together with other experts involved. These can serve as the basis for a first cost estimate and are used to check the requirements for granting planning permission. Depending on the type of planning and the task, preliminary design drawings must not always be drawn to scale.

Preliminary design drawings should include at least:

- Integration of the building in its environment
- Representation of the structure on the site
- Indication of the main thoroughfare
- North point
- Representation of the floor plans, main floor and sections such as the design of the building and its facades
- Space allocation plan (allocation of the rooms)
- Approximate dimensions of the building and rooms that serve as the basis for the calculation of base-areas and volumes of buildings
- Construction details
- Representation of the design concept and the spatial effect with perspectives and models

Preliminary design drawing for a doctor's practice
Source: Meuser Architekten

Working Tools
Basics and Standards
Types of Architectural Drawings

Design and Building Instruction Drawings

As a general rule 1:100/1:200

Design drawings are drawings depicting the overall design for a proposed structure. These originate from the preliminary design with consideration of the advice of other experts involved in planning. Due account should also be taken of requirements stemming from urban design, design and construction. The perceptibility of design and construction components must be given. Design drawings also serve as the basis for the calculation of costs. Depending on the type of planning and the task, preliminary design drawings are usually depicted at a scale of 1:100. With larger objects this is 1:200.

Design drawings should include at least:
Floor plans:
- Dimensions of the location of the building in the site
- References to building entrances
- North point
- Dimensions of the building and construction components
- Clear room dimensions of the shell
- Height above sea level of the building
- Room areas in m²
- Indication of the building type and essential construction materials
- Colour scheme and lighting design
- Building joints
- Door and window openings with the opening direction
- Stairs and ramps with an indication of the rise-to-run ratio, the number of risers and the rise direction (walking line)
- Chimneys, conduits and shafts, facilities of the technical outfitting
- Operational fitments and furnishings
- In the event of changes in the construction, the new components to be obtained and removed
- The number of trees and the proposed design of open spaces on the site (traffic areas/green corridors)
- Section planes

Sections:
- The existing and proposed lay of the ground (part of the land)
- The height of the ground floor slab in relation to the site (usually, the finished floor level of the ground floor is defined with ± 0,00 as the height reference point)
- The height of the finished floor level floor above ± 0,00 of the other floors
- Height above sea level of the structure
- Height between floors, clear floor ceiling heights, if necessary
- Constructive details on the foundation and roof system
- Stairs and ramps with an indication of the rise-to-run ratio and the number of risers
- The wall height as defined in the building regulations
- Roof heights and slopes, as well as the roof system
- Connections to the adjacent existing buildings, if necessary

Elevations:
- Structure of the facade including building joints
- Window and door divisions
- Gutters and rainwater downpipes
- Chimneys and other technical installations
- Roof overhangs
- The wall height as defined in the building regulations
- Roof heights and slopes, as well as the roof system
- The existing and proposed lay of the ground and eventually the gradient of the road
- The subsequent development to be taken into consideration, if necessary; at least two window axes of the neighbouring buildings should be illustrated

Building instruction drawings evaluate the construction project within the scope of a legal review. This particularly concerns information on building guideline regulations and/or regulations for other design drawings supplemented by legal procedures. As a general rule, building instruction drawings are to be created at a scale of 1:100.

Right:
Building application drawing for a one-family house
Source: Meuser Architekten

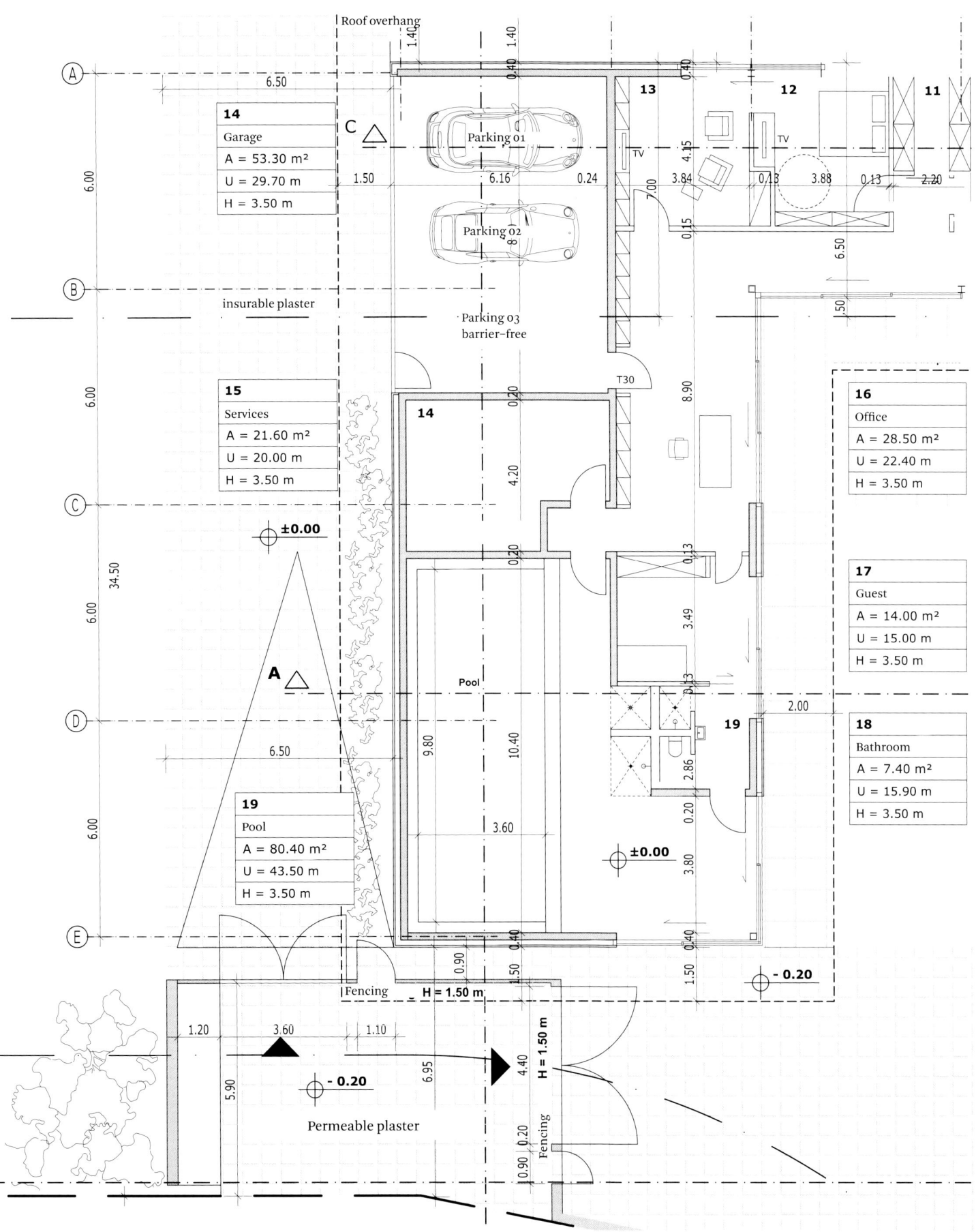

As-Built Drawings
Floor Plans

As a general rule 1:50/1:20

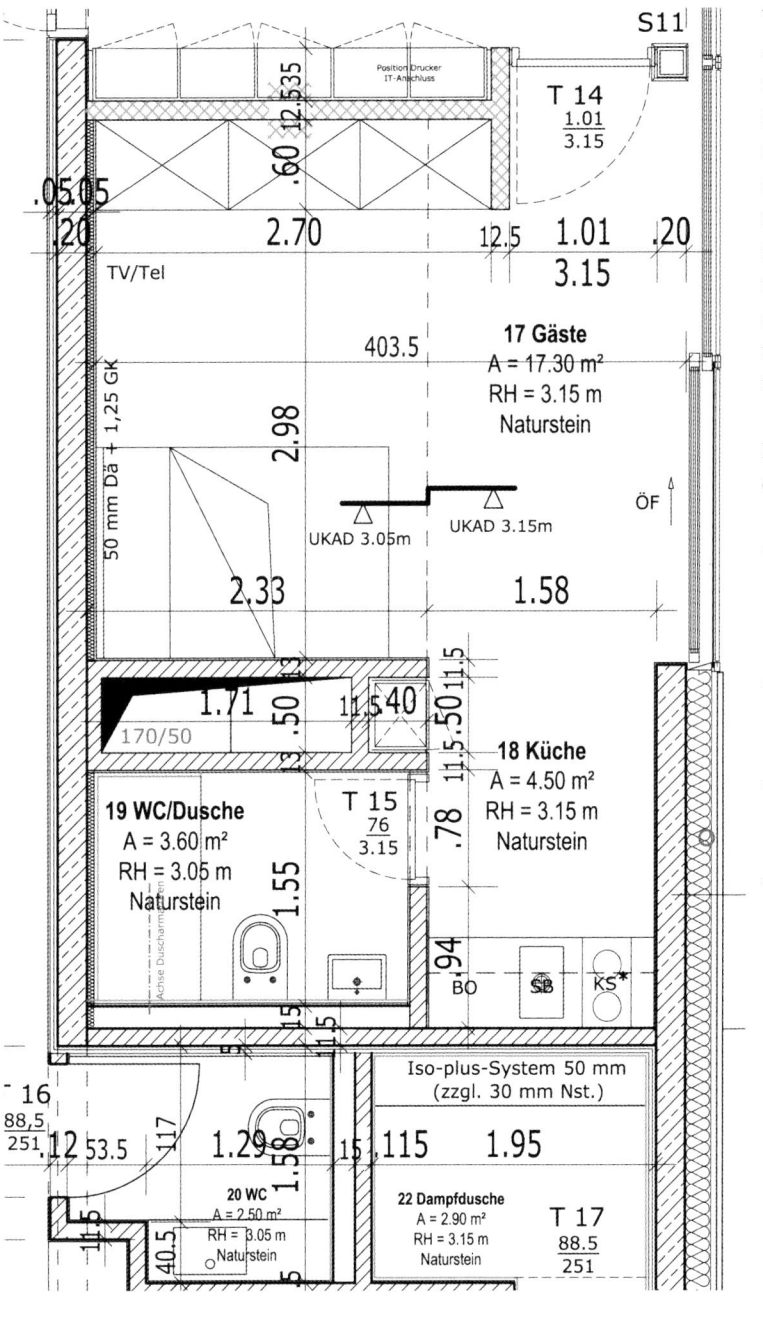

When planning the execution of a project, the planning results of the earlier draft design or approval planning are worked through to the point that the construction project can be realised. This is done with account taken of urban, creative, functional, technical, construction-physical, economic, energy-industry and ecological requirements, including contributions from other experts involved in planning. This is until a solution ripe for execution can be found. The execution planning provides the basis for the preparation of tender documents, contract specifications and the cost calculation. As-built drawings are usually drawn at a scale of 1:50/1:20. The drawings and information must be clearly arranged and co-ordinated to one another.

Depending on the nature and scope of the project, as-built drawings should contain at least:

- All relevant information necessary for the execution of the project, such as dimensions, tolerances, material specifications, information on the quality and nature of the materials, operation instructions
- All details necessary for the execution of the project, e.g. final and complete as-built, detail and design drawings at a scale of 1:50 to 1:1
- Depending on the nature of the project, outside facilities at a scale of 1:200 to 1:50 – particularly planting schemes – with the necessary written observations
- In the case of spatial extensions, a detailed presentation of rooms and room sequences at a scale of 1:25 to 1:1 with the necessary written observations and material prerequisites

Top and right:
As-built drawing for a one-family house in Germany (excerpt)
Source: Meuser Architekten

Working Tools
Basics and Standards
Types of Architectural Drawings

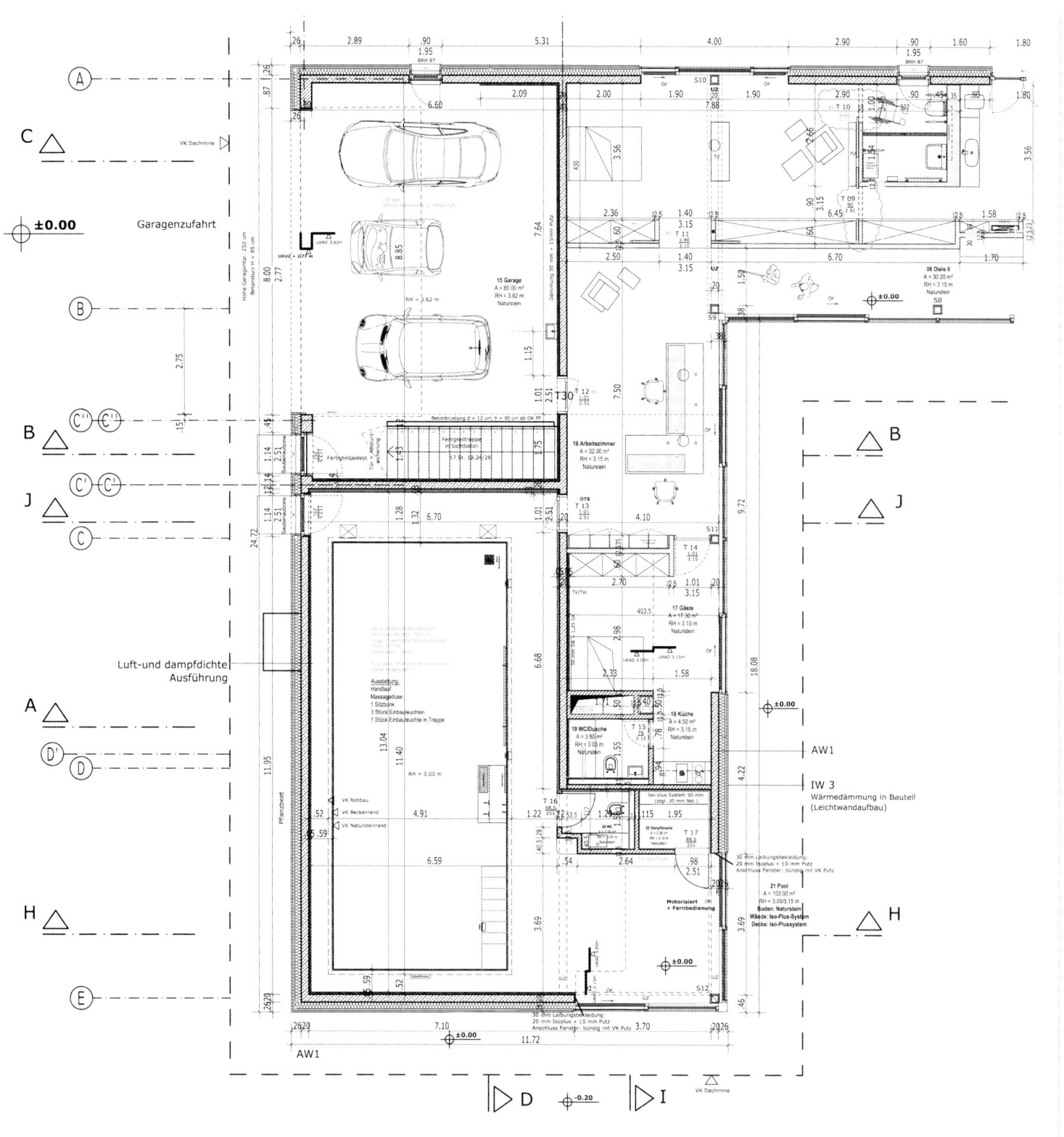

As-Built Drawings
Elevations and Sections

As a general rule 1:50/1:20

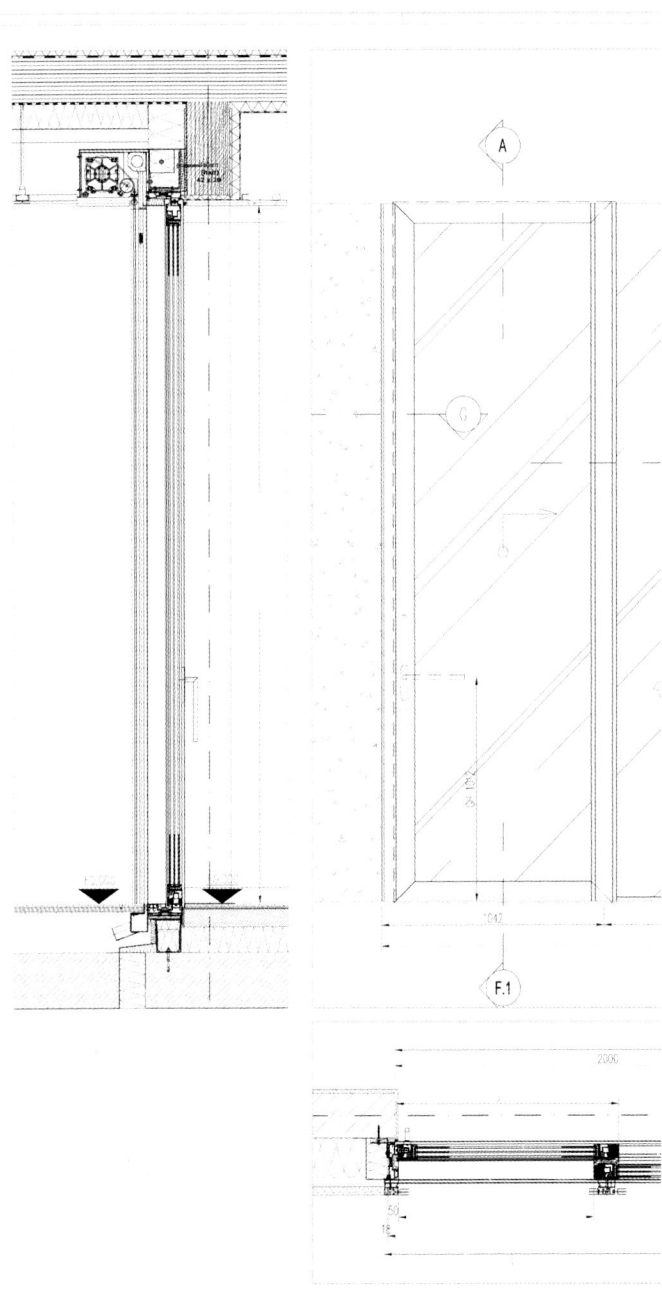

Elevations

Elevations should contain at least:

- The structure of the facade including the representation of joints
- Dimensions and elevations
- Concealed floor slabs and bases situated behind the facade
- Windows and doors with an indication of the division and types of openings
- Gutters and rainwater downpipes
- Chimneys and other technical installations
- The subsequent development, if necessary

Sections

Sections should contain at least:

- The height between floors and clear room heights
- Heights of floors and ceilings with an indication of shell construction dimensions, final dimensions, landings, parapets, beams etc.
- Dimensions of components
- Indication of the building type and essential construction materials
- Stairs with an indication of the number of risers, rise-to-run ratios and the rise for ramps
- Indication of the position and levelling of the waterproofing
- Recesses
- Areas with height indicators
- Information on drainage
- Fixtures
- Information on other detail drawings

Top and right:
As-built drawing for a one-family house
Source: Meuser Architekten

Working Tools
Basics and Standards
Types of Architectural Drawings

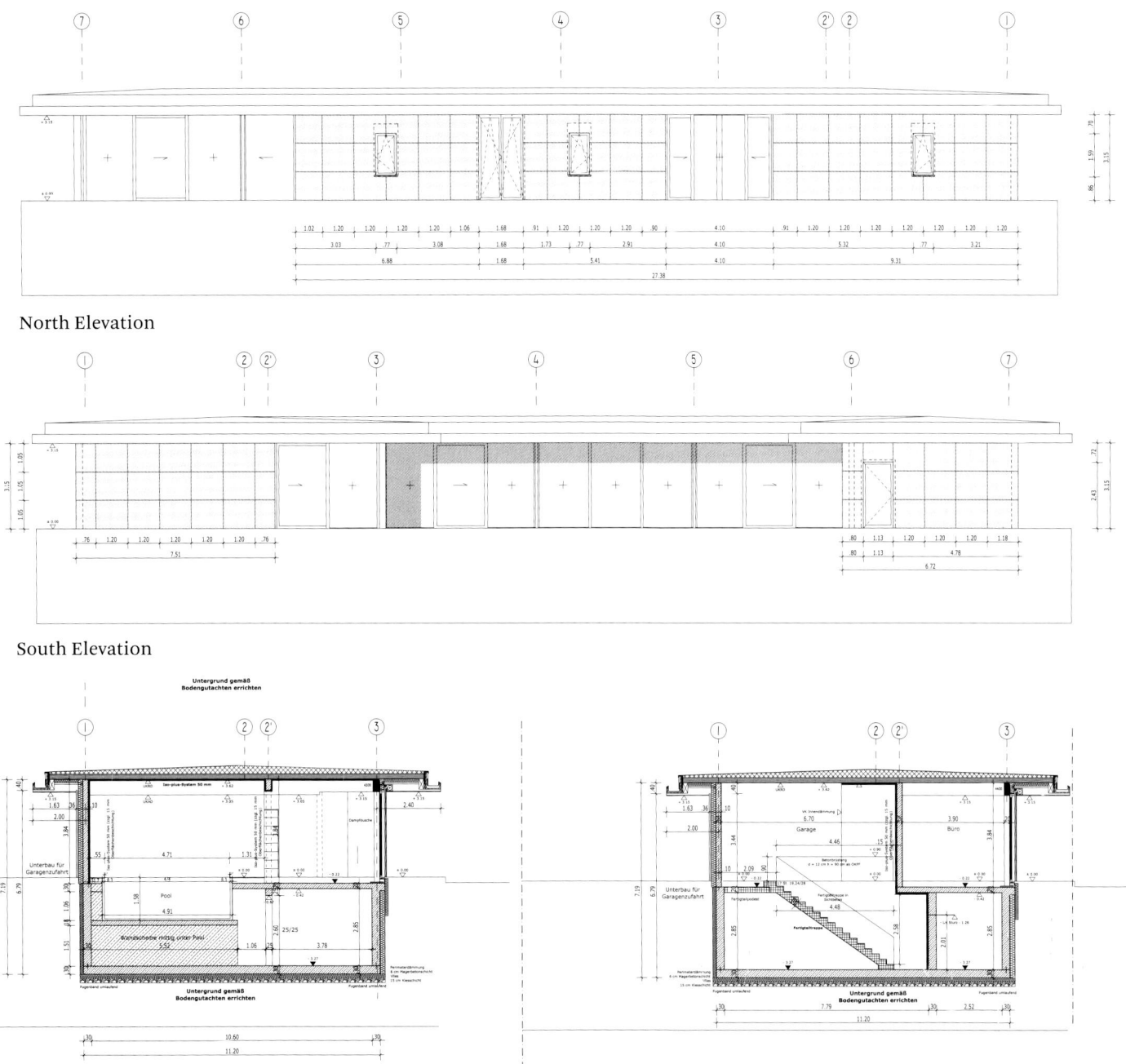

North Elevation

South Elevation

Section H–H

Section B–B

Detail and/or Component Drawings

1:20 to 1:1

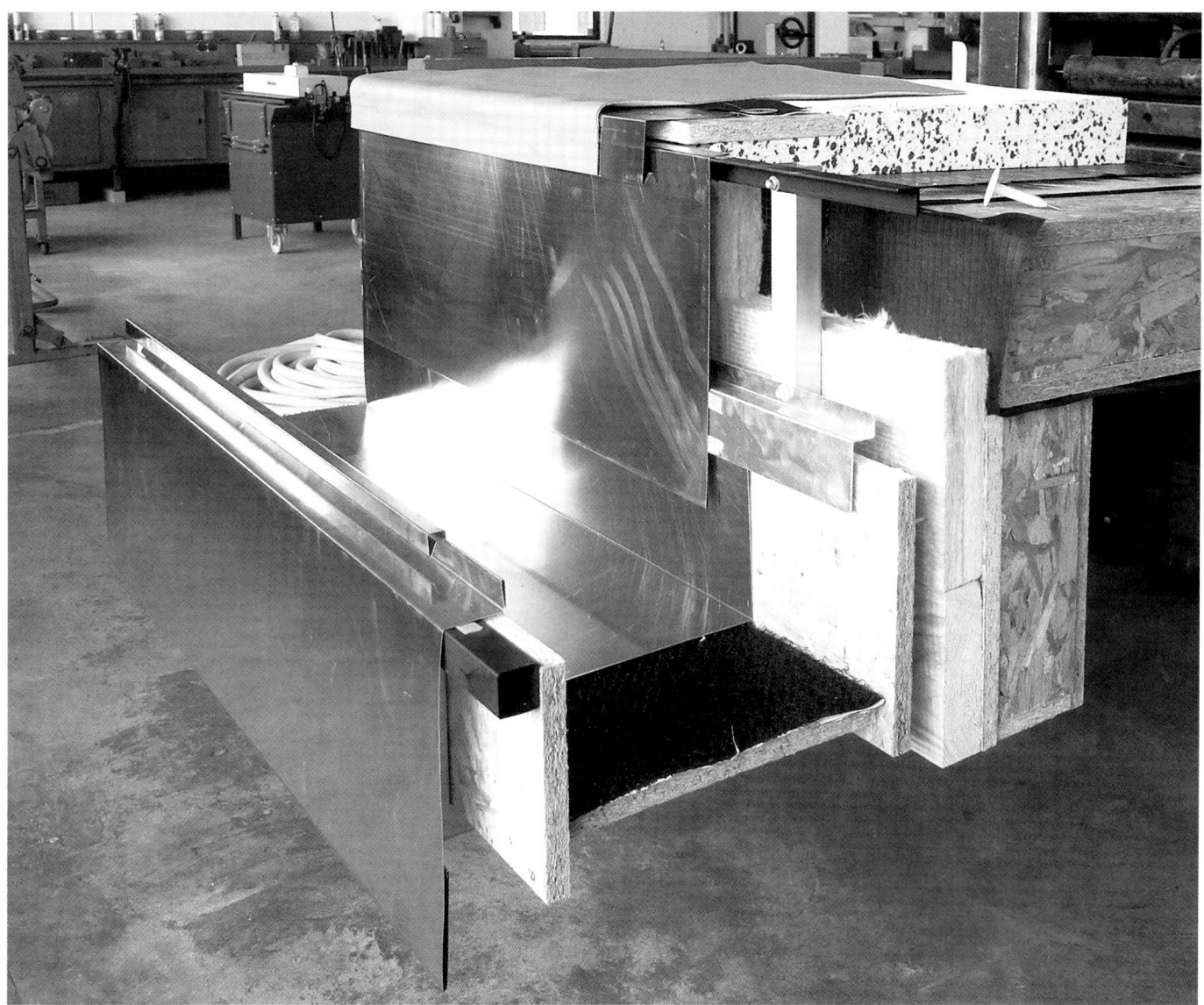

A model of a roof element as shown in the detail drawing right (not to scale)

Detail drawings
Detail drawings expand on working drawings in certain sections by providing additional information. They are drawn to a scale of 1:20/1:10/1:5/1:1 and must be indicated in as-built drawings.

Working Tools
Basics and Standards
Types of Architectural Drawings

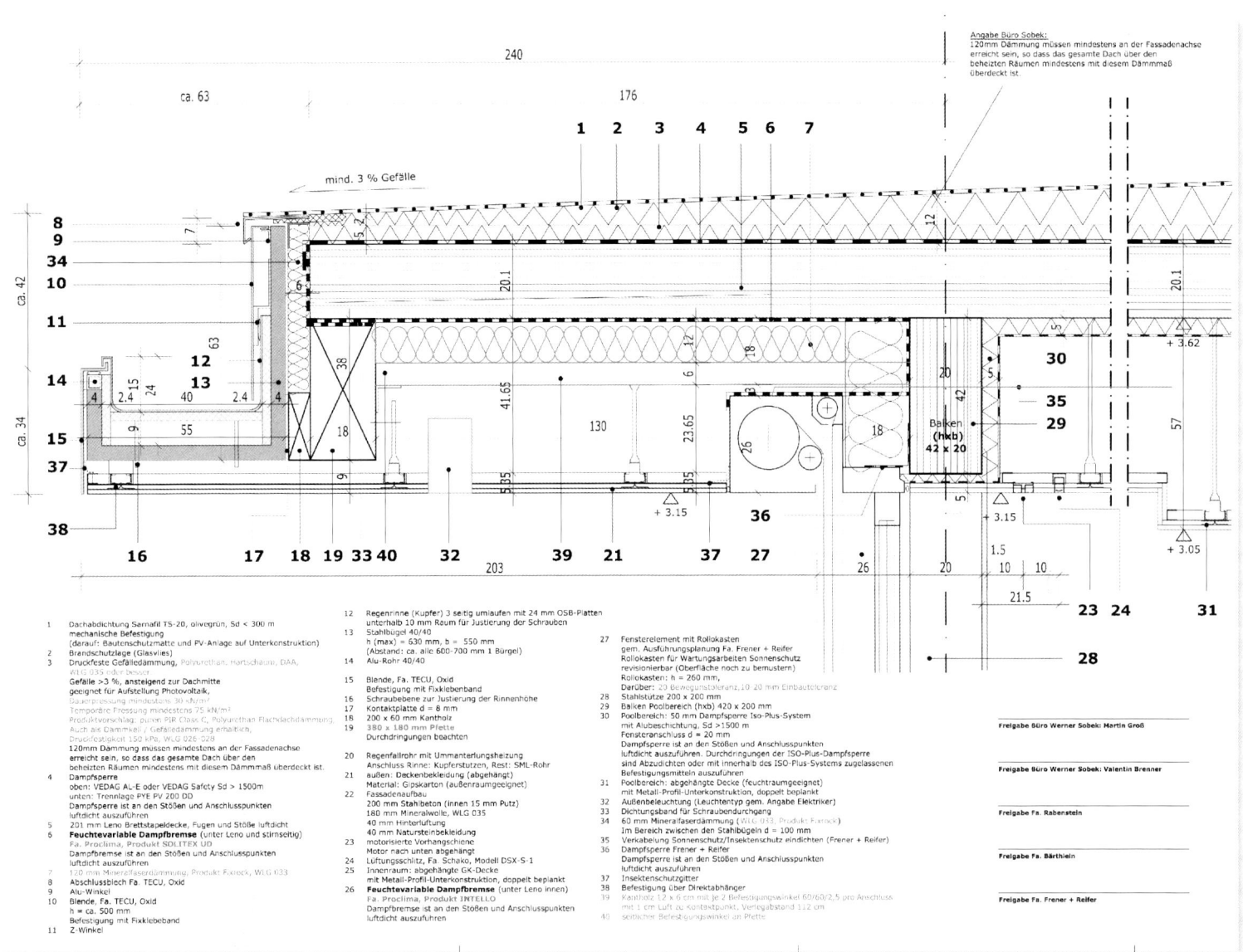

As-built drawing for a one-family house,
Detail drawing for a roof cantilever
Source: Meuser Architekten

»Architecture is the learned game, correct and magnificent, of forms assembled in the light.«

Le Corbusier

Discussion

181 Drawing between History and Digital Innovation
Fabrizio Avella

181 The Plan
185 Orthogonal Projections and Flat Section
194 Perspective
206 The Axonometric Projection
212 Paper
214 Techniques
227 Permanence and Variations in Computer Science Design

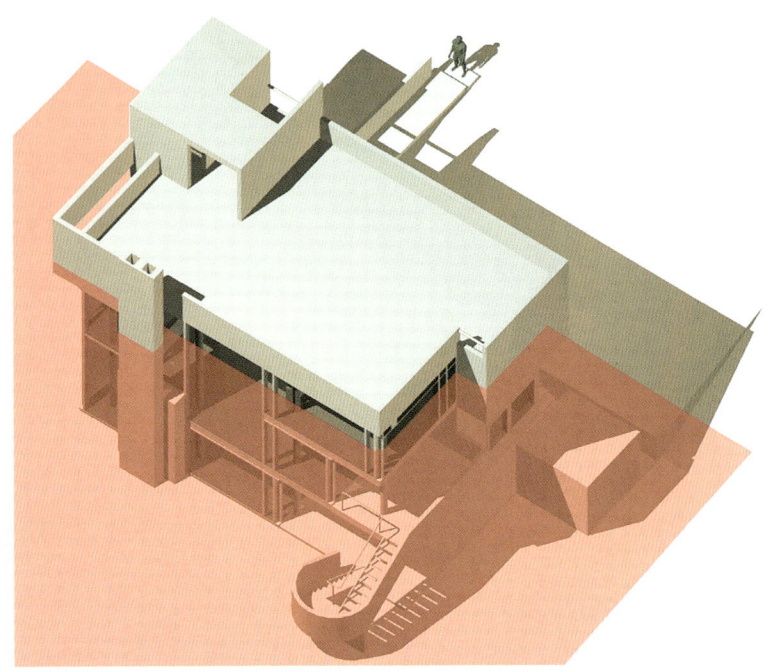
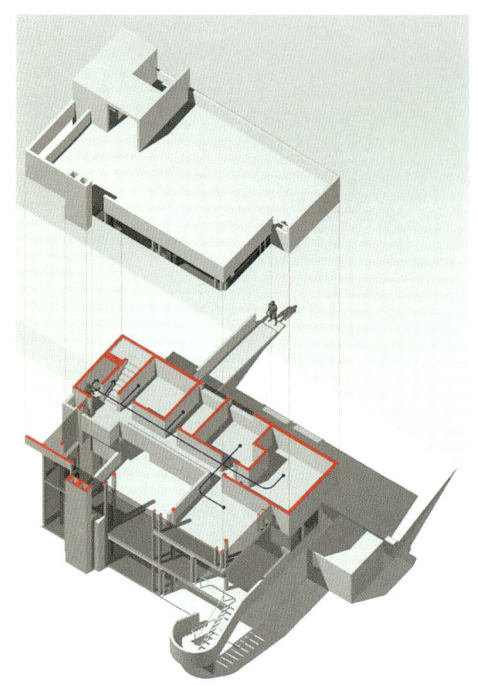
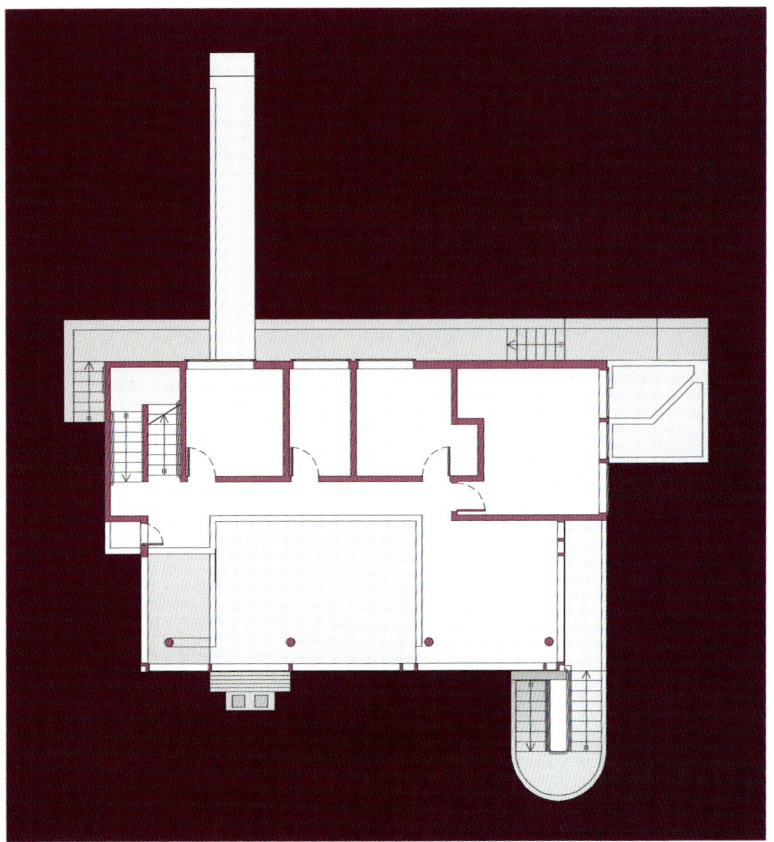
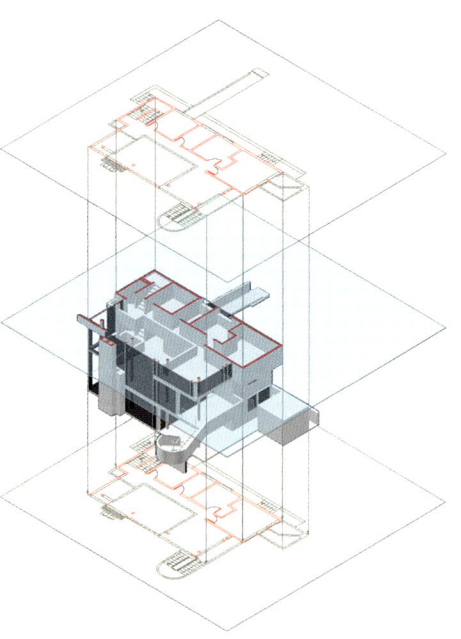

Bernardo Augello,
Smith House by Richard Meier,
2006

180

Drawing between History and Digital Innovation
Fabrizio Avella

The introduction of digital processing techniques in architectural drawing has, in recent years, shaken the foundations of the drawing discipline. The aim of this essay is to determine what, conceptually, has remained unchanged compared to the codes of the manual drawing and how much it proposes itself as the new structure of thought. Considering technique as a dimension that creates thought with a set of bi-univocal reports, one wonders if and how the use of new skills can influence and change the way we represent, and, therefore, think about architecture. In order to do this it is necessary to reflect on the codes of the methods and techniques of representation, focusing on those aspects which may help us to understand whether and how these codes have been impaired or accepted in the processes of digital drawing.

The plan

It is very difficult to determine how long the plan has been used to describe architecture. The first method of representation mentioned by Vitruvio is *iconography*, the footprint of an object left on the soil, and traces of this method are found as early as 7200 BC.[1] The plan is a drawing that requires a high level of abstraction on the part of those who carry it out and by whom it is interpreted: we must imagine cutting an object with a huge plane, to eliminate the entire upper portion above a giant knife and, as if that were not enough, we must imagine looking at what is left from a point an infinite distance away.

The sequence of images extracted from a study by Bernardo Augello on some architecture by Richard Meier shows what the process leading to the drafting of a plan is. Yet, despite being probably the most analogical design and least mimetic invented by man, it remains the most familiar and easy to interpret even to the inexperienced eye, not used to drawing diagrams: subway maps, information boards for tourists and diagrams of emergency exits of public buildings are drawn in plan; estate agents provide photos and plans, but never an axonometric section; a client, even if not trained, can understand the intentions of the architect by looking at the plans of a project since information is conveyed in a clear and comprehensible manner.

It is not easy to determine the reasons for this familiarity, but certainly anyone who has studied design has been introduced early to this kind of drawing: in any book of art history the Greek temples are classified in *monoptera, pseudo-diptera, diptera*, depending on how many rows of columns surround the naos, or hexastyle, octostyle depending on the number of columns on the main front, and has learned to recognise churches with central plan or longitudinal plan.

The plan drawing was well known and used in Roman times. Besides the aforementioned Vitruvio, there are fragments of a stone plan of Rome during the Imperial age, dated between 203 and 211 AD. *The Forma Urbis* or *Marble Map of Rome* is a set of marble slabs showing a rectangular portion of the city 4.3 by 3.2 km, on a scale which reduces the plan to approximately 18×13 m.[2] The construction technique and the accuracy of the survey, which is very high if we consider the tools available, suggest that a very high quality of representation was already being used, coded and implemented to allow such a vast and complex operation to take place.

The easy stroke for the wall is not misleading, as it is due, probably, to the scale of the drawing and the technology. Consider that the plan was built by cutting marble slabs with a stylus, where the size of the representation did not allow exact scale

Forma Urbis Romae, 203–211 AD
Tav. 53 della Forma Urbis Roma,
Stanford University e Sovraintendenza ai Beni
Culturali del Comune di Roma,
Rome (Italy)

Pianta del Tempio di Castore e Polluce presso il circo Flaminio, 2nd century AD
Museo Nazionale Romano, inv. 365105,
Rome (Italy)

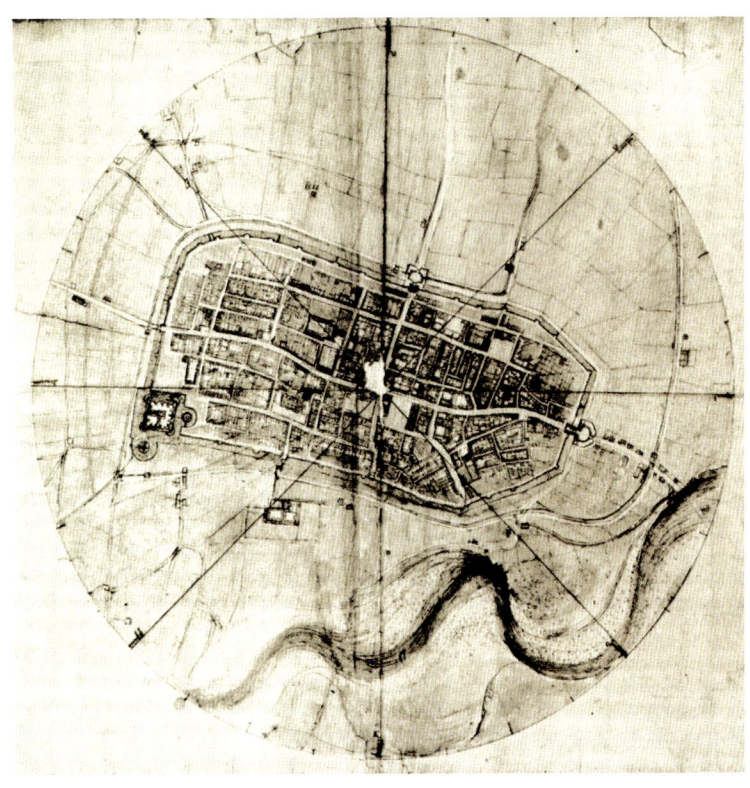

Leonardo da Vinci (1452–1519),
Pianta di Imola (Italy), 1502
Windsor Castle, Royal Library, RL 12284r,
Windsor (UK)

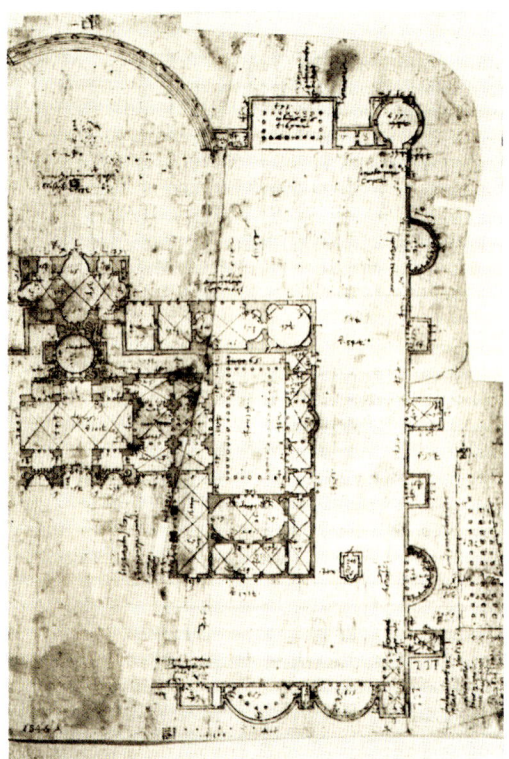

Giuliano da Sangallo (1445–1516),
Pianta delle terme di Diocleziano a Roma (Italy),
date unknown
Gabinetto delle Stampe degli Uffizi, Florence (Italy),
Photo: Pineider

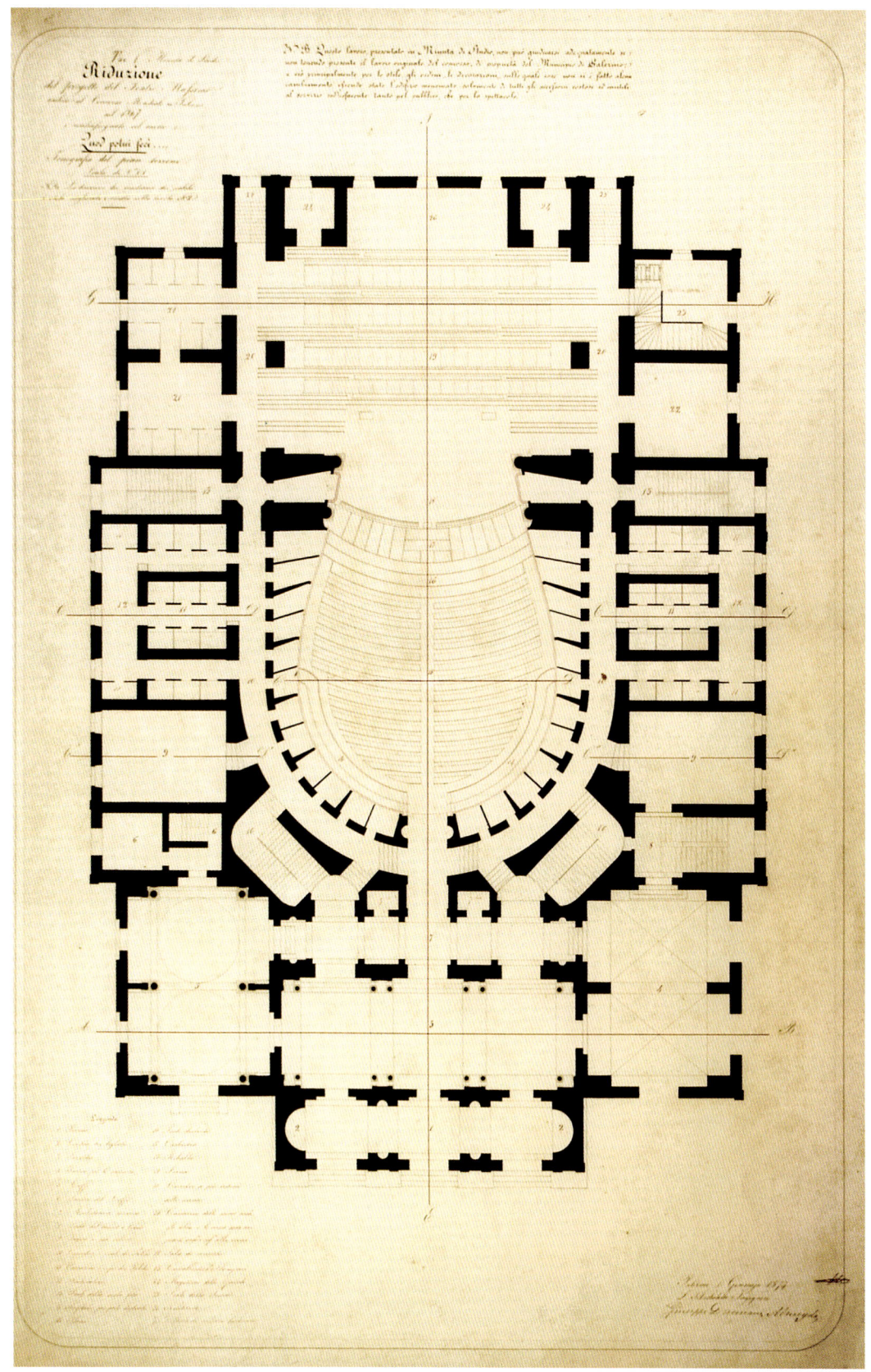

Giuseppe Damiani Almeyda (1834–1911),
Project for Teatro Massimo in Palermo.
Plan of the first floor, 1874
Archivio Damiani, Palermo (Italy)
Photo: Fabrizio Avella, post-processing: Fabrizio Avella, Giuseppe Dalli Cardillo

reproduction of the thickness of walls. A representation of walls by parallel signs can be seen in the plan of a portion of the Castor and Pollux Temple, made prior to the *Forma Urbis*, in which the technique for rendering the section is quite similar to the one used today.

The *marmorea plan* represents a simplification of graphics due, probably, not to a simplification of the code, but a limit set by the techniques used. The operation becomes even more impressive when one considers that in order to find a perfect planimetric representation in orthogonal projection with an acceptable level of accuracy, we have to go forward approximately thirteen centuries, to Leonardo da Vinci's map of Imola of 1502. Considering that apart from the plan of Imola, pseudo-perspective or pseudo-axonometric representations in topographic maps are not found until the seventeenth century, the scientific nature of *Forma Urbis* is appreciated even more.

There are no reasonable sources of doubt that the plan was used as a method of representation in medieval times, but to find codes closer to those we use today, we had to wait until the fifteenth century. It is worth noting, in this respect, the survey of the Diocletian baths by Giuliano da Sangallo, in which the distinction between the cut portions of the wall and the projection of the vaults above is clearly visible.

The reproduction of the plan did not undergo any specific innovations in the following centuries, except for refinements of techniques for making distinctions between the drawing of the section parts and projection parts. From a purely theoretical point of view, there is no difference between the plan of the project for the city's Teatro Massimo of Palermo by Giuseppe Damiani Almeyda, and the plan study of Casa Smith by Richard Meier, achieved through a common CAD software: both plans assumed to cut the building with a secant plane positioned at a certain height, to remove the top and look at the remaining portion from an infinite, zenithal distance. They both also betray the choices made by the designer to clearly distinguish the portions of wall cut from what, by contrast, is represented in orthogonal projection.

The descriptive power of the plan, perhaps determined by its abstract, low mimetic nature, was so strong that it was subsequently chosen to define the typological characteristics of architecture. Consider, for example, the tables of Durand,[3] and, more recently, the interesting essay by Carlos Martí Aris on the concept of type in architecture. In both cases, the purpose of defining types of architecture leads to extensive use of the plan as fully sufficient to define the types in question.[4] Moreover, the upheavals created by the formal and spatial Modern Movement were not able to undermine the importance of the plan, if Le Corbusier felt the need to identify it as one of the five principles which generate architecture.

Even today, despite the fact that we have definitely abandoned the idea of typology and accepted that contemporary architecture moves toward complex forms, the plan remains among the forms of representation still used and all BIM programmes provide more or less automatic procedures for extracting plans from three-dimensional models, regardless of the complexity of their configuration.[5]

Villard de Honnecourt, *Front view and section of the nave of the cathedral of Reims*, c. 1220/1235
From *Livre de Portraiture*, Codex ms. Fr. 19093, Fol. 31. National Library of France, Paris (France)

Facade of Strasbourg Cathedral
(Plan A1), c.1275
Musée de l'Œuvre Notre-Dame,
Inv. No. 2, Strasbourg (France)

Orthogonal projections and flat section

Almost all the texts dealing with the history of representation apay a tribute to the original section of the nave of the Cathedral of Reims, dated around 1230, reported in the *Livre de Portraiture* of Villard de Honnecourt. Commenting on its importance, Frommel notes how the role of the architect transformed in the Gothic period, in that as well as being the master-builder, the head of the building site with great technical skills. His need to visualise the building required not only *in-situ* sketches, but also drawings with which to organise the project.[6] This drawing is also interesting because it fits together the exterior view of the building (the facade) with the interior view (the section), juxtaposing facade and section to highlight similarities and variations, revealing an analytical capacity of the highest quality.

Another graphic tribute to a Gothic cathedral is given on the design of the facade of the cathedral in Strasbourg, dated between 1250 and 1260, in which there is a more correct orthographical projection than the one on the sheet of Palinsesto of Reims. These drawings are historic as the first European examples of sections and facades on parchment, using a projective code similar to that which we are accustomed to in the modern era. Certainly, the complexity of the Gothic construction site and the strong attention given to constituent elements such as doors, windows, pinnacles, and the refined geometries which they underpin could give legitimacy to the systematic use of the front view. The method was probably already known and used. Consider, for example, that Vitruvio had already combined orthography, now called elevation, with iconography, *the drawing in plan*. The lack of evidence does not necessarily mean that there was no *orthographic* drawing during the early Middle Ages.

The importance of these medieval drawings must be attributed not to the fact that they reveal the use of this system during the Middle Ages, but that they represent the rare few pieces of evidence that have survived to this day. While, in fact, we have evidence of the existence of the plan in Roman times, there is no equivalent to the front elevation with a clearly identifiable code similar to the one existing today.

There may be various reasons for this. Among those considered likely, we should recall that, in medieval construction sites, the *magister* (master) made *ephemeral* drawings on non-durable media, such as boards surrounded by wooden planks, where he would *draw* – or better rabble – with a steel or wooden stylus on a layer of lime. These drawings were actually an empirical tool for solving problems of implementation. They were necessary for the *magister* in order to communicate with apprentices. Once the problem was solved, the drawing could be removed and the *sheet* could be reused.

The elevation drawing, like the plan, underwent a refinement during the Renaissance. One reason that may have played a role in this process lies in the education of the Renaissance architect, which included study through the survey of buildings, in order to infer compositional rules and codes. In painting the ancient building, little by little, orthogonal projection turned out to be even more effective, because it allowed the architectural

Anonymous French artist,
Tempietto di San Pietro in Montorio, date unknown
Cod. Destailleur D, I, Hdz. 4151, Fol. 103 recto,
Staatliche Museen, Kunstbibliothek, Berlin (Germany)

order to be drawn and described with geometrical and impartial accuracy. If an architect begins to use a method of representation in order to understand ancient architecture, it is likely that he will also use it to think about the architecture to be built. Referring to specific essays on the role of drawing tools for developing architecture from the early Renaissance, it is useful to follow some of the steps.[7] In the fifteenth century, the need to control the design process through drawing was already felt, and it is no coincidence that the treatises devote space to specific thoughts on the methods of representation.

In *De re aedificatoria* Leon Battista Alberti feels the need to give specific prescriptive guidance for architectural drawing that is intended for construction only, without yielding to the temptation of performing pictorial representations.[8] The architect needs a metric precision that the painter does not and he must strive to design 'the shape and extent of each front and each side using real angles and non-variable lines: like one who wants his work to be judged not on a deceptive semblance, but precisely on the basis of verifiable measures'.[9]

In the early Renaissance, the perspective, despite its strong value for *measuring* space, was not used in architecture because it often produced an *illusory appearance* and for three-dimensional representation wooden models were preferred, as they were indispensable tools for the verification of what was to be built, an important stage of the design process.

Thus, the model became in fact a method of representation,[10] also praised by Leon Battista Alberti, who appreciates its metrical accuracy, to the point of considering its accuracy as one means of expenditure control: a sort of three-dimensional cost estimate.[11] Thus, a method for architectural design emerged: the use of detailed and metrically controllable drawings. These needs were met by the plan, by the elevation in orthogonal projection, and by the wooden model in scale which allowed three-dimensional control even before the invention of axonometric projection. However, the process is not linear and there is a phase in which the earlier perspective studies re-enter the vocabulary of architectural drawing: this is the case with those drawings where pseudo-perspective betrays a lack of control in the process of rationalisation of the orthogonal projection. Look at the section and elevation of Bramante's Tempietto of San Pietro in Montorio; while the elevation drawing on the left depicting the front is quite correct, the section succumbs to the temptation of perspective in the drawing of the external ambulatory, whose columns are viewed from an angle.

A mixture of orthogonal projection and perspective is far from rare in architectural drawing during the Renaissance, but there is a progressive refinement of the method and a greater respect for heartfelt Albertian prescription.

The orthogonal triad, which involves both the combined and closely correlated use of plan, elevation and section is thus an achievement of the mature Renaissance. Raphael, in the letter sent in 1519 to Leo X, gives very specific requirements regarding the drawing of architecture: 'The drawing, and thus the building relevant to the architect, is divided into three parts – the first of which is the plan, or we say the *plan drawing*, the second is the outside wall ... the third is the inside wall ... which is as necessary as the other two, and is made in the plan with parallel lines – like the outside wall – and shows half of the building inside, as if it were divided in half.' Although not all historians are in agreement on the attribution of the famous letter to Leo X, it is, however, very probable that the author meant the need for control of construction through

Antonio da Sangallo il Giovane (1484–1546),
Progetto per San Pietro, 1516
Galleria degli Uffizi, A 66,
Florence (Italy)

clear and shared graphic signs, with notations, that do not lead to perspective distortion. A strong impetus to codify the orthogonal projection was, without doubt, the construction of the St. Peter's Basilica. The control of such an ambitious and complex work had to be supported by precise, metrically controllable graphics. The site, given the magnitude of the work, the design complexity and symbolic importance, was the perfect opportunity to codify the architectural drawing. Here, therefore, the requirement of the plan, of the *outside wall* and *inside wall*, is that of the elevation and of the section. The need was felt by Raphael, who grappled with the complexity of the work and who understood that he could not make use of perspective to address and solve the complex problems of the construction of St. Peter's.

The role played by Antonio da Sangallo the Younger in coding the section and the orthogonal projection is underlined by Wolfgang Lotz, who reminds us of his education as a *faber lignarius* (a carpenter): a non-philosophical education which can be seen in Sangallo's strength in implementing a drawing method more useful to a carpenter than a painter.[12] He introduced (or re-introduced) it in the drawing of architecture with a dignity equal to that of perspective, which, while effectively describing space, is not ideal for metrically controlling the size of a column or a wall, or for controlling the architectural order.[13]

Marking some of the stages of this long and winding path, we may stop at Leon Battista Alberti, who suggested the use of the plan and model as methods for accurate representation of architecture, at the letter to Leo X, in which the author relied on the accuracy of the orthogonal projection and the vertical section, and at Antonio da Sangallo the Younger, who seems to collect these suggestions and implement the use of the section for the construction of St. Peter's.

Here, then, plan, elevation and section – the orthogonal triad – are as closely related one to another as three feet of a stool, describing the building with the precision of a surgeon in order to monitor its construction. This code was enhanced with a special type of projection in which a half of the elevation was accompanied by half the cross section. This method, which assumes perfect symmetry in the building may have been the result of practical needs: the cost of paper, although not comparable to that of parchment, was still high, and, in addition to the use of both sides of the sheet, the representation can be optimised by putting together the two portions of the building. The axial symmetry also ensures that the information contained in this type of drawing is quite comprehensive.

The theory that is today known as the theory of architecture owes its strength to the Renaissance, entirely independent of the architecture built: a set of theoretical concepts which were perfect models to be pursued, a set of rules underlying a new idea of architecture that is not necessarily indebted to real buildings of the past.

One way to structure the theory of architecture, thanks to the possibilities of printing on paper and the new techniques of graphical representation, was certainly the treatise, which widely used the triad (plan, elevation and section), and which would be a powerful medium for the dissemination and study of the theory of architecture. We will see later what were some of the reasons that led to the development of the treatise; for now it is important to note how the orthogonal triad became a shared set of rules: the techniques of engraving had changed, and shaken off the uncertainties of the pseudo-perspective of the early Renaissance. Taken together, these projective methods lend themselves perfectly to the description and control of the

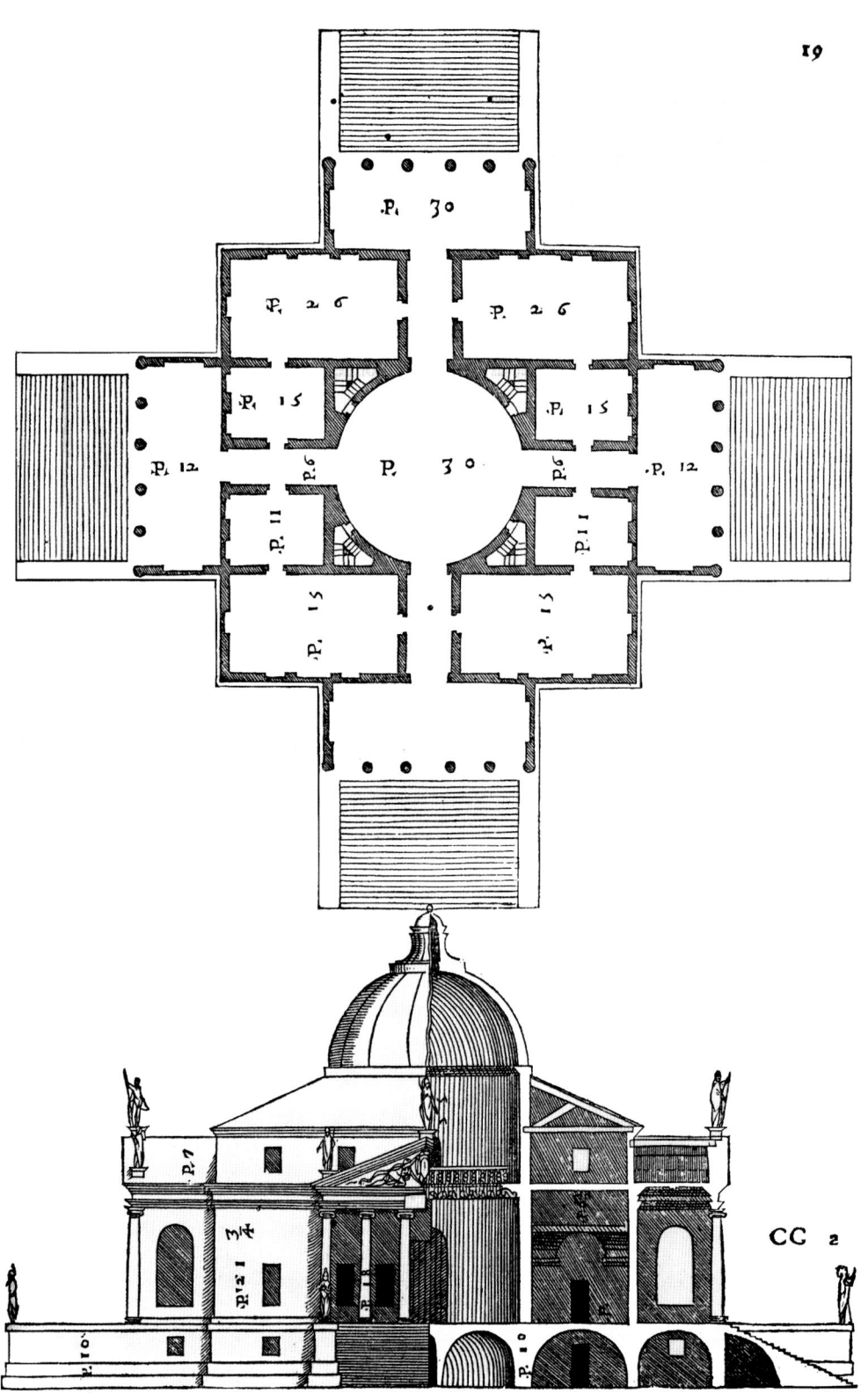

Andrea Palladio (1508–1580),
La Rotonda, 1570
From *I quattro libri dell'architettura* (Libro Secondo),
Venice (Italy)

Jacopo Barozzi da Vignola (1507–1573),
Trabeazione e capitello di ordine corinzio, 1562
From *Regola delli cinque ordini dell'architettura*, tav. XXVI,
Rome (Italy)

Vincenzo Scamozzi (1552–1616),
Elementi decorativi di architettura di ordine dorico, 1615
From *L'idea dell'architettura universale*, Parte II, Libro VI,
Venice (Italy)

Guarino Guarini (1624–1683),
Chiesa di San Filippo Neri a Casale, 1737
From *Architettura Civile*, tav. XXV,
Turin (Italy)

Domenico De Rossi (1659–1730),
Chiesa di San Carlo ai Catinari, 1721
From *Studio d'Architettura Civile*, III, fol. 23
Photo: Biblioteca Hertziana, Rome (Italy)

Giuseppe Damiani Almeyda (1834–1911),
*Progetto per il teatro Massimo di Palermo,
prospetto principale*, 1874
Archivio Damiani, Palermo (Italy)
Photo: Fabrizio Avella,
post-processing: Fabrizio Avella, Giuseppe Dalli Cardillo

Giuseppe Damiani Almeyda (1834–1911),
Padiglione centrale del Gran Caffé, prospetto, 1890
From *Istituzioni Architettoniche*,
Archivio Damiani, Palermo (Italy)

Bernardo Agnello,
Saltzman House by Richard Meier,
elevation, 2006

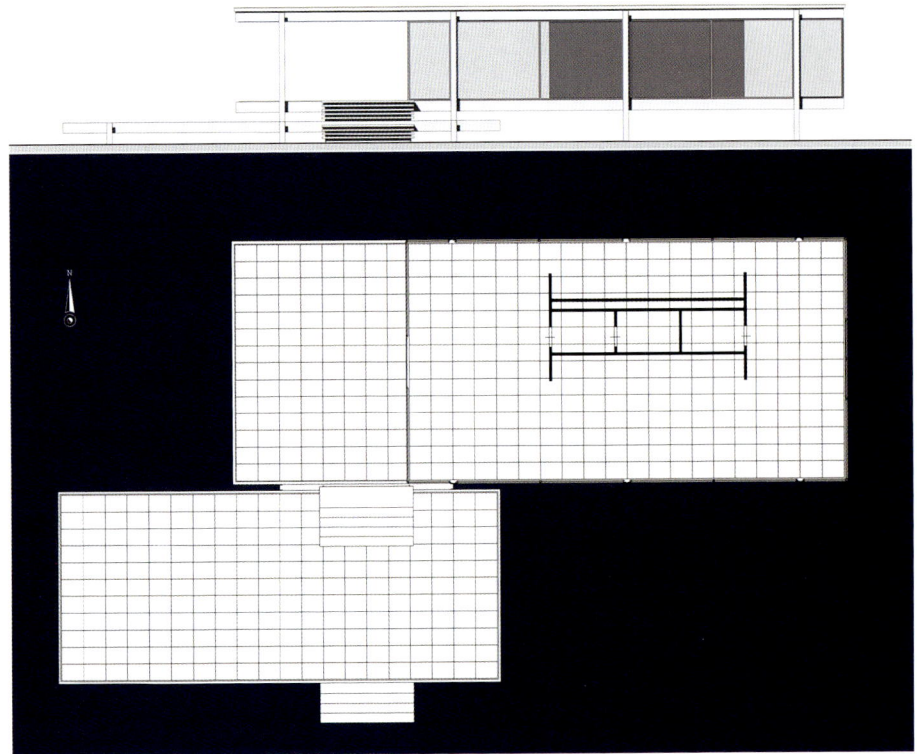

Fabrizio Avella,
Farnsworth House by Mies van der Rohe,
plan and elevation, 2006

founding parameters of Renaissance architecture: *ordo, dispositio, symmetria, proportio* of the whole and its parts. The regular pattern of plan and type, the proportional pattern in elevation, and the proportional order need a precise system of representation and, conversely, a codified system of representation allows the development of a theory of architecture based on that order. The planimetric indication, the description of architecture via orthogonal projection, and, if necessary, the *inside wall* is a group capable of providing clear guidance for the configuration of architecture. Axonometric projection, perspective, mimetic simulations of space are not necessary: the specifications of the plan, and the signs of the *inside wall* are enough to fully describe a work of architecture without room for misunderstanding or misinterpretation. Plan, section and elevation remained substantially unchanged during the Baroque and late-Baroque period, as well as in treatises through until the twentieth century, having been included in the Mongian code which is still widely used today.

It could be precisely the power of the code of the orthogonal projection, reinforced by the work of Gaspard Monge, that allowed them to remain until the early decades of the twentieth century: the concept of *facade*, *front elevation* and *side elevation* as well as the permanence of architectural order.

The *drawing, the outside wall and the inside wall* is therefore also a form of thought. Even the concept of the modern movement, based, however, on orthogonal planes, has not weakened this position: Le Corbusier felt the need to include the free plan among his five points and to control the *Modulor* in the elevation; the plan and the elevation lend themselves to *classicism* and the proportional severity of Mies van der Rohe.

As far as the influence of the projection system on the thought of architecture is concerned, Vittorio Gregotti notes: 'As a first rough approximation we can say that the systems of representation that we used are generally related to the structure of Euclidean space and its geometric representation for projections and sections, a system that has some significant limitations.'[14]

The system of orthogonal projections, in point of fact, is able to represent architecture when it has certain characteristics: the facade of a Renaissance church is drawn on a plane parallel to the front, perpendicular to the main axis. The sections lie on vertical planes parallel to those of the elevations and any elevation belongs to planes which are all perpendicular to the plan. This system of projections reproduces (and inspires) features such as *axiality* and *perpendicularity* between axes and planes, referring to axes x, y, z, which are orthogonal to each other. These features, though within complex space systems, have remained in many examples of modern and contemporary architecture. The spatial, formal and volumetric complexity of the emblematic architecture of the twentieth century from Rietveld to Loos, from Mies to Meier is, however, to be considered as a highly structured system of orthogonal planes. As far as digital design is concerned, nothing new was introduced, apart from a procedural point of view: the elevation is not a drawing to be attached to the plan, which generates the information needed for its construction, but is one of the infinite elaborations that can be drawn from a three-dimensional model. It is a two-dimensional set of three-dimensional information. It can be realised as an autonomous two-dimensional model, but the tendency is to cut it from a three-dimensional model and submit it to a subsequent post-processing, where information can be added, such as dimensions, notations or other technical information.

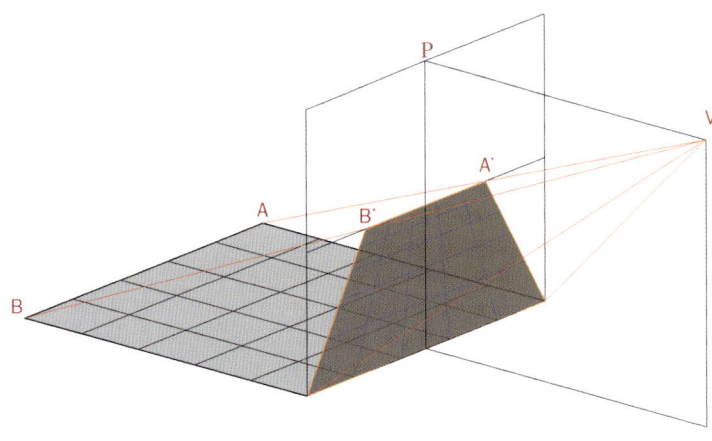

Fabrizio Avella, *Construction of a perspective* (axonometric diagram)

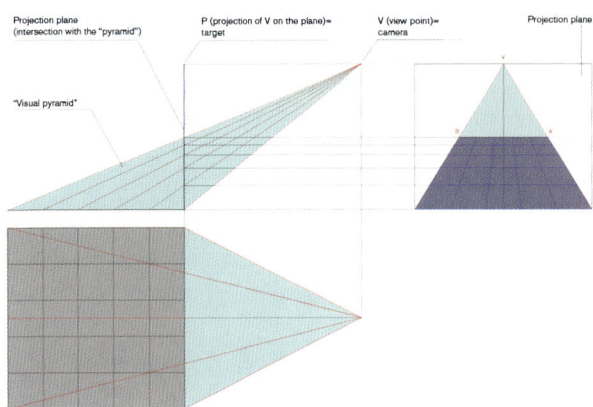

Fabrizio Avella, *Perspective construction according to the method of Leon Battista Alberti*

Perspective

Anyone wishing to find out the genesis of perspective can draw on essays of unsurpassed completeness: from the now *classic* essay by Erwin Panofski *Perspective as Symbolic Form*,[15] to the most recent work by Martin Kemp, *The Science of Art*,[16] to Henry Millon and Vittorio Lampugnani Magnago's, *Rinascimento da Brunelleschi a Michelangelo. La rappresentazione dell'architettura*,[17] to name only the most famous. Beyond the various approaches of the works cited and other essays on the topic, it seems that today we can agree on some points. First of all, as we have seen for orthogonal projections, the perspective that we know today is the result of a long process of codification, which had a strong push in the early fifteenth century. This is not to say that it did not exist previously: Panofsky points out that every era had its own perspective, a system to represent the depth of space. From the vertical axis perspective with *fish bone* vanishing point perspective, to the mere juxtaposition of an array of Byzantine plans, sufficient to understand what is *in front* and what is *behind*, each era chose its own way of representing space. Even masters of painting, such as Giotto and Lorenzetti, had begun to explore different ways to represent the volume and placement of figures in the depths of space, to overcome the long standing problem of the representation of the *n* dimensions of phenomenal reality on the two dimensions of the surface to be painted. The interest in perspective was very strong both in the pictorial as well as architectural fields and the two areas overlapped in the fifteenth century, and lost their disciplinary boundaries: it is not clear whether the perspective was borrowed from pictorial studies or if the pictorial painting absorbed a method developed to draw a rational space like that of the Renaissance. Early studies on the definition of a method can be seen in the work of one architect, Filippo Brunelleschi, who, in 1413, drew on a board the famous Baptistery of Florence; Leon Battista Alberti wrote about the perspective in *De Pictura* of 1436, to emphasise the fact that perspective does not belong to architectural design. The ideal city of Baltimora is dated after 1470, but it would be questionable if it is a framework or an architectural representation. *De prospectiva pingendi* by Piero della Francesca was produced in 1482, during his stay in Rimini, after completion of his major paintings, which are often framed in architectural spaces, and, in the same year, the presence of Donato Bramante in Milan is documented for the construction of the choir of Santa Maria in San Satiro, which owing to a perspective was able to simulate a depth similar to that seen for the transepts, deceptively expanding a space that was, as an actual matter of fact, relatively small.

One could continue at length, but simply to highlight some aspects: the *perspectiva artificialis*[18] focuses on the positioning of a point of view from a measurable distance, coinciding with the eye of the observer, from which the visual rays start and, intersected by a plane, give life to the representation of perspective. Point of view (V), projected perpendicular to the framework, determines the position of principal point (P), i.e. the vanishing point of lines perpendicular to the plane. Studies by Brunelleschi, the method of L. B. Alberti (*Intersection*

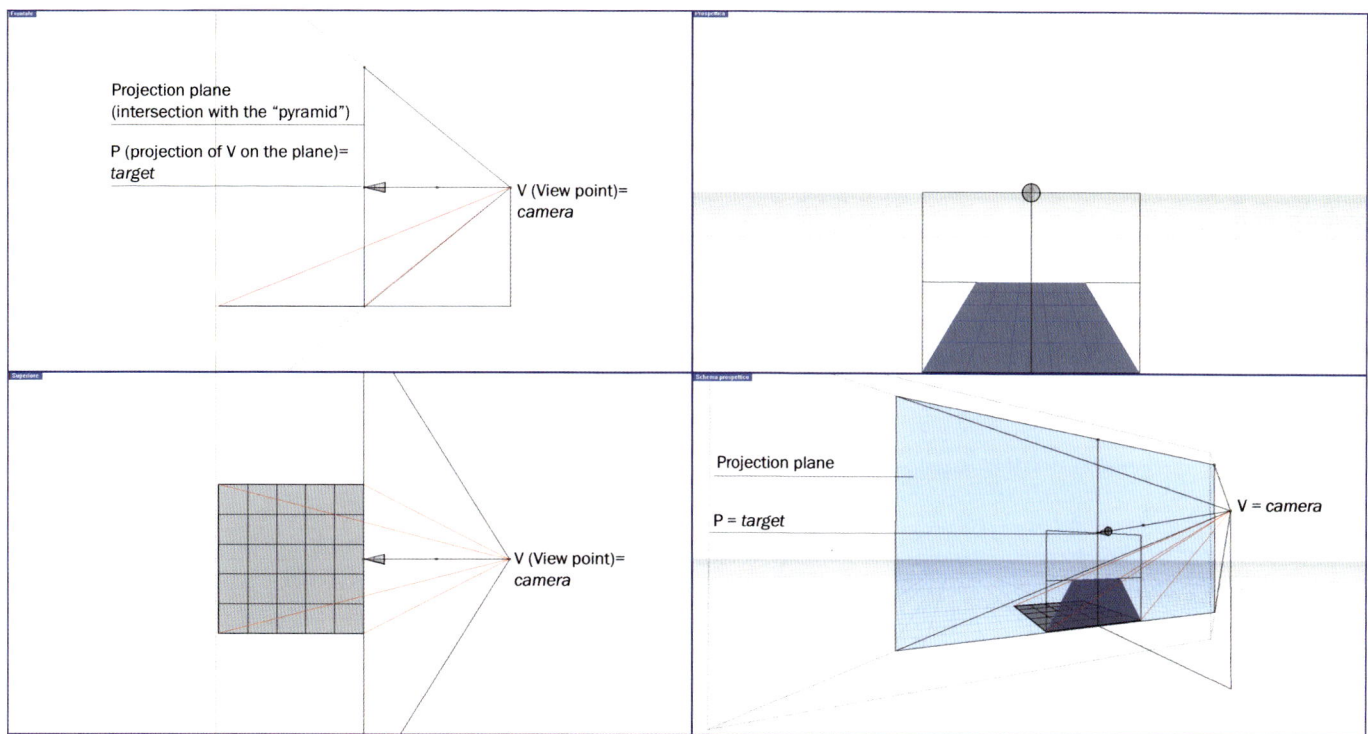

Fabrizio Avella, *Perspective construction according to the method of Leon Battista Alberti performed with a CAD software*

of the visual pyramid), the experiments of Albrecht Dürer, the optical chamber of Canaletto, are all based on the same concept: given a centre of projection, the image of infinite points in space can be determined if, interposing a plane between this centre and objects in space, it is possible to draw (on the plane) the intersection between the plane and the *pyramid* of visual rays. Hoping not to disappoint the supporters of innovation, the concept is identical to that which is encoded in the algorithms underlying the perspective view in a CAD programme: the centre of projection, or point of view, coincides with the camera, its projection on the plane coincides with the target. The perspective which is created with a CAD programme perfectly follows the rules codified by Brunelleschi and Alberti. Try to draw a regular pattern and to obtain its perspective according to the Albertian method of intersection of the visual pyramid. The viewpoint is positioned at V and its projection on a representation at P.

According to the method advocated by Leon Battista Alberti, in order to obtain the perspective of a regular pattern made of squares it is sufficient to find the intersection of visual rays (red) with the perspective plane cutting the *pyramid* of visual rays convergent in the point of view (V). The frontal view of the framework shows that these intersections will close as you move toward the horizon line. The intersection with the traces of straight lines perpendicular to the framework and, therefore, convergent at the *central* vanishing point, will result in the perspective. The perspective path shown in the figure will then be extracted.

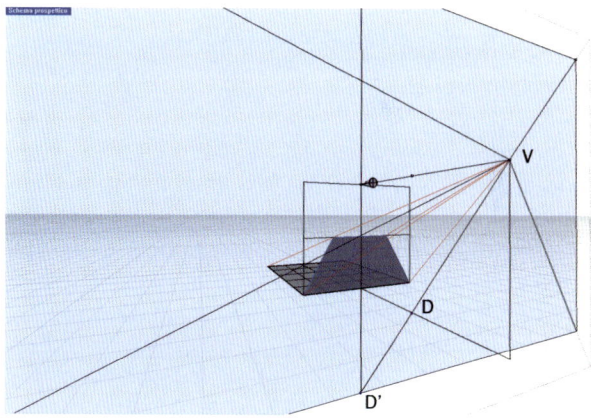

Fabrizio Avella, *Perspective scheme which extends the width of the visual field*

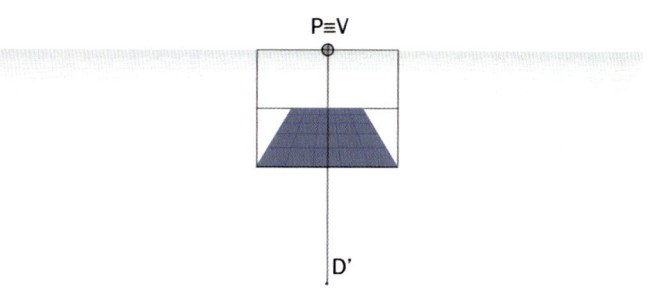

Fabrizio Avella, *Perspective of the previous scheme*

195

Albrecht Dürer (1471–1528),
Man Drawing a Lute, 1525
Bibliothèque Nationale de France,
Paris (France)

Albrecht Dürer (1471–1528),
Man Drawing a Reclining Woman, 1525
Bibliothèque Nationale de France,
Paris (France)

If a camera is placed in correspondence with the point of view and what in many programmes is called the target is placed at the projection on the point of view, you can see how the two constructions coincide perfectly.

It should be noted, however, that if one extends the field of view of the plane of projection, marked in blue, over the ground line, on a monitor the perspective view will make the parts placed in front of the projection plane visible, resulting in distorted perspective or aberration. You can, for example, vertically extend the framework to include the projection of point D in front of the framework itself. The effect is shown in the figure, where D is the projection of D at the bottom of the perspective view. Again, construction perspective follows all of the rules of descriptive geometry that continue to have importance and meaning.

However, even if the software applies an algorithm that would have pleased Brunelleschi, Alberti, Dürer and Monge, it is easy to find today perspectives with horrible aberrations which provide a distorted representation of space. This happens for one simple reason: the construction of perspective is made intuitively and without control. We can momentarily reconsider the Renaissance perspective: in order to draw it, it is essential to have perfect control of the positioning of the view in the plan, the plane was often positioned vertically and it was always possible to determine the position of the point on the perspective from the combination of planimetric and altimetric information.[19] A system of thought such as that of the Renaissance focused on the *central perspective*, that is the perspective where the point of view, and hence the vanishing point, was centrally located in the composition. It was the human eye, placed on *the centre* of humanist thought. The central perspective may also have the advantage of enhancing the asymmetry, as in the drawing of the Farnsworth House by Mies van der Rohe, where the glass window on the left side balances the right wall with the chimney. The centrality of perspective in this case also serves to highlight the spatial rhythm of the perspective through the use of the rigid pattern of tiles in the floor. It is probably no coincidence that the Renaissance principles of drawing describe the simple space of modern architecture as well, since both classical and modern architecture converge in the quest for simplicity. Contrastingly, the central and centred perspective in House N by Sou Fujimoto shows strong asymmetry of the architecture, albeit in a highly rational composition characterised by orthogonal planes.

Even if most of the Renaissance architects (and artists) started drawing a lot of perspective with central vanishing point, soon they felt the need to break this symmetry. In the same way, the *rule* of order was changed, broken and transformed by architects such as Palladio and Bramante,[20] even the centrality of the perfect design or iconic composition are called into question: the vanishing point can therefore be decentralised, as in Cigoli's perspectives, or be placed almost in line with the floor, as in Galli Bibiena's drawings; in some cases it even goes outside the sheet, which is hardly an acceptable solution for Leon Battista Alberti and Piero della Francesca.

The perspective is always *with one only vanishing point*, but the image is cropped so as to decentralise the positioning. Perspectives made in this way gives a sense of dynamic space, the

Raffaello Sanzio (1483–1520),
Studio di prospettiva, date unknown
Galleria degli Uffizi,
Florence (Italy)

Ludovico Cardi, called Cigoli (1559–1613),
Prospettiva di un passaggio, date unknown
Galleria degli Uffizi,
Florence (Italy)

Hans Vredeman de Vries (1527–1609),
Hall with colonnades on two floors, c. 1560
Albertina Gallery, Vienna (Austria)

Paul Landriani (1755–1839),
Ingresso ad una galleria con imponente scalone,
date unknown
Castello Sforzesco,
Milan (Italy)

Paul Landriani (1755–1839),
Interno monumentale con soffitto cassettonato, date unknown
Castello Sforzesco, Milan (Italy)

Fabrizio Avella,
Farnsworth House by Mies van der Rohe,
perspective, 2006

Denise Ippolito,
House N by Sou Fujimoto,
2008

eye runs towards the vanishing point and the weight of the image becomes unbalanced, a condition which was attractive to artists who were beginning to think about a new, non-static idea of space that would lead to Baroque and late Baroque compositions.

The decentralisation of the vanishing point is a criterion that went on to be used until the twentieth century, where representation accentuated the longitudinal axis of the space, whatever the style or other architectural features. A new variable: the rotation of the plane of projection. The world is changing its image. It is possible to maintain, perfectly undisturbed, the already existing conditions, as long as the eye does not look over a wall, or at a compositional axis, but looks toward a corner, then something extraordinary happens: the vanishing points become two, the space becomes faster, and the calm, reassuring symmetry of the Renaissance is overtaken by the complexity of space in the Baroque era.

If, then, architecture is conceived as a composition of volumes that do not necessarily follow rhythmic and axial compositions, if space is no longer marked by the constant repetition of parallel planes, then looking in a corner is a good way to obtain a lot of information and capture the essence and articulation of those volumes. Although the concept of space had not yet been upset by the Modern Movement, the first decades of the twentieth century were undoubtedly fertile in proposing new concepts of composition and volumetric space, thanks also to the accidental perspective which became the preferred method for three-dimensional representation until axonometric projection was invented. The factory at Purmerend, by Jacobus Johannes Pieter Oud, consists of simple volumes, rendered perfectly by using accidental perspective,[21] which was even successful in representing the Fallingwater House by Frank Lloyd Wright or *La Maison Spatiale* by Jean Gorin. This is not to state a similarity between those architectures, but to highlight the effectiveness of this method for rendering them (even if they present different features). This method was also perfect to render the futuristic perspectives of Antonio Sant'Elia, Mario Chiattone and Tullio Crali, whose architectural visions longed for buildings with complex volumes and the expressive power of the cultural revolution that crossed Europe during those years. As for with other nuances, Chernikhov's choice of perspective shows without any doubt some similarities, at least with regard to the representation of utopia.

Just as rotating the framework of an azimuthal angle is enough to change the outcome of a perspective, rotating the framework on a vertical plane changes something again, the result is a sloping perspective, which is particularly suitable for drawing large vertical buildings.

Jacobus Johannes Pieter Oud (1890–1963),
Factory at Purmerend, 1919
Nederlands Documentatiecentrum voor de Bouwkunst,
Amsterdam (the Netherlands)

Frank Lloyd Wright (1867–1959),
The House on a Waterfall – Fallingwater (Kaufmann House), 1935–37
Frank Lloyd Wright Foundation, Taliesin, Wisconsin (USA)

Jean Gorin (1899–1981),
La Maison Spatiale, 1964
Musée National d'Art Moderne – Centre Pompidou, Paris (France)

Ferdinando Galli Bibiena (1657–1743),
Prospettiva di un interno con passaggi multipli di arcate sorrette da pilastri a bugnato, date unknown
Accademia di San Luca, Rome (Italy)

Tullio Crali (1910–2000),
Palazzo delle scienze, 1930
MART, Museo d'Arte Moderna e Contemporanea di
Trento e Rovereto, Rovereto (Italy)

Mario Chiattone (1891–1957),
Construzioni per una metropoli moderna, 1914
Università di Pisa, Dipartimento di Storia dell'Arte,
Gabinetto di disegni e stampe, Pisa (Italy)

Right:
Yakov G. Chernikhov
(1889–1951)
Composition No. 86
From Architectural Fantasies:
101 Compositions
Gouache on paper,
24.2 cm × 30.3 cm,
Collection Dmitry Y.
Chernikhov (Russia)

Antonio Sant'Elia (1888–1916), *La città nuova.*
Casamento con ascensori esterni, galleria, passaggio
coperto, su tre piani stradali, 1914
Museo Civico di Palazzo Volpi, Como (Italy)

Fabrizio Avella, *Tensione*, 2005

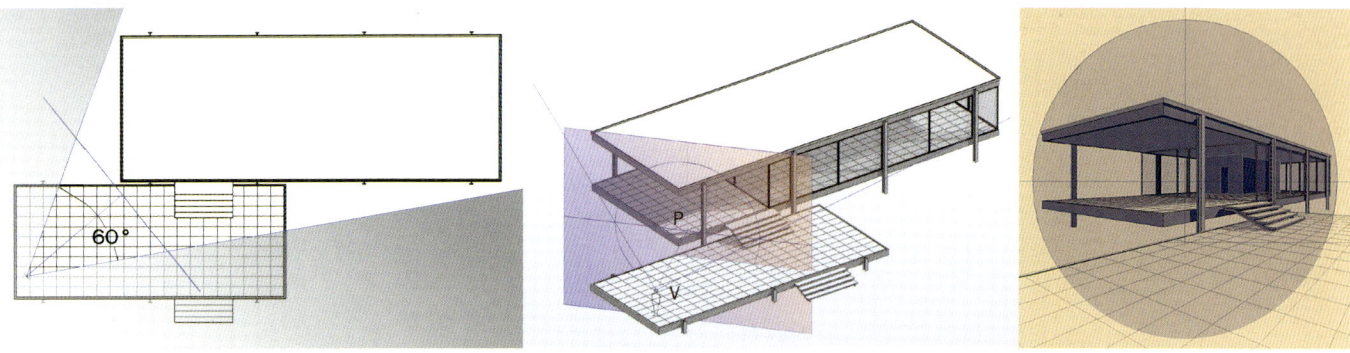

Fabrizio Avella,
Farnsworth House by Mies van der Rohe,
perspective studies, 2007

From these considerations an important aspect becomes clear: the perspective is not simply a mechanical operation aiming at a three-dimensional view on the plan, it is also, and perhaps above all, an expressive code. It is seen as the variation of the concept of space, it changes the settings of the perspective, the positioning of the main point, or the rotation of the perspective's plane. One wonders what, today, in digital drawing, has changed in the perspective representation. Considering that, as shown, the algorithm that handles the setting of the perspective with CAD programmes follows a logic which perfectly coincides with the constructions of Leon Battista Alberti and Brunelleschi, it is not possible to attribute responsibility for the loss of control in perspective representations to these programmes. If liability is to be sought in the programming, it can be found in the simulation of the photo, which, apart from having many things in common with the perspective, actually introduces parameters such as convexity of the lens outside the flat representation. That means that if we want to render the perspective of a three-dimensional model, we do not need to directly settle the position of the projection plane, its rotation or its inclination. Often the only operation required is the positioning of the camera (coinciding with the point of view or centre of projection) and a target (projection of the point of view on the plane), but, this way, the plane is not visible. Alternatively, it is even easier to *orbit* around an object and change the setting from *parallel* to *prospective*. Almost no CAD user worries about how the perspective is created, and begins to flounder between the various zoom parameters, distance and pan until a view that comes close to that expected is obtained. The results are generally disappointing.

Among the most common are the aberration of the perspective and the inclination of the framework. Aberration happens when a too extensive portion of the visual field is included in the framework. Inclination of the framework often happens because, while fixing the camera, one does not see the plane itself (because most CAD software does not visualise it). It is, as a matter of fact, very simple to obtain both a pleasant and controlled perspective.

We begin from the perspective's plane: CAD software, it is said, does not allow you to visualise it, which is essential in the manual construction. How do you resolve the problem? Noting that the right vector joining the camera (the point of view, V) with the target (projection point of view on the framework, P) is none other than the main visual axis that, by definition, is perpendicular to the plane, we determine the camera-target axis, i. e. the vector VP and indirectly but unequivocally, the positioning of the plane. We must, however, decide what portion of the model we want to render. According to an empirical rule for manual construction, we should draw the portion of the object that is included in the dihedral angle whose apex is the centre of projection. This angle, about 60°, is defined as an optical cone: on the inside, the peripheral aberrations do not cause aberration in the perspective view.[22] As you move away, the perspective suffers aberrations which become, at times, unbearable to the eye. The succession of figures that render some perspectives of Farnsworth House by Mies van der Rohe allows us to observe how, to increase the visible portion and avoid peripheral aberrations, we just need a simple trick: moving the projection centre (the view point) away from the model, while keeping the

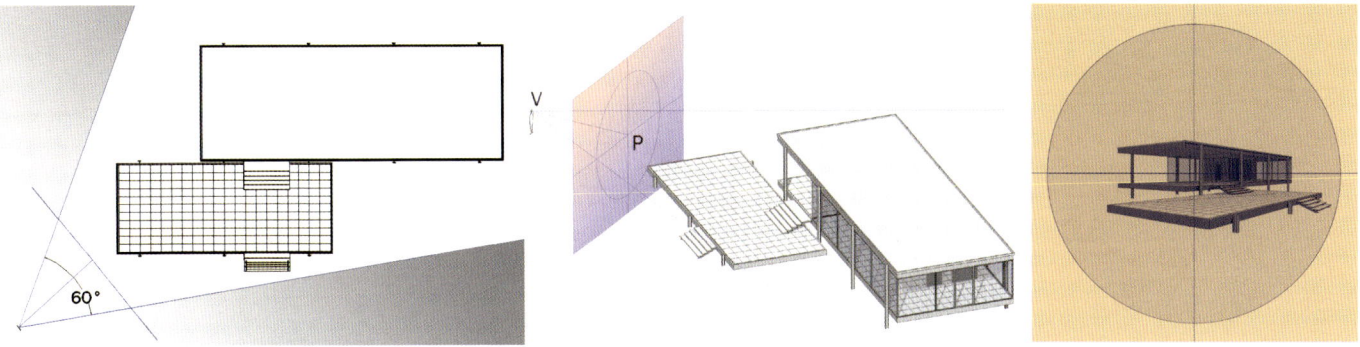

Fabrizio Avella,
Farnsworth House by Mies van der Rohe,
perspective studies, 2007

camera-target distance unchanged. This will avoid the deleterious effects of the zoom function, which often automatically change the distance of the point of view from the plane, therefore increasing the visible portion, but also including those portions which present peripheral aberrations.

The same considerations apply to the plane inclination. If the inclination of the plane can be useful, for example, when rendering a skyscraper seen from below, the same will probably not work when rendering a horizontal building. The perspectives with vertical plane, easier to draw by hand than the ones with tilted plane, are, paradoxically, less immediate in CAD software, because it is not easy to control the positioning. It is true that in reality our visual axis is rarely perfectly horizontal, but the charm of perspectives with vertical plane, is perhaps due to the abstraction of this particular condition. The aforementioned perspectives of Sant'Elia, Chiattone and Chernikhov, whilst the buildings are drawn with vertical development, are not drawn with tilted plane. Moreover, the perspective with vertical plane respects a very strong natural condition: the perpendicularity of the axis of the human body compared to the earth, resulting in visual horizontality. It is, therefore, necessary to choose which effect to obtain and, again, this can be done through the control of the camera-target: locating the two points in space on the same coordinate of the z-axis, the camera-target axis will be horizontal and, consequently, the drawing will be vertical. Tilting the axis tilts the drawing, too. Simple. What has failed in the common digital drawing is the need for *a priori* thinking that involves choices about *what* to see, *how* to see it, and *why* see it in one way rather than another.

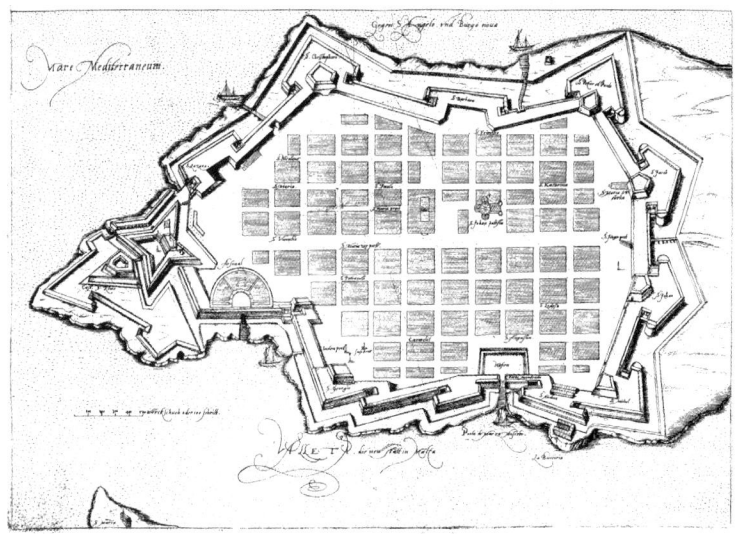
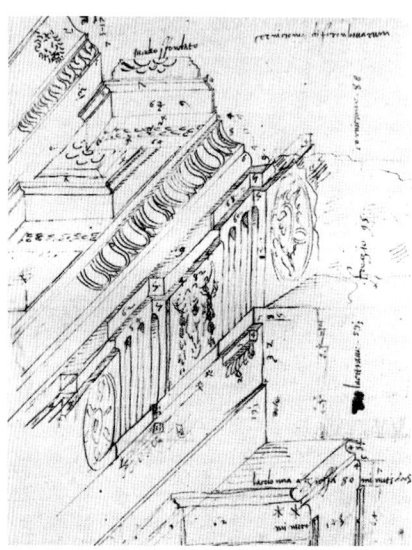

Daniel Speckle (1536–1589), *Valletta map*, 1589
From *Architectura von Vestungen*,
Tab. 15 before fol. 84 (ed. 1608),
Strasbourg (France)

Antonio da Sangallo il Giovane (1484–1546),
Dettaglio di trabeazione, date unknown
Gabinetto delle stampe degli Uffizi,
Florence (Italy)

The axonometric projection

In order to give a short history of axonometric projection, we must surely remember the impact that the introduction of gunpowder had on military strategies in Europe, both in attack and defence. The defensive strategy involved the need to redesign the system of city walls. An attack carried out with ladders and arrows could be effectively contained by high, relatively thin walls, but the advent of long-range artillery required a reconfiguration of the walls, which were transformed into low, wide embankments contained by thick, solid walls to cope with such shocks. The study of ballistics also gave some guidance on geometric trajectories, giving preference to bastions with sloping walls, which were very effective in diverting projectiles, while allowing the insertion of defensive positions. The form of the fortifications was complicated, the perimeters of fortified towns became jagged, geometrically they became triangular, hexagonal, pentagonal. In elevation drawings the walls had to be well designed: their profiles had to be tilted to contain the embankment and to absorb and deflect projectiles; and the study of the ditches and the distance between the outer and internal walls demanded attention too.

The control parameters become, in this way, numerous and complex and require new methods of representation. As in the case of religious architecture, the wooden model could perform this task perfectly, but presents some difficulties, as it is cumbersome and not always easily transportable. One can try, then, to draw a complex object on a flat surface, like a model but without the distortions that occur in perspective. One can try to obtain a design that may include planimetric indications of the plan and altimetric ones of the profile.

If such a method existed it would have considerable advantages: it could completely control the planimetric form and model how the walls would react to an offensive, how troops could move along the walls, and how the walls relate to the road layout and the city behind. One could also understand precisely what elevated forms should be used in order to minimise the risks. It is therefore a matter of putting together information about the plan with information about the profile.[23] Therefore, what is called today, not by chance, military axonometric projection, originates where heights are shown in true form and size on a layout scheme lacking in angular and metric distortions.[24] Simple. Inspired. Effective.

It is likely, however, that axonometric projection had little success because, as already mentioned, the interest of the Renaissance architect was perfectly satisfied by the orthogonal triad, the wooden model and perspective. The axonometric projection was unnecessary and, ultimately, useless; it added little to the design of architecture in its entirety, to an eye used to the possibility of *real-time orbit* around the wooden model. The *3D view* was, in the Renaissance, entrusted to the wooden model for proper control of the scale dimension, and to the prospective for spatial simulation. The axonometric projection could have been suitable, at most, for the design of architectural details and the design of machines. When, however, the architect becomes a military planner, an adequate system of representation

Giuliano da Sangallo (1445–1516),
Macchine per ingegneria, date unknown
Biblioteca Apostolica Vaticana,
Vatican City

is developed. Consider also that in the sixteenth century Italy was the scene of continuous clashes of European powers, fragmented into many political entities involved in whirling game of alliances, betrayals, campaigns and attacks: a perfect laboratory to develop increasingly sophisticated defensive architecture and rapid and effective ways to design.

To see the axonometric projection enter into the design of civil and religious architecture, one needs to wait until the seventeenth century. For the Baroque architect it is no longer sufficient to determine the type, the architectural system and order, he is no longer content with the platonic solid approach, but feels the need to intersect, overlap, and warp simple forms in search of complex spaces. The workers are unprepared, the architects stress their ability to build the project: if it is true that the plan, elevation and perspective still work well for describing general information, architectural order and spatial effect in the Baroque, it is also true that any of the above mentioned techniques were sufficient to describe the way to cut the stones and how to put them together to obtain the complex three-dimensional forms of the Baroque building.

Once again a graphical method is needed to solve new and complex problems. Once again architects need to match the information coming from the plan with that resulting from the elevations, they need to understand how to position a form in a precise position, without running the risk of juxtaposing pieces with faces that do not match. The architect must be able to say with precision to the craftsman how to carve the stone, in a way the craftsman can understand it. But before reaching this stage,

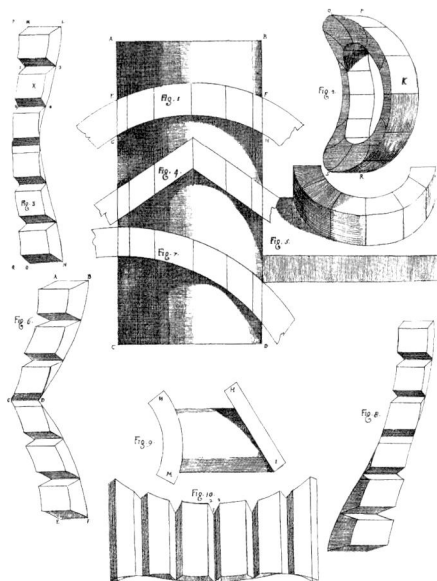

Guarino Guarini (1624–1683),
Scomposizione in conci di porzione cilindriche, 1737
From *Architettura Civile*, tab. XXXI,
Turin (Italy)

the architect must be able to very accurately prefigure the shape of the individual stone and its positioning in the determination of the overall shape.

Today we call this science *stone carving*, and it can be said that in the post-Renaissance era it introduced the use of axonometric projection to the graphic language of the architect even in a non-military field, contributing to studies that converge in what we today call descriptive geometry. The treatises of architecture are enriched by this form of representation and it becomes customary to insert tables explaining how to obtain the intersection of curved, spherical and conical surfaces and everything else necessary to turn into stone the fervent imagination of Baroque and late Baroque architects. The axonometric projection, sometimes shaded, joined with equal dignity plans and prospects, but only to explain the technical and constructive aspects. Until the nineteenth century axonometric projection remains, however, an effective way to represent components of architecture, construction aspects, geometry of portions of buildings, but not yet architecture in its entirety. It is the way Auguste Choisy used, in the tables of his famous *L'art de bâtir chez les Romains* and *L'art de bâtir chez les Byzantins* and Jean-Baptiste Rondelet in *Traité théorique et pratique de l'art de bâtir*.

In architectural design, the capability of axonometric projection to describe components and volumetric relations of an object is a feature that meets the needs of a new coming reality in the nineteenth century: that of industrial production. A machine cannot be designed by drawing a perspective (because of its misleading visuals) and needs to be controlled with unassailable accuracy in all components, in the way they are assembled and what they become once assembled.[25] The technical drawing becomes an instrument of thought and control, an essential component of the production process, functional to the precision requirements of mechanised production.[26] Since then the use of the axonometric projection design associated with the planning and performance of the industrial product has never ceased to impose itself. Even today kits for model building and the explanations for the assembly of kits, toys and electrical components are drawn in axonometric projection.

The military axonometric projection, in the moment it moves from a military field to a civil one, loses its ability to control the design and becomes a code of expression for drawing components, parts, be they made out of stone, wood, steel or cast iron. To see the axonometric projection become a method of representation able to describe the entire architectural complex (and not just one part of it) one must wait until the thought is affected by a profound transformation, that a world war destroys an apparent order, that concepts such as architectural order, rhythm of a facade, and decorative arrays are swept away by the irrepressible force of Futurism, Cubism, and the Modern Movement. Everything is called into question politically: democracy, economic growth, visual arts, literary patterns. The point of view and perspective disappear from painting. Pictorial

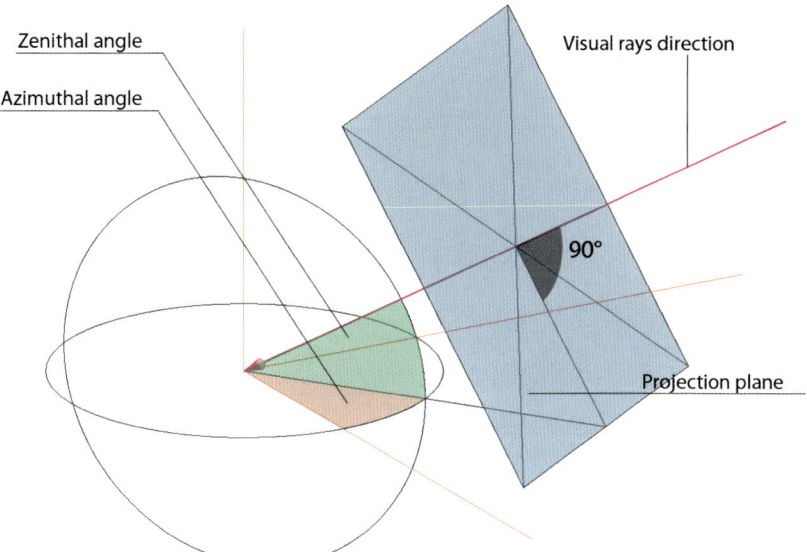

Fabrizio Avella,
Projective conditions of orthogonal axonometric projection with CAD software

space is no longer measurable. Architectural order is banished: it is not appropriate in a world that seems to reject the order of things. It seems, moreover, that after fanciful interpretations made by architects and imitators from the Renaissance onwards, it had used up its expressive and significant strength. The beginning of the twentieth century presented fertile ground for the displacing of axonometric projection from the design of machines to that of architecture. This occured for several reasons: in the Modern Movement, architecture is considered a *living machine*. If I have to draw a car, I need a method already successfully tested in the design of machines. Modern architecture rejects *style*, order, decoration, facade,[27] in favour of a concept of space and form that tends to trap, intersect, split simple volumes, collecting the pieces in new compositions and re-assembling them, preferably, however, on plans and Cartesian systems.[28] The axonometric projection is perfect: a machine is designed with no decorative frills, which are now considered intolerable, it decomposes the elements, provides the cold lucidity of mechanics, and allows the composition of pieces to be observed with detachment. The method has been passed down to us and is included among those available to design technique. But a clarification is to be made regarding the type of axonometric projection. While the axonometric construction made by hand may vary between oblique and orthogonal axonometric projection, almost all programmes for digital design will use orthogonal axonometric projection. The reason is simple: the algorithm that manages orthogonal projection is also perfectly applicable to axonometric projection in the sense that the calculation for drawing an object on the projection plane depends on the relationship between projecting rays and plane, not between framework and object position.

It is quite irrelevant, therefore, whether the plane is perpendicular or oblique with respect to the face of an object; actually, the planar orthogonal projection can simply be considered a special case of generic orthogonal projection. The mathematical relationship that determines the calculation of the reduction factors on the axes is a trigonometric function depending on the azimuthal and zenithal angles that define the visual axis. A projection in elevation, therefore, is fully described by the algorithm that handles this function, in which the direction of view axis is perpendicular to the plane in which the elevation lies. A plan is the result of a visual axis perpendicular to the horizontal plane and so forth. Nothing new. All you need is basic knowledge of descriptive geometry to know that orthogonal projections and orthogonal axonometric projections have identical projective conditions.

The problem of *digital thinking* is that axonometric projection is not consciously chosen as a form of expression, but it is only one way that someone has pre-determined for us to see an object in three dimensions. What remains, however, is the ultimate usefulness of viewing an object from different points of view without undergoing the laborious axonometric construction that design by hand requires.

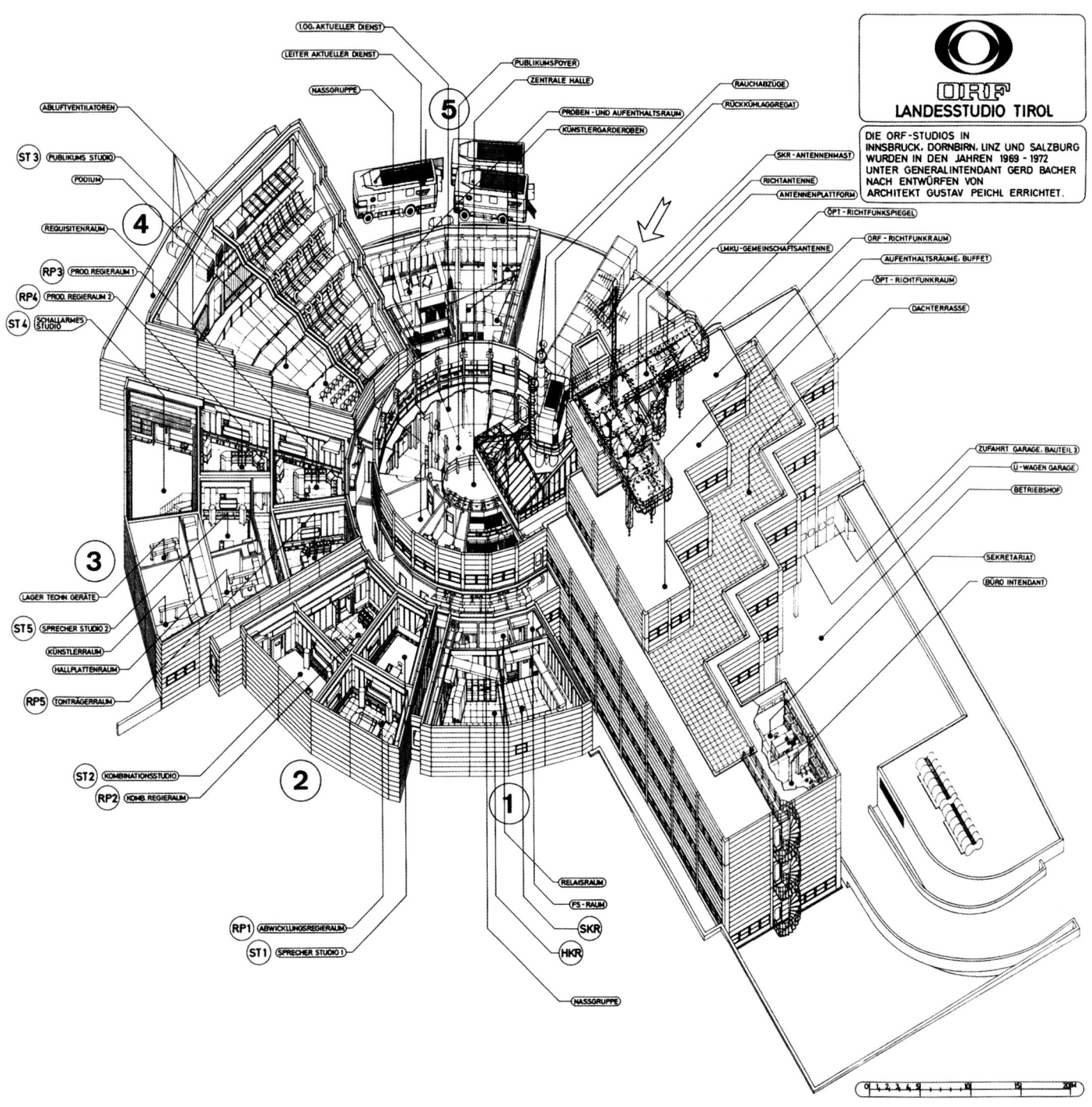

Gustav Peichl (1928–),
ORF regional studio Tyrol, 1969
Innsbruck (Austria)

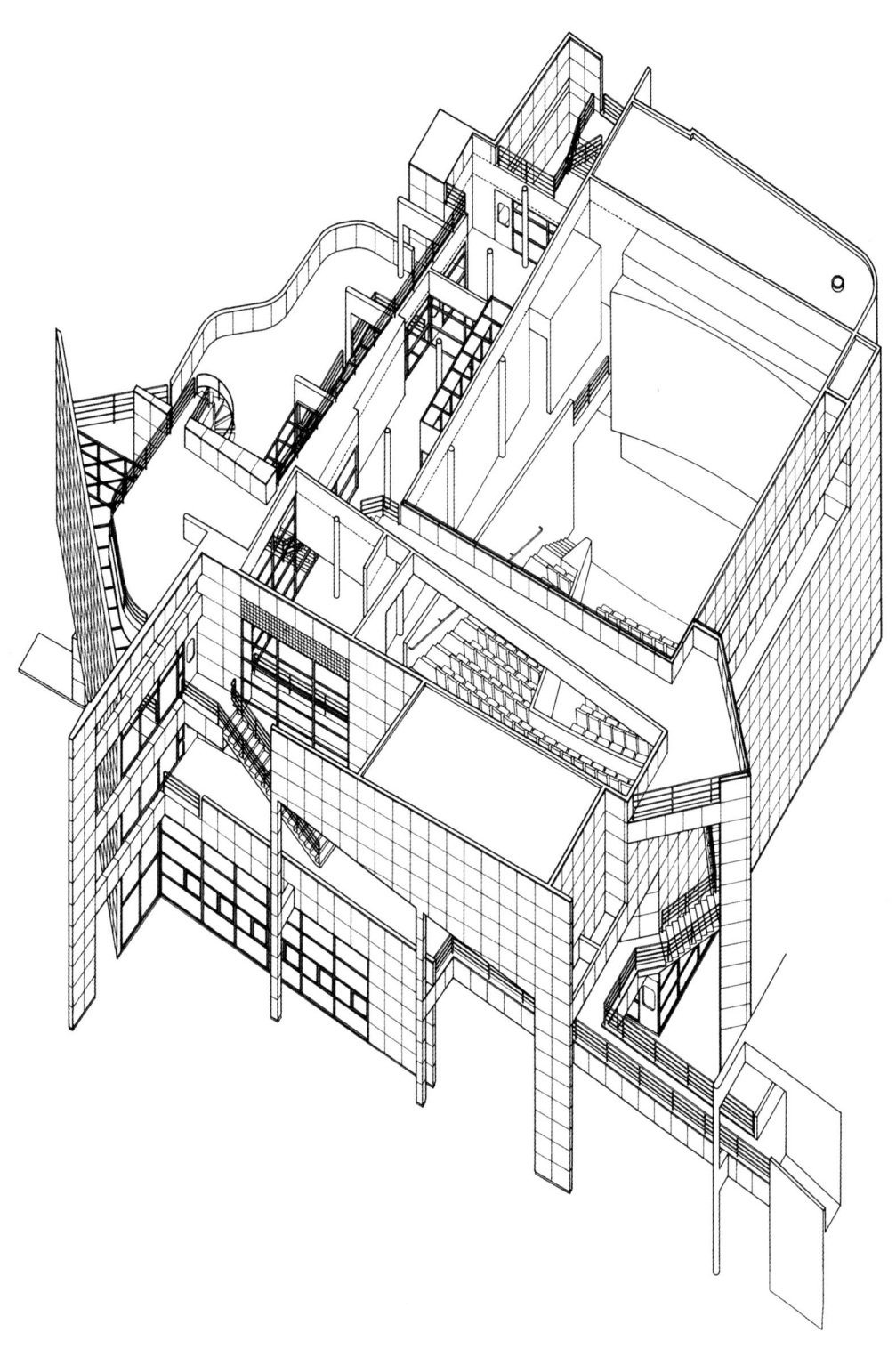

Richard Meier (1934–) and Partners,
The Atheneum, 1976
New Harmony, Indiana (USA)

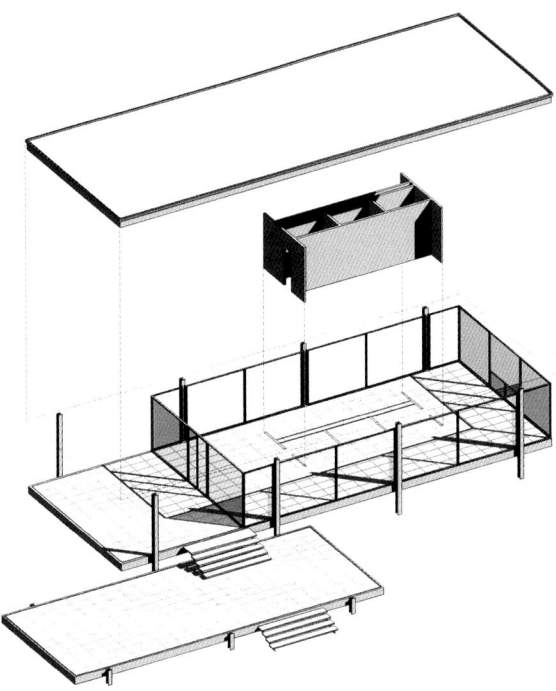

Fabrizio Avella,
Farnsworth House by Mies van der Rohe,
axonometric projection, 2006

Paper

This brief and incomplete overview of methods of representation cannot conclude without considering a determining aspect for the history of drawing: the introduction of paper in Europe. The fact is anything but minor and not merely a technical change in habits: the implications are indeed far-reaching. It was mentioned how in medieval building sites ephemeral media were used for the preparation of construction drawings. In this case the drawing was used to explain a specific detail or part of the building, and was no longer needed once its execution had been completed.

It is not surprising that this approach is not too worried about projective accuracy, which is probably not believed to be necessary for effective and qualitative information. Drawings, that not had only a functional quality, but for some reason had to preserve and pass on information, were done on parchment, which had a very high cost and required laborious preparation.[29] The introduction of paper in the fourteenth century did not immediately undermine the use of parchment, due to its initial high costs, and because, as always, new techniques and new habits need time to undermine those already known and consolidated. The custom of using wooden tables appropriately prepared for inscribing using a metal stylus was still widespread among artists in the fifteenth century. In 1437, Cennini Cennino described in detail the preparation of wooden tables on which lay a mixture of crushed and incinerated animal bones, mixed with saliva and smoothed to provide a surface which could be marked using a metal stylus. Once a drawing was finished, the table could be used again by removing the substrate and spreading a new one out.

Paper has, however, significant advantages, and by the mid-fifteenth century, papyrus was already used almost exclusively for special occasions.[30] Having a substrate on which to execute a drawing that can continue to exist even after having performed its function means that the same drawing may become the subject of study by both the executer and others. Having paper means being able to draw from true monuments of antiquity, which is essential in architecture education during the Renaissance. The increasing availability of paper, at a more accessible cost, facilitated developing project proposals and coding architectural orders. These conditions led to architects beginning to use architectural drawing not only when building something new, but also during education, for studying existing architecture, raising the matter that today we call architectural surveying, and conceptualisation of the design process.[31]

Paper makes a unique contribution to the theory of the birth of architecture, a study unthinkable without the help of the drawing, and probably you can now see how the discipline of drawing does not necessarily require the creation of a painting, a fresco,

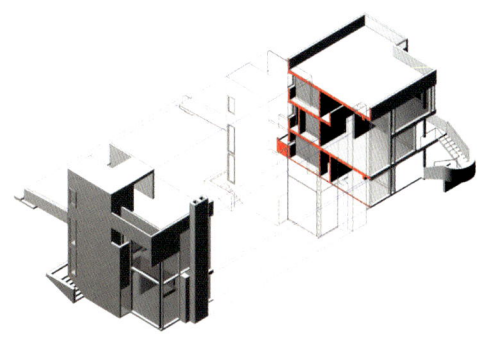

Bernardo Augello,
Smith House by Richard Meier,
axonometric projection, 2006

a statue, or a building.[32] Now think about another aspect: it was seen that both medieval construction site and preparatory techniques for painting required to trace signs on a surface, bounded or not, that was actually flat. The use of paper lying on a table does not call into question this consolidated habit: it continues to provide a flat surface to draw. Also familiarity with the execution of paintings on canvas, is to be considered as a habit of drawing on a flat surface.

Perhaps these aspects, together with other considerations of conceptual levels, pushed the designers of the fifteenth century to try to codify the drawings on the plane. Perhaps, these were the reasons that led to the codification of what we know today as flat projection methods. Perhaps this mental habitus leads to the logical consequence of Cartesian space. Perhaps.

Paper certainly plays an important role in the growth of architectural drawing discipline and in the encoding of methods of representation. Paper goes down in price. In addition to the historic mills of Fabriano, other paper mills are set up. The techniques optimise the process. Some think that, in addition to executing the drawing, you can also reproduce, not only through the copy, but also through techniques that allow several copies to be obtained using a matrix. At the beginning of the fifteenth century Johannes Gensfleisch (better known as Gutenberg) develops printing techniques. Now you can reproduce a text without the hard work of copying scribes. Paper is cheaper, methods of representation begin their arduous path to codification, the techniques of reproduction such as woodcut and intaglio allow a number of copies of a drawing etched with a stylus into a slab of wood or copper to be reproduced on paper, the study of classical architecture teaches that orders are categories to be interpreted: here are all the ingredients to give rise to an explosive mixture.

It is the birth of the treatise: architecture is studied not only through the surveying of classical monuments, but also through books, on the pages of treatises containing various *modern* interpretations. Architectural drawing in the Renaissance is not only for building, but becomes an instrument of knowledge and interpretation of architectural thinking, a new language that needs shared coding, which provides rules to be respected as it becomes a page that can be accessed at a later time. Its communication load does not end with the resolution of a constructive problem, it goes still further. It cannot therefore afford the randomness of spoken language, it needs precise grammatical and syntactical rules.

Coding can be considered completed with the work of Gaspard Monge, who, while not having invented the methods of representation, certainly played a significant role in the definition, classification and nomenclature. He imposed order on what had already happened, clearly defining the codes that are still in use today.

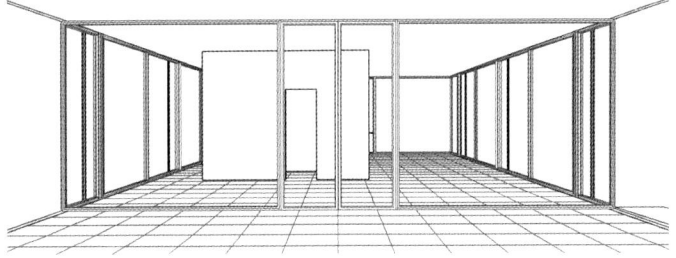

Fabrizio Avella,
Farnsworth House by Mies van der Rohe,
axonometric projection, 2006

Karl Friedrich Schinkel (1781–1841),
Hall of Neues Museum Berlin (Germany), c. 1828
From *Sammlung architectonischer Entwürfe, enthaltend theils Werke, welche ausgeführt sind, theils Gegenstände, deren Ausführung beabsichtigt wurde*, ed. Karl Friedrich Schinkel, Berlin 1828, Notebook 18, p. 103.

Techniques

Thought goes to use of technique, technique influence thought. The two chase each other in circular paths in which one becomes a child to the other. Coming to the end of these thoughts about drawing we cannot neglect the technical realisation of a drawing, in its purely instrumental-material aspect, but also extending the concept to that of expressive technique, taking into account the semantic implications that the choice of a technique entails. Perhaps the most immediate way to draw is to leave a mark, a trace on a surface: a piece of wood on wet sand, a finger on a fogged glass, a pencil on a sheet of paper.

In this case, *not figure* has the same background as the figure: a trace that makes only the apparent contour has the function of distinguishing what is the form from what is the surrounding space, but the background is the same, the grain and the colour of the medium do not change.[33] For someone who draws, feeling the need to describe the plasticity of the object is not necessary, merely to give information about its shape and its dimensions. The drawing is analytical, schematic, descriptive of crucial points but in all disinterested in plastic, volumetric or material reports. It is the preferred technique of technical drawing, of executive drawing, little inclined to research chromatic character. The issuing subject, a designer, for example, transmits to the receiving person (a master, a worker, a carpenter, a blacksmith), simple and essential information to tell him where to build a wall, at what height end and insert the frame, how fit two pieces of wood, where and how to put a hole in a metal pillar.[34] At this stage it is not necessary to know that the wall will be plastered and painted red, that the wood will be teak or rosewood, or that the metal will undergo a process of satin chrome. It is the drawing in which the focus is on the form as abstract concept, on the model as a reproduction of an idea, a concept, not necessarily reported or projected in the real world.

One of the aspects that require such a choice is related to the techniques used to perform and reproduce the drawing. It is no coincidence that such an expressive criterion has been used, for example, for reproduction techniques that *hollow out* such as a woodcut, where the printing plate is carved in relief, leaving what will be the stroke of the drawing. The executer carves the part that will not be drawn, the *line* is obtained by subtraction of matter and is therefore already very onerous to achieve an apparent contour drawing.[35] Bringing additional information would make the technique even more cumbersome and, in fact, Renaissance woodcuts in many treatises often present drawings of architectural orders only by the apparent contour.[36] There are, in fact, woodcuts showing shadows that contravene this rule, as in the case of the treatise by Scamozzi, but it is easier to find images, as in the treatise by Serlio, that simply describe only the apparent contour.

In more recent times the same result can be achieved by drawing on a sheet of glossy paper with China pens or ink pens, while in the digital environment you can use t*he hidden* visualisation technique which allows you to hide everything that is in

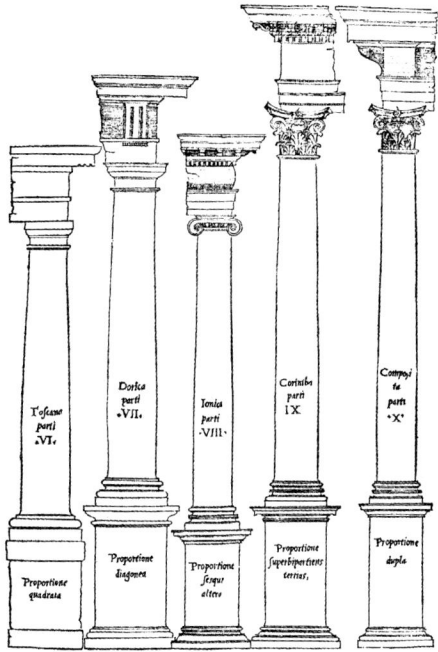

Sebastiano Serlio (1475–1554),
Ordini di colonne, 1619
From *Tutte l'opere d'architettura et prospettiva*,
book IV, p. III, Venice (Italy)

James Stirling (1926–1992),
Derby City Centre, 1970
Drawing by Leon Krier

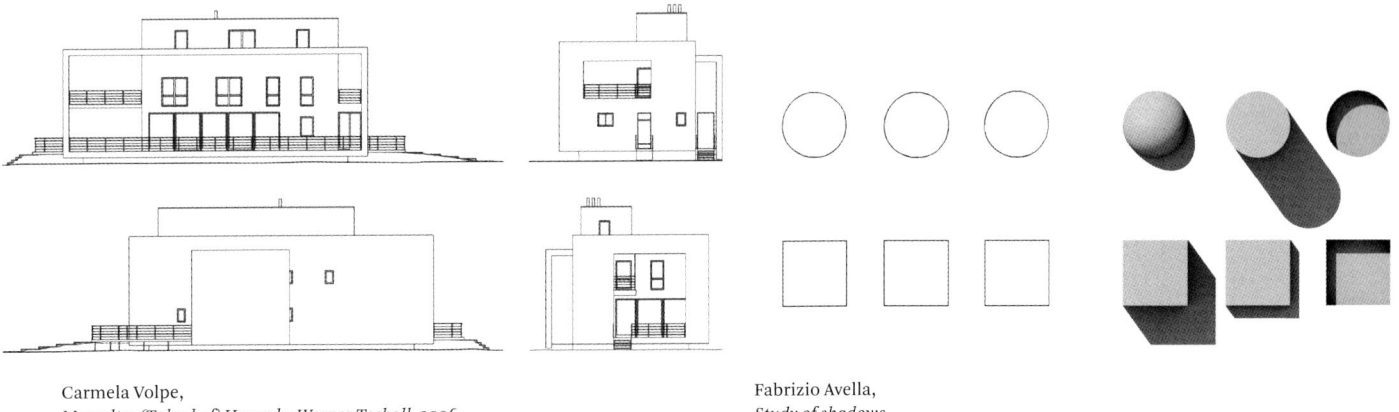

Carmela Volpe,
Mumelter (Taberhof) House by Werner Tscholl, 2006

Fabrizio Avella,
Study of shadows

the background relative to the positioning point of view – and therefore *hidden* to the eyes of the passive observer. The apparent contour drawing is limited to distinguishing the limits of the object, it does not give any other information. You can then add the shadows, introducing to the drawing of architecture techniques already used in preparatory drawings for painting: charcoal drawing, white lead, and blood become part of the lexicon as the architect provides an excellent introduction to a new parameter, shadow. By simulating the presence of a light source something changes: the volume is no longer just a form distinct from other forms and from the space in which it is immersed. It projects and casts shadows on itself, on another volume, on its support. Its edginess is manifested more clearly and becomes more recognisable than the soft roundness of the ball that it is next to. Moreover, even in spoken language we use the term *shed light on something* to invoke clear understanding of obscure issues. But for the sake of clarity there need to be shadows to give us information.[37] The forms remain abstract but are no longer described only by straight or curved sections. Three squares and three circles on a white field: the shadows tell us that the first is a hemisphere, the second a cylinder, the third a hole, and the squares are the projection of two blocks of different heights and a hole in square form. The shadows informs us of the roundness of the surface, the height of solids, and furthermore the depth of the holes.

Shadows add a lot of information: what remains to be determined is how to represent them. To this aim, it is useful to distinguish drawings that do not need to be reproduced from those which should be. If today, in fact, given the reproductive techniques, the distinction is negligible, in previous eras reproducibility became a parameter choice for technique and, consequently, graphic rendering suffered. The problem was strongly felt in the original editions of the treatises, in which the drawings were to be reproduced to complement and explain the text. The desired effect can be achieved thanks to the spread of *relief* techniques, including the *etching*, a technique used for the reproduction of images of the treatise by Vignola, which allow for a more subtle and dotted drawing. Unlike the woodcut, the drawing is reproduced using signs that actually will be inked, removing with a metal tip (hence the name, in some cases, *puntasecca*) a thin layer of wax that covered the plate. Metal parts that were no longer protected by wax corroded when immersed in a mixture of water and nitric acid. After cleaning and inking, the paper surface was pressed to the plate. With this procedure, the

Giuseppe Dalli Cardillo,
Study of shadows, 2008

Bernardo Augello,
Smith House by Richard Meier,
shaded perspective, 2006

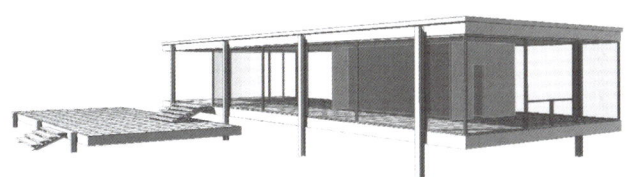

Fabrizio Avella,
Farnsworth House by Mies van der Rohe,
shaded perspective, 2006

lines can be made with very fine tips, for the benefit of reduced thickness of the final mark. Here, however, drawings appear in the treatises, with shading obtained through a combination of parallel lines, sometimes overlapping and cross-hatched, which thicken in darker areas and thin out in the most clear. A similar effect, visible in the table of Perrault, was obtained by reproducing a matrix engraved on copper.

The problem does not exist when the drawing need not be reproduced; here you can use pen or the India ink on paper and get the shading by using pencil, charcoal or watercolour or tempera. This is the case of the drawing by Ludovico Cardi (Cigoli), made with pen and brown ink with watercolour on white paper. The shadows can be homogeneous and their intensity is obtained from a greater or lesser presence of water. Shading is widely used in digital design, as it is possible to simulate the presence of light sources on the scene. The total absence of problems in the reproduction of shaded images means that not only are the shadows produced by homogeneous background hatching, but you can even achieve very good levels of shading simulation also on curved surfaces with nuances that turn from intense black to startling white, passing through a very high number of stages of grey intensity.

The different rendering engines also allow the simulation of clear shade that simulates the crisp light of the sun on a beautiful day, or nuanced, as obtained from diffused light or from the interaction of light sources, and many more different reflections of light rays.[38]

But the shadows might not be enough: colour could be needed. Where there are no impediments related to reproduction or where *chromo-lithographic* techniques permit it, the design of architecture is enriched with information by the use of colour. The techniques used, in some cases borrowed from paintings, have been manifold, ranging from drawing to watercolour to tempera to coloured pencils. Watercolour is used a lot, as it allows various intensities of colour, more or less saturated depending on the amount of colour and dilution, and allows a good drawing on paper of proper thickness; no deformations occur as they would with other types of paint. Tempera, more rarely used in architectural drawings, allows similar results, but with very diluted paint used very carefully. The *facade* of the competition project for the Teatro Massimo by Damiani Almeyda, in the second half of the eighteenth century, and the perspective of Wagner's villa, at the beginning of the twentieth century, are two examples of drawing on watercolour paper.

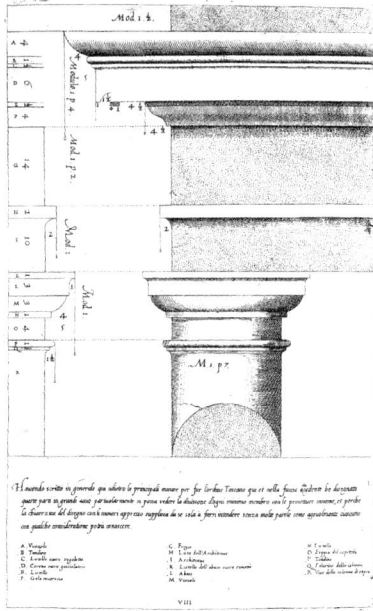

Jacopo Barozzi da Vignola (1507–1573),
Trabeazione e capitello di ordine toscano con indicazione precisa del modulo, 1562
From *Regola delli cinque ordine d'architettura*, tab. VIII, Rome (Italy)

Claude Perrault (1613–1688),
Base, capital and entablature and details of ionic column, 1683
From *Ordonnance des cinq espèces de colonnes selon la méthode des anciens*, tab. 4, Paris (France)

Ludovico Cardi, called Cigoli (1559–1613),
Disegno per apparato effimero, date unknown
Galleria degli Uffizi,
Florence (Italy)

Giuseppe Damiani Almeyda (1834–1911),
*Project for the Teatro Massimo in Palermo,
front elevation*, detail, 1874
Archivio Damiani, Palermo (Italy)
Photo: Fabrizio Avella, post-processing:
Fabrizio Avella, Giuseppe Dalli Cardillo

Otto Wagner (1841–1918),
Villa Wagner, 1905
Historical Museum of the City of Vienna,
Vienna (Austria)

Another technique that spread in the twentieth century was that of gouache, which gave the possibility to create uniform coloured surfaces, and to obtain shades.[39] Like the techniques for watercolour and tempera, it could be used on drawings in pencil, pen or ink on paper or cardboard.

Chromatic simulation has already been included in digital drawing, simply by colouring volumes or surfaces which are transformed into polygonal surfaces by the rendering engine. The image of the museum of Corciano was obtained via insertion of light sources and colouration of the faces of the solids used for modelling. On the individual faces the effect can be seen of light rays that make the tone darker in shade, and dark grey if the surface is deprived of colour connotations. The use of colour in manual drawing has opened the way for an additional level of information: the material simulation. Just as colour can be used to obtain the shade of a wall, it can equally be used for the same techniques, to simulate the material aspects. Borrowing painting techniques, the nineteenth century architect has surveyed the expressive possibilities of colour to produce not only the different degrees of brightness and saturation of a colour depending on how much light it gets, but also to simulate the characteristics of material surfaces. Stone, wood, marble, decorated walls, and even marble slabs for flooring, as in the splendid drawing by Damiani Almeyda, which depicts a burial chapel. Please note that polychrome design became widely used after archaeological studies brought to light the Pompeian architecture, whose polychromy became the model for many architectures of the nineteenth century. The technique lends also itself to the representation of architecture full of ornamental aspects, as with the experiments of what today is called *Eclecticism*, but it is also perfectly effective for the design of Art Nouveau ornaments.

At the beginning of the nineteenth century, Alois Senefelder, already the inventor of lithography in 1796, perfected the process and laid the foundations for *chromo lithography*, which allowed the reproduction of shades and nuances. They fall, therefore, within the limits of reproductive technology and colour can be achieved even when we know that it must be reproduced for educational or teaching purposes. The colourful design suffers a setback with the Modern Movement, which bans, among other things, the decoration and does not like the colour, preferring simple volumes, preferably white, or, at most, unplastered material or concrete. Such a simple architecture does not need to be drawn in colour. One apparent contour

Giuseppe Damiani Almeyda (1834–1911),
Cappella sepolcrale, 1890
From *Istituzioni Architettoniche*, Archivio Damiani,
Palermo (Italy)

Yakov Chernikhov (1889–1951),
Hydroelectric power station, From Fundamentals of Modern Architecture, tab. 149, 1931
Yakov Chernikhov International Foundation
Moscow (Russia)

Fabrizio Avella, Guglielmo Acciaro,
Pepe Vasquez Reina,
Archaeological Museum of Corciano (Italy), 2002

Anthony Saladino,
Chiesa di San Lorenzo in Trapani (Italy),
rendering by Mirco Cannella, 2007

drawing and, at most, a bit of shade are enough to show the volumetric composition. Today, the colourful and *mimetic* drawing has taken the place it deserves, thanks to the introduction of techniques for rendering, which, in addition to simulating the impact of rays of light, can simulate the material aspect by calculating engines. The rendering engine allows the simulation of material aspects, such as reflection, mirrored reflection, grain,[40] matte or shiny appearance. Besides that you use the textures,[41] which can faithfully reproduce patterns of materials such as wood or marble veins, the pattern of a wall of bricks, the irregularity of a wall of stone, etc.

Even an untrained eye can recognise, in the drawings, that in some cases the figure is more abstract, analytical, with a code that requires more skills for interpretation by the receiving entity, while in other cases, the similarity with the perception is greater and the drawing is more mimetic.[42] Between mimesis and the symbol there may be different levels, and codes may overlap mimetic analogue codes. It may occur, for example, that an interior of Mies can be described by overlapping the design in black and white, perfect for the representation of modular scanning, with images of furniture and outside vegetation, whose realism, achieved through a photographic superposition emphasises the transparency of glass surfaces. It is possible that the shapes of people, cut from photographs and, therefore, with a mimetic code, are incorporated into designs that deliberately have cartoon-like graphics, or, conversely, the photo of a panel, from the mimetic code, positioned on an interactive wall of a display module, co-exists with the black silhouettes of stylised human figures. Or well-simulated stone walls co-exist with trees that stand out against the backdrop of an unreal white sky.

Denise Ippolito,
Interior of a residence, 2007

Fabrizio Avella,
Farnsworth House by Mies van der Rohe, perspective, 2006

Angela Finocchiaro,
Housing, 2007

Giuseppe Dalli Cardillo,
Banca Popolare di Lodi (Italy) by Renzo Piano, perspective, 2006

Denise Ippolito,
Conference room, 2007

Giuseppe Dalli Cardillo,
Banca Popolare di Lodi (Italy) by Renzo Piano, perspective, 2006

Angela Finocchiaro,
Housing, 2007

Claudia Di Carlo, Giuseppe Trapani, Luca Viccica,
Modulo espositivo, 2008

Aldo Baldo, Giuseppe Dalli Cardillo,
Salvatore Mandracchia,
Restoration of the Ospedale dei Bianchi in Corleone (Italy), 2007

Ernesto Basile, *Palazzo per l'esposizione nazionale di arti e industrie in Palermo*, c. 1891
Archivio Basile, Universitá degli studi di Palermo,
Facoltá di architettura,
Palermo (Italy)

The balance of possibilities may also decisively indicate a technique which is far from mimesis. The surfaces show strange striations, or hatches which are thickened where the light changes to shadow without any indication of materials or colours that will be perceived in that space.

To conclude to this exploration of the techniques of representation we consider a symbolic drawing by Ernesto Basile: the elevation of the National Palace of Arts and Industries of Palermo, in which mimetic code and analogical code co-exist in the image almost perfectly. It seems you can see the different levels of attention given by the architect to the study of the facade: from the geometric trace to the game of geometric projection of light decorative bands, from the penumbra of the voids to the chromatic valences determined by pigmentation or by different materials assumed for the columns or for the building structure.

Permanence and variations in computer science design

It was chosen in this essay to address the complex problem of two-dimensional representation by distinguishing the representation methods from the techniques of construction. The two are not separable for the proper interpretation of an image, but the distinction may be useful to identify similarities and innovations in digital drawing vis-à-vis manual. In regards to the methods of representation, it has already been pointed out how computer technologies for flat representation have not introduced any changes to the codes already known: a section of a building is conceptually similar to the section of St. Peter's by Antonio da Sangallo the Younger, just as a front elevation is obtained by algorithms that use identical projective conditions to those shown and used in the facade of the Rotonda di Palladio. About axonometric projection, it has already been pointed out what the limitations of digital drawing are; it does not allow, except in rare cases, the development of oblique axonometric projection. This restriction, in fact, has a small impact on the draftsman: oblique axonometric projection had significant advantages during the construction phases as it allowed the entities to be kept in true shape and size, limiting dimensional changes to the oblique axes. It was easy, therefore, to build and control three-dimensional elements. If, however, it is possible to achieve orthogonal axonometric projection without special efforts, the loss of oblique axonometric projection seems to be an acceptable price. The problem of post-dimensional control, a user-friendly solution for the oblique axonometric projection where simple factors were used (1:2, 1:1), can be overcome through the many commands for distance analysis, angles, areas made available in CAD programmes. As for perspective, it has already been pointed out that it is easy to demonstrate that the algorithm for calculating the perspective is actually quite close to that of Brunelleschi and Alberti, and certainly Monge would not be displeased either. What has changed profoundly is the implementation procedure and the concept of the geometric model. In hand drawing, each drawing is a two-dimensional model of a multi-dimensional reality: a plan, an elevation, a perspective, are two-dimensional transpositions of a multidimensional object, drawn according to a shared code of descriptive geometry which today we call methods of representation. The use of different models that are related one to each other forces you to think carefully about the method you are using, whether or not it is appropiate for expressing the meaning and describing the right information. It has been seen that this has resulted historically in a long and arduous path of choice of coding methods. It has also been seen that the method was also associated with a structure of thought. Paraphrasing Panofsky, the plan, the section, the orthogonal projections, the axonometric projection, the perspectives are all *symbolic forms*. Anyone who has done only a cube with a CAD programme knows that the process is reversed: it constructs a model in a virtually infinite space, from which infinite projections are derived. It is not necessary, therefore, to reason too much about which method of representation you are using. The important thing is to see the object. It is not uncommon to see talented modellers who manage to obtain models of even complex shapes that do not pose a problem if they are looking at the object in axonometric projection or perspective. Ironically, the ease of immediacy of the visualisations has generated a digital split from the building of the model and its representation. A problem that is easily seen when teaching is to make students understand that even if they make a perfect model, the exercise is not completed, they still must *draw* it. In hand-drawing, construction and manual representation of the model are two coinciding phases. In computerised design they are not: building and monitor display coincide, but the representation is left to a stage where some control was lost. The process can be legitimate when it passes directly from a CAD model to a CAD or CNC implementation,[43] which does not need any drawing on paper and representation in a not so distant future, and will allow numerically controlled sites. Then we could debate the utility of disciplinary issues. Considering that, for various reasons, the static plan representation could be needed for a long time, it was necessary to make some reflections. The possibility of having, in a few moments, infinite points of view of a model is, for those who have experienced physical pain and strained their eyesight building an axonometric projection or a perspective, is simply breathtaking. The invitation is to ensure that the representation of a digital model occurs after the brain has been switched on, recalling that representing means choosing, and avoiding that someone else (the programme or the limits on its use) chooses for us. The positive aspects of digital design include the *revenge* of the perspective, thanks to its *ease* of execution. You look back to architecture *from below* and not just in axonometric projection (whose manual construction is more immediate), and this can only be good for a design in which man is *inside* architecture, not simply looking at his absurdly shaped shiny technological object from infinity.[44] The drive towards the prospect is also a desire for immersive viewing. Panofsky had already raised the issue of limitation of the perspective plan, and one might wonder whether the computer cannot give a boost to the passing of this method. Projection systems on cylindrical surfaces are already on the market, and it is possible that these systems may have, in the near future, a greater spread. And the possibility of spherical projection systems is not to be excluded. The drive could come from the display systems for virtual simulation in military operations and for video games. The game has begun and it is already possible to find projectors or helmets with monoscopic or stereoscopic displays with viewing angles of 150°, a value near the horizontal view of our eyes. As for the techniques of representation, the reasoning to be done is between technique and thought: if I can paint colour I can think of colours, if I want to make a white object I choose to leave the colours in the tray. Thanks to rendering, the drawing goes back to being *in colour*, and this is great. Thanks to rendering the photorealism often becomes the end, and this is not necessarily great. One thing is certain: the concept of the model is changing and, therefore, the way it summarises reality. The model is no longer a set of abstract geometric shapes that combine to reproduce an idea: Renaissance design and Alberti's wooden model did not worry about providing additional information. They described the shape and this was already sufficient to give the necessary information. The authority, the Pope, the duke or lord, knew that the implementation would involve the choice of stone, plaster, wood, paintings, frescoes to change that work into abstract spaces, floors, sometimes columns. There was no need to render.

Today, the wooden model is no longer enough. At the conclusion of a process that began with the eighteenth century vedutistica, architectural design is enhanced by the pictorial meanings that horrified Alberti, but, inevitably, are irresistibly attractive. Today a customer, often far from the artistic preparation that the Renaissance patron had, is unable to interpret an abstract design. The culture of the image in which we are immersed has lost the common sense capacity of abstraction, we must look to understand and we must see something that is as close as possible to reality. Manufacturers of video games began a race a long time ago, no holds barred, to obtain the most realistic result; TVs now have a resolution that can be compared to a view through a microscope. No longer satisfied with seeing a football match, we must see the beads of sweat on the player, each individual hair and the tattoo printed on the shoulder when the player takes off his shirt, rejoicing after a goal. Even the animation industry has introduced, within a few years, increasingly sophisticated techniques aimed at realistic representation: we have all been fans of Nemo's father and we have forgiven Dori for his thoughtlessness; we hoped for the victory of the Incredibles, and we hoped that Scrat in *Ice Age: Dawn of the Dinosaurs* would finally get his acorn. All this surrounded by beautiful scenery where the ocean depths, tropical forests and glaciers were presented with impeccable craftsmanship. So the acceleration that is occurring in research and applications related to realism and virtual reality is normal and expected. The problem is that we are confusing media with the goal. The representation cannot do without symbolic codes and photorealism cannot be the ultimate goal. Hoping not to have the same fate as the protagonists of *Until the End of the World* by Wim Wenders,[45] we will soon be users of immersive visualisation systems and display systems will diffuse to increase reality: we will be able to see a digital model overlapped perfectly with phenomenal reality through displays with semi-transparent lenses. The method is already widely used in industrial design, and is likely to expand rapidly to the visualisation of architecture. In this way, the desire for realism will be satisfied and we will not be able to distinguish what really exists from what is the fruit of our imagination. Perhaps all this follows an atavistic impulse towards mimetic reproduction: its efforts to obtain drawings in perspective, the techniques of reproduction, photography, first in black and white, then colour, Muybridge's attempts to reproduce motion, cartoons, the growth of video games from aseptic white rectangles on a black background bouncing a rectangular white ball to football video-games that reproduce the appearance of real players, and more, deliver the pursuit of realism. It is undeniably amazing what you feel when dealing with reproductions, not only visual, which can simulate reality. The historic success of Madame Tussauds wax museum in London is one of many confirmations that the concept of the faithful copy is fascinating to man. Perhaps it is a way to feel capable of owning reality,[46] rather than being subjected to it: the higher the degree of *precision* with which I reproduce reality, the greater the illusion of control and possibly, at the same time, the lower the sense of frustration that I face when I realise that however sophisticated technologies become, reality is not reproducible.

But man needs symbol, abstraction. Perhaps this awareness of the introduction of new techniques will, however, lead to new forms of abstraction. Equally strong is, in fact, our need to create symbols to represent codes of non-immediate interpretation. None of the techniques mentioned affect the success of *The Simpsons*, or *South Park*, and we will continue to watch with pleasure the *Pink Panther* cartoons and *Mickey Mouse*. It seems disappointing, then, that the digital representation is unable to resolve the dilemmas: mimesis and abstraction? Hyperrealism or new areas of expression? Finally, if the model is no longer an immutable object, but can become an information system that interacts with the user, I must be able to exert even stronger control over its construction and its representation, be it analogue or iconic, symbolic or mimetic, static or dynamic. Whatever its result, I must know how to control, manage the model. The possibilities of digital representation are enormous and are influencing the way we interpret and represent reality, whether existing or in project. What does not change and what we should always keep in mind, is that to draw, to represent, means to choose, to decide. Better do it with awareness.

Appendix

232 Index
234 Sources

Index

Index of Names

Adam, Robert 38
Alberti, Leon Battista 13, 136f., 194ff., 204
Asisi, Yadegar 67-75
Augello, Bernardo 180, 213, 217
Avella, Fabrizio 181-229, 240
Böhm, Paul 67, 76-79
Brunelleschi, Filippo 194, 196, 198, 204, 227
Canal, Giovanni Antonio 38
Cennino, Cennini 212
Challe, Charles Michel-Ange 38, 43
Chambers, Sir William 38
Chernikhov, Yakov Georgievich 46
Chipperfield, David 37
Choisy, Auguste 18
Destailleur, Gabriel-Hippolyte 26
Durand, Jean-Nicolas-Louis 17
Eisenman, Peter 24
Fensterbusch, Curt 15
Francesca, Piero della 194, 196
Fuksas, Doriana 67, 80-83
Fuksas, Massimiliano 67, 80-83
Gadamer, Hans-Georg 21
Gilly, David 26
Gilly, Friedrich 26
Gonzaga, Pietro di Gottardo 38
Gregotti, Vittorio 193
Gropius, Martin 26, 31
Hadid, Zaha 67, 84-87
Haftmann, Werner 64
Hecker, Zvi 67, 88-93
Heidegger, Martin 22
Holl, Steven 48
Honnecourt, Villard de 11
Huntley, Roger 37
Jones, Inigo 26
Joseph Michael Gandy 38, 44
Klein, Bruno 14
Kohtz, Otto 32
Kollhoff, Hans 21
Krier, Rob 67, 94-97
Langhans, Carl Gotthard 28
Le Corbusier 17, 22, 57, 60f., 179, 184, 193
Leatherborrow, David 11
Mattern, Hermann 36
Meier, Richard 79, 180f., 184, 192, 211, 213, 217
Mies van der Rohe, Ludwig 21, 63, 192f., 196, 200, 204f., 212, 214, 217, 223
Monge, Gaspard 193, 196, 213, 227
Moore, Charles 56
Nägelke, Hans-Dieter 7, 26-37, 240
Palladio, Andrea 17
Panini, Giovanni Paolo 38, 41
Panofsky, Erwin 194, 227f.
Penther, Johann Friedrich 17
Percier, Charles 45
Peruzzi, Baldassarre 16
Piranesi, Giovanni Battista 38
Pittner, Heinrich 52f., 56ff., 61, 65, 240
Poelzig, Hans 22, 35
Powell, Helen 11
Prix, Wolf D. 67, 98-101
Quarenghi, Giacomo 38
Radoske, Alexander 112-115
Raschdorff, Julius 26
Ridingers, Georg 17
Sangello, Giuliano da 182, 184, 207
Sattler, Christoph 67, 106-109
Schaudt, Johann Emil 34
Scheurer, Ludwig 33
Schinkel, Karl Friedrich 16, 21, 26, 29, 214
Senefelder, Alois 220
Simon, Hans 35
Soane, John 26, 38, 39
Speer, Albert 22
Stüler, Friedrich August 30
Sturm, Leonhardt Christoph 17
Tchoban Foundation 39
Tchoban, Sergei 38-39, 49, 115
Thomon, Jean-Francois Thomas de 42
Vasaris, Giorgio 26
Vinci, Leonardo da 7, 15
Vitruv 15
Wolters, Rudolf 22
Zuccari, Federico 38

Index of References

A
Abstraction 11, 58, 60, 64, 229
Academy drawing 11
American National Standards Institute (ANSI) 133
Angular dimensions 145
Arris 156f.
As-built drawing 140, 144, 161, 172, 174, 176f.,
Attic 156
Axonograph 123
B
Ballpoint pen 126
Bauakademie 26
Bay 14
Border 135
British Standards Institute (BS) 133
Brush 55, 121f., 125
Building instruction drawing 160, 170
Burmester template 122
C
Canvas 123, 130, 213
Carcass drawing 161
Card stock 134
CD-Rom 131
Ceiling opening 2, 154, 162
Change index 136
Charcoal 33f, 49, 76ff., 112, 121ff., 216f.
Choir chapel 13
Circle 15, 21, 58, 61, 123, 144, 145, 216
Clock tower 14
Colour theory 62
Compass 11, 15, 123 24
Component drawing 140, 176
Composition 60
Computer Aided Design 129
Computer keyboard 23
Computer workstation 129
Construction administration 26
Contour line 157
Computer monitor 21
Construction plan 11, 119, 135
Cross section dimension 145
Cube 58, 227
Curvatures 122
Curved cells 13
D
Date of amendment 137
Deconstructivism 23
Deconstructivist 24, 67,162
Depth 13, 56, 154, 165
Design drawing 160, 168, 170, 172
Detail drawing 140, 174, 176f.,
Development plan 140, 166
Diagrams 160, 168, 181
Digital drawing 129f., 138
Digital pen 130, 131
Dimensioning 144ff.
Dimensioning guidelines 144
Divider 123
Document status 136
Door frame 153
Door hinges 153
Door opening dimensions 153
Doors 152
Dormer 156
Drawing board 64, 121f., 125, 129
Drawing paper 125, 134
Drawing pencil 124
Drawing scales 140ff.
Drawing table 121
Dusting brush 122
E
Eave corner 156
Eave height 157
Elements 7, 57, 185, 209, 227
Elevation drawing 135, 165, 186, 206
Ellipse 122
Emergency overflow 156
Eraser 122f.
Eraser pencil 122
Erasing shield 123
Euro-Asian Council for Standardisation, Metrology and Certification (EASC) 133
European Standard (EN) 133
Exploded-view drawing 164
Exterior elevation 11
F
Felt-tip 109ff., 126
Fire protection closure 153
Flash drive 131
Flat roof 149, 156
Folding 135
Font size 146
Formwork drawing 161
Freehand perspective 59
French curve 122
Full section 164
G
Gable 156
Geometry set square 122
German Institute for Standardisation (DIN) 133
Golden ratio 61
Graph paper 134
Graphics tablet 121, 129ff.
H
Height dimension 145
Hip eave 156
Hip rafter 156
Hip roof 156
I
Ichnography 162
Illustration 7, 138
Indian ink 53
Ink pen 126, 214
International Standard (ISO) 133
Isometric representation 154
L
Labelling 135, 138, 144, 146f., 154
Laptop 131
Layered section 164
Leader line 143, 145f.,
Lean-to roof 156
Line thickness 146, 162
Line types and line widths 143
Lintel 2, 145, 152ff.,
Lockable plastic rail 121
M
Main eave 156
Mansard roof 156
Margin 135
Measured drawing 160
Modifications to drawings 136
Modulor 57, 61, 193
Mouse 53, 129ff.
Museum of Architecture 7, 27-30, 39, 240
N
Niches 154
O
Oblique projections 145
Oil pastels 109
Opening 2, 144, 152ff., 154, 161f., 170, 174
Opening dimensions 153
Oral presentation 138
Orthogonal projection 13, 184ff., 209, 227
Outlet 156
P
Paper and drawing sheets 134f., 138, 140
Paper weight 134
Parabola 122
Parapet 2, 145, 153, 174
Partial hip roof 156
Partial section 164
Pastel chalk 121
Pencil 121
Pencil sharpener 122
Perception 49
Permanent marker 126
Perspective 9, 75, 134, 164, 168
Photo camera 131
Pigment pen 126
Planning permission 160, 168
Plat 166
Plein-air drawing 65
Plotter 129, 131
Preliminary design drawing 160, 168, 170
Presentation drawing 138
Printer 53, 129, 131
Prism scale 122
Proportion 23, 39, 52f., 55ff., 138, 165, 193
Pyramid 58,195
R
Rainwater downpipe 170
Recess 154f, 161, 174
Recess in the wall 154
Reference lines 145
Reinforcement drawing 161

Renderings 22, 24, 126, 129
Representation methods 227
Resistance class 153
Ridge 156f
Roof design 157
Roof slope 157

S
Saddle roof 156
Scaenographia 15
Scale 140
Scanner 129, 131
Screen 129
Section drawing 164
Set square 121
Settlement drawing 161
Shading 124f., 143, 148, 157, 217
Shed or saw-tooth roof 156
Side view 138, 165
Site plan 140, 166
Sizes 134ff.
Sketches 11, 22, 26f., 38, 53, 64f., 119,
    126, 140, 160, 185
Sketching paper 123, 131, 134
Slot plan 154
Soffit 138
Speed square 122
Sphere 58
Stairs 150f
Standard lettering lines 146
Standards 133
Steeple roof 156
Styles of roof 156
Symbol 121, 149, 158, 222, 229

T
T-rails 121
Taskbar and start menu 130
Tented roof 156
Title block 135, 140
Tracing paper 123, 125, 134
Triangle 121f., 145, 149, 155
Triangular scale 122

U
User interface 130

V
Valley 156f.
Vanishing point 59, 194ff.
Verge 156
Vertical section 16, 187
Volume model 129

W
Wall thickness 2
Window 129, 145, 152f., 157, 170, 174
Window height 153
Working drawing 161
Working tools 121

The History of Architectural Drawing
Klaus Jan Philipp

1   Josef Ponten: *Architektur die nicht gebaut wurde*, Stuttgart 1925 (Reprint with a preface by Frank Werner, Stuttgart 1987).

2   Joachim P. Heisel: *Antike Bauzeichnungen*, Darmstadt 1993.

3   Peter Pause: 'Gotische Architekturzeichnungen in Deutschland', Diss. Bonn 1973; Roland Recht (ed.): *Les Bâtisseurs des Cathédrales gothiques*, exhibition catalogue Straßburg 1989; Wolfgang Schöller: 'Ritzzeichnungen. Ein Beitrag zur Geschichte der Architekturzeichnung im Mittelalter', in: *Architectura* 1989, p. 36-61; Johann Josef Böker: *Architektur der Gotik*, Salzburg 2005.

4   'Piet Lombarde: New Techniques for representing the object': Hans Vredeman de Vries and Hans van Schille, in: Heiner Borggrefe und Vera Lüpkes (eds.): *Hans Vredeman de Vries und die Folgen*, Marburg 2005, p. 101-108; Josef Ploder: *Heinrich von Geymüller und die Architekturzeichnung*, Vienna 1998; Werner Oechslin: 'Geometrie und Linie: die Vitruvianische »Wissenschaft« von der Architekturzeichnung', in: *Daidalos*, 1, 1981, p. 20-35; Werner Oechslin: 'Architektur, Perspektive und die hilfreiche Geste der Geometrie', in: *Daidalos*, 11, 1984, p. 39-54.

5   Carl Linfert: 'Die Grundlagen der Architekturzeichnung', in: *Kunstwissenschaftliche Forschungen*, 1, 1931, p. 133-246; Elisabeth Kieven: *Von Bernini bis Piranesi. Römische Architekturzeichnungen des Barock*, Stuttgart 1993; Adolf Reinle: *Italienische und deutsche Architekturzeichnungen 16. und 17. Jahrhundert*, Basel 1994.

6   Werner Oechslin: 'Émouvoir - Boullée und Le Corbusier', in: *Daidalos*, 30, 1988, p. 42-55; Winfried Nerdinger, Klaus Jan Philipp, Hans-Peter Schwarz (ed.): *Revolutionsarchitektur. Ein Aspekt der europäischen Architektur um 1800*, Munich 1990.

7   *Visionen und Utopien. Architekturzeichnungen aus dem Museum of Modern Art*, exhibition catalogue, Frankfurt am Main, Kunsthalle Schirn, Munich 2003; Horst Bredekamp: Die Architekturzeichnung als Gegenbild, in: Margit Kern, Thomas Kirchner und Hubertus Kohle (ed.): *Geschichte und Ästhetik. Festschrift für Werner Busch zum 60. Geburtstag*, Munich 2004, p. 548-553; Jürgen Paul: 'Der Architekturentwurf im 20. Jahrhundert als kunsthistorisches Arbeitsfeld', in: Stephan Kummer (ed.): *Studien zur Künstlerzeichnung. Klaus Schwager zum 65. Geburtstag*, Stuttgart 1990, p. 308-321; Carsten Ruhl: 'Im Kopf des Architekten: Aldo Rossis La città analoga', in: *Zeitschrift für Kunstgeschichte*, 69, 2006, p. 67-98.

8   Ekhart Berckenhagen: *Architekturzeichnungen 1479-1979 von 400 europäischen Architekten aus dem Bestand der Kunstbibliothek Berlin*, exhibition catalogue, Berlin 1979; Winfried Nerdinger: *Die Architekturzeichnung. Vom barocken Idealplan zur Axonometrie. Zeichnungen aus der Architektursammlung der Technischen Universität München*, Munich 1985; Werner Broda (ed.): *Dreiecks-Verhältnisse. Architektur- und Ingenieurzeichnungen aus vier Jahrhunderten*, Nürnberg 1996; Jürgen Döring (ed.): *100 Ideen aus 200 Jahren. Architekturzeichnungen des Barock, Klassizismus und Historismus*, Hamburg 2003.

9   Project by Bibliotheca Hertziana, Rome: http://lineamenta.biblhertz.it/; Project by Deutsche Fotothek Dresden: http://www.deutschefotothek.de/?ARCHIV_ARCHITEKTUR; project by TU Berlin: http://www.architekturmuseum-berlin.de.

10 For example: Heinrich Wurm: *Baldassarre Peruzzi. Architekturzeichnungen, Tafelband, Tübingen 1984; Michelangelo e il disegno di architettura*, Centro Internazionale di Studi di Architettura Andrea Palladio ... A cura di Caroline Elam, Venezia 2006; François Fossier: *Les dessins du fonds Robert de Cotte de la Bibliothèque nationale de France: Architecture et décor*, Paris 1997; Helge Bofinger und Wolfgang Voigt (ed.): *Helmut Jacoby. Meister der Architekturzeichnung*, Tübingen 2001.

11 See Roland Recht: *Le Dessin d'architecture. Origine et fonctions*, Paris 1995. This is simply a collection of essays on medieval and Renaissance architectural drawing, as is the volume edited by James S. Ackerman and Wolfgang Jung, *Conventions of Architectural Drawing: Representation and Misrepresentation*, Cambridge, Mass. 2000, which contains essays mainly on issues of modern architectural drawing. On the problem in general: Margaret Richardson: 'Architectural drawings, problems of status and value', in: *Oxford Art Journal*, 5,2, 1983, pp. 13-21; Werner Oechslin: 'Rendering - Die Darstellungs- und Ausdrucksfunktion der Architekturzeichnung', in: *Daidalos*, 25, 1987, pp. 68-77.

12 Kieven 1993, Von Bernini bis Piranesi, p. 9.

13 Wolfgang Kemp: *Die Räume der Maler. Zur Bilderzählung seit Giotto*, Munich 1996.

14 Hans W. Hubert: 'Architekturzeichnung', in: *Enzyklopädie der Neuzeit*, Vol. 1, Stuttgart- 2005, pp. 614-624.

15 Werner Jacobsen: *Der Klosterplan von St. Gallen und die karolingische Architektur. Entwicklung und Wandel von Form und Bedeutung im frankischen Kirchenbau zwischen 751 und 840*, Berlin 1992.

16 James S. Ackermann: 'The origins of architectural drawing in the Middle Ages and Renaissance', in his: *Origins, Imitation, Convention. Representation in the Visual Arts*, Cambridge 2002, p. 27-65.

17 Wolfgang Schenkluhn: 'Inter se disputando. Erwin Panofsky zum Zusammenhang von gotischer Architektur und Scholastik', in: Franz Jäger und Helga Sciurie (ed.): *Gestalt, Funktion, Bedeutung. Festschrift für Friedrich Möbius zum 70. Geburtstag*, Jena 1999, p. 93-100; Wolfgang Schenkluhn: 'Die Grundrissfiguren im Bauhüttenbuch des Villard de Honnecourt', in: Leonhard Helten (ed.): *Dispositio: der Grundriss als Medium in der Architektur des Mittelalters*, Halle 2005, p. 103-120.

18 Klaus Jan Philipp: 'Sainte-Waudru in Mons. Die Planungsgeschichte einer Stiftskirche 1449-1450', in: *Zeitschrift für Kunstgeschichte*, 52, 1988, p. 372-413.

19 Böker, *Architektur der Gotik*, p. 176 (inv. no. 16.872v) and 421 (inv. no. 105.064).

20 Villard's sketchbook also contained two 'perspective' drawings of the choir chapel interior and exterior.

21 Wolfgang Lotz: 'Das Raumbild in der italienischen Architekturzeichnung der Renaissance', in: *Mitteilungen des kunsthistorischen Instituts Florenz*, 7, 1956, pp. 193-226.

22 Cited in ibid. p. 194.

23 DIN 1356-1:1995-02, p. 3, paragraph 4.3.1. As an alternative, 4.3.2 offers a mirrored view from beneath the upper part of a horizontally sectioned building.

24 In the case of DIN 1356-1, this is represented by a building model by the American architect Charles Gwathmey.

25 Bruno Klein: 'Der Fassadenplan 5 für das Straßburger Münster und der Beginn des fiktiven- Architekturentwurfs', in: Stefanie Lieb (ed.): *Form und Stil. Festschrift für Günther- Binding zum 65. Geburtstag*, Darmstadt 2001, pp. 166-174.

26 Böker, *Architektur der Gotik*, p. 27; Böker is primarily correcting Wolfgang Lefèvre: 'The emergence of combined orthographic projections', in his (ed.): *Picturing machines 1400-1700*, Cambridge, Mass., pp. 209-244.

27 Vitruvius I, 2,2: 'Species dispositionis, quae graece dicuntur ĐĐĐĐĐ [ideas], sunt haec: ichnographia, orthographia, scaenographia. Ichnographia est circini regulaeque modice continens usu, e qua capiuntur formarum in solis arearum descriptiones. Orthographia autem est erecta frontis imago modiceque picta rationibus operis futuri figura. Item scaenographia- est frontis et laterum abscedentium adumbratio ad circinique centrum omnium linearum responsus.' See also Maria Teresa Bartoli: 'Orthographia, ichnographia, scaenographia', in: *Studi e documenti di architettura*, 8, 1978, pp. 197-208.

28 Assessing the various translations and interpretations of this passage by Vitruvius is no easyy task. In the translation by Rivius (pp. XXIV–XXV), it reads: 'Aber Scenographia bezeichnet auch in solcher auffziehung die neben seiten / nemlichen wie sie sich nach der satzung des puncts Perspetivischer weise verlieren oder abstellen mit allen neben linien.' In Claude Perrault's 1673 translation, it reads (p. 10): 'Et la Scenographie fait voir l'Èlevation non seulement d'une des faces, mais aussi le retour des costez par le concours de toutes les lignes qui aboutissent au centre.' August Rode proposes the following in his translation of 1796 (p. 25f.): 'Die Aussicht endlich ist der Fronte und der abgehenden Seiten schattierte Zeichnung – adumbratio –, so dass alle Linien in Einem [sic!] Augenpunkte – centrum – zusammentreffen.'

29 Most recently, Georg Germann: 'Raffaels "Denkmalpflegebrief"', in: Volker Hoffman et al. (eds.): *Die Denkmalpflege vor der Denkmalpflege, Akten des Berner Kongresses 30. Juni – 3. Juli 1999*, Bern 2005, pp. 267–286; Christoph Thoenes: 'Vitruv, Alberti, Sangallo. Zur Theorie der Architekturzeichnung in der Renaissance', in: *Opus incertum.- Italienische Studien aus drei Jahrzehnten*. With an introduction by Andreas Beyer, Horst Bredekamp and Peter Cornelius Claussen, Munich 2002, pp. 317–341; Christof Thoenes:- '"architectus docet". Über Imagination und Realität in italienischen Architektur-zeichnungen der Renaissance', in: Sylvia Claus et al. (eds.): *Architektur weiterdenken. Werner Oechslin zum 60. Geburtstag*, Zürich 2004, pp. 142–153.

30 Franz Graf Wolff Metternich and Christof Thoenes: *Die frühen St.-Peter-Entwürfe 1505–1514*, Tübingen 1987, p. 83, fig. 85.

31 Wolfgang Jung: 'Verso quale nuovo S. Pietro? Sulla prospettiva a volo d'uccello U2A di Baldassare Peruzzi', in: Gianfranco Spagnesi (ed.): *L'architettura della basilica di San Pietro: Storia e costruzione*, Rome 1997, pp. 149–156.

32 On Palladio's reasons for his reductive, somewhat fragmented procedure, see Bernhard Rupprecht: 'Prinzipien der Architektur-Darstellung in Palladios I Quattro Libri dell'Architettura', in: *Vierhundert Jahre Andrea Palladio (1580–1980)*, Colloquium der Arbeitsstelle 18. Jahrhundert, Gesamthochschule Wuppertal, Heidelberg 1982, pp. 11–43.

33 Jean-Nicolas-Louis Durand: *Precis des leçons d'architecture*, Paris 1819, p. 32.

34 Andreas Haus: 'Architektonische Schatten', in: *Archithese*, 27, 1997, 1. edition, pp. 4–11; Andreas Haus: 'Karl Friedrich Schinkel "Der schöne notwendige Zusammenhang" – Architektur-bild und schwankende Übergänge zwischen "Klassizismus" und romantischem "Historismus"', in: Sylvia Claus et al. (eds.): *Architektur weiterdenken. Werner Oechslin zum 60. Geburtstag*, Zürich 2004, pp. 232–239.

35 See also Wolfgang Lefèvre, Jürgen Renn et al. (eds.): *The Power of Images in Early Modern Science*, Basel 2003.

36 Jacques Androuet du Cerceau: *Leçons de perspective positive*, Paris 1586; Jacques Perret: *Des fortifications et artifices. Architecture et perspective*, Paris 1594; see also Robin Evans: *The Projective Cast. Architecture and its Three Geometries*, Cambridge, Mass. 1995.

37 Georg Ridinger: *Architektur des Schlosses Johannisburg zu Aschaffenburg*, facsimile of the Mainz 1616 edition, edited with an explanatory note by Hans-Bernd Spies, Aschaffenburg 1991 (published by the Geschichts- und Kunstvereins Aschaffenburg e.V. Reihe Nachdrucke, Vol. 2).

38 Augustin-Charles d'Aviler: *Ausführliche Anleitung zu der ganzen Civil-Baukuns*t, trans. Leonhard Christoph Sturm, Augsburg 1725.

39 Johann Friedrich Penther: *Anleitung zur Bürgerlichen Baukunst*, Vol. 1, Augsburg 1744, pp. 17–21, article: 'Baurisse'.

40 William Farish: 'On Isometrical Perspective', in: *Transactions of the Cambridge Philosophical Society*, Vol. 1, 1822, pp. 1–20; Bernhard Schneider: 'Perspektive bezieht sich auf den Betrachter, Axonometrie bezieht sich auf den Gegenstand', in: *Daidalos*, 1, 1981, pp. 81–95.

41 Penther 1744, p. 20.

42 Walter Gropius: 'Idee und Aufbau des Staatlichen Bauhauses', in: *Staatliches Bauhaus*, Weimar 1919–1923, Weimar and Munich 1923, pp. 7–18.

43 Yves-Alain Bois: 'Metamorphosen der Axonometrie', in: *Daidalos*, 1, 1981, pp. 40–58; Yves-Alain Bois: 'Avatars de l'axonométrie', in: *Images et imaginaires d'architecture: dessin,- peinture, photographie, art graphiques*, Paris 1984, pp. 124–134; Thierry Mandoul:- 'Entre raison et utopie. Auguste Choisy et la projection axonométrique', in: *Les cahiers de la recherche architecturale et urbaine*, 17, 2005, pp. 139–150.

44 Auguste Choisy: *Histoire de l'architecture*, Paris 1899, p. 7.

45 Le Corbusier: *Ausblick auf eine Architektur (Vers une architecture 1923)*, Gütersloh 1969, p. 47ff.

46 This is referred to in Bruno Reichlin, Introduction, in: Jacques Gubler (ed.): *Alberto Sartoris*, exhibition at ETH Zürich, Lausanne and Zürich 1978, pp. 8–25 and Mandoul, 'Entre raison et utopie'.

Architecture for Keyboard Instruments Only
Augusto Romano Burelli

1 Martin Heidegger first held his renowned lecture titled *The Question Concerning Technology* in summer 1953 at the meeting *Arts in the Technical Age* at the Bavarian Academy of Fine Arts in Munich. Friedrich Georg Jünger, Werner Heisenberg, Ernst Jünger and José Ortega y Gasset also attended the event. Heidegger brought his well-received speech to a close with the words: "Denn das Fragen ist die Frömmigkeit des Denkens" which means "questioning is characterised by the piety of thinking."

2 Rüdiger Safranski with reference to Friedrich Georg Jünger, in: *Ein Meister aus Deutschland. Heidegger und seine Zeit*, Frankfurt am Main 2001, p. 438.

3 This phrase is attributed to Ludwig Mies van der Rohe who, however, apparently never uttered it. It probably comes from the works of St. Thomas Aquinas' which were found in Mies' library.

4 Theodor W. Adorno: *Ästhetische Theorie*, Frankfurt am Main 1973, p. 334.

5 This recalls Herder's aphorism which describes how man, an imperfect being, had to invent language as a form of compensation.

6 Martin Heidegger: *Aufenthalte*, Frankfurt am Main 1989, p. 32.

7 Three architectural firms – Meinhard von Gerkan and Volkwin Marg, Paola Gennaro and Augusto Romano Burelli as well as Petra and Paul Kahlfeldt – were involved in the construction project with the unusual name of Upper East Side Berlin.

8 Planungs AG Neufert Mittmann Graf Partner drew up the implementation plan in accordance with Frank O. Gehry's design of the south facade of the DZ Bank situated on Berlin's Pariser Platz. Gehry's design was substantially modified so that it was possible to construct the facade in the first place. The creator of the design praised it at the inauguration and what is more, was serious. He obviously could not remember his original design.

9 The impossibility to implement complicated forms in hand drawings makes me think of the way in which Antonio Canova, the great classical sculptor, prepared the marble replica of the plaster model of one of his works. He pierced the model with hundreds of small nails which he then connected with a thin wire so that the plaster statue was swathed by a mesh of triangles. The marble block was grinded along this multiangular mesh - a task which was carried out by scholars with the greatest of care. The stone that was to be removed was held in place by the mesh of triangles, yet the body of Niobe had still not appeared: Only the master himself would strip the last coating of the statue and polish its silky-smooth skin.

Sources

Collecting Architectural Drawings
Hans-Dieter Nägelke

Further reading: For the history of the collection of and the preoccupation with architectural drawings see Ursula Baus: *Zwischen Kunstwerk und Nutzwert. Die Architekturzeichnung, gesehen von Kunst- und Architekturhistorikern seit 1850*, Diss., Stuttgart 1999. For an overview of the history of the collection see Eva-Maria Amberger: 'Von der Kunst- und Wunderkammer zum Architekturmuseum. Architektursammlungen im Spiegel der Zeit', in: *Westfalen und Italien. Festschrift für Karl Noehles*, Petersberg 2002. The collection history of individual buildings has frequently become a theme of representations: For different Berlin collections see: *Die Hand des Architekten. Zeichnungen Berliner Architektursammlungen*, exhibition catalogue. Berlin 2002. For Munich, see Winfried Nerdinger (ed.): *Die Architekturzeichnung. Vom barocken Idealplan zur Axonometrie. Zeichnungen aus der Architektursammlung der Technischen Universität München*, München 1987 idem. (ed.): *Architekturschule München 1868–1993. 125 Jahre Technische Universität München*, München 1993; for Karlsruhe: 'Querschnitt. Aus den Sammlungen des Südwestdeutschen Archivs für Architektur und Ingenieurbau' (ed.) *Südwestdeutschen Archiv für Architektur und Ingenieurbau*, Karlsruhe 2006; finally, for the Architectural Museum in Berlin, Hans-Dieter Nägelke (ed.): *Architekturbilder. 125 Jahre Architekturmuseum der Technischen Universität Berlin*, Kiel 2011. References on digitalisation can be found under www.architekturmuseum-berlin.de and on the Federation of German Architecture Collections under www.architekturarchive.de

Freehand and Technical Drawing
Natascha Meuser

1 The Barkhofen, Eva-Mari: Gustav Peichl. *Die Zeichnung ist die Sprache der Architekten. Bauten und Projekte für Deutschland*, Berlin 2013: Akademie der Künste.

2 Batran, Balder; Born, Alexandra; Frey, Volker; Gustavus, Beatrix; Hansen, Hans-Jürgen; Köhler, Klaus et al.: *Bauzeichnen*, Stuttgart 2011.

3 Bauakademie Berlin (ed.): Die Hand des Architekten. Zeichnungen aus Berliner Architektursammlungen, Cologne 2002.

4 Bingham, Neil R.: *100 Years of Architectural Drawing. 1900–2000*, London 2013.

5 Blaser, Werner: *Architektur und Natur. Das Werk von Alfred Caldwells*, Basel 1984.

6 Böhm, Gottfried; Raev, Svetlozar; Schmidt, Hans M.; Müllejans, Rita: *Der Architekt Gottfried Böhm. Zeichnungen und Modelle*, Cologne 1992.

7 Bott, Gerhard; Dee, Elaine Evans (ed.): *Idee und Anspruch der Architektur. Zeichnungen des 16.–20. Jahrhunderts aus dem Cooper-Hewitt Museum*, New York; Wallraf-Richartz-Museum und Museum Ludwig 1979–1980, Cologne 1979.

8 Broda, Werner: *Dreiecksverhältnisse. Architektur- und Ingenieurzeichnungen aus vier Jahrhunderten*, Nürnberg 1996.

9 Ching, Frank: *Die Kunst der Architekturgestaltung als Zusammenklang von Form, Raum und Ordnung*. Revised and extended edition, Augsburg 1996.

10 Dahmlos, Heinrich-Jürgen: *Bauzeichnen. Grundlagen, Baukonstruktionszeichnen, Bauentwurfszeichnen, Perspektivzeichnen, Schattenkonstruktionen*, 17. edition, Hannover 1996.

11 Damisch, Hubert: *Der Ursprung der Perspektive*, Zürich 2010.

12 Deutsches Institut für Normung: *DIN-Normen für den Unterricht*, Berlin et al. 1985.

13 Documenta III, internationale Ausstellung: *Handzeichnungen*, Kassel 1964.

14 Dürer-Gesellschaft: *Der Traum vom Raum. Gemalte Architektur aus 7. Jahrhunderten; eine Ausstellung der Albrecht Dürer Gesellschaft*. Nürnberg, Marburg 1986.

15 Feireiss, Kristin: *Hand-drawn worlds. Handgezeichnete Welten*, Berlin 2003.

16 Ferriss, Hugh: *Architectural renderings of General Motors Technical Center.* C. 1920–1940.

17 Fucke, Rudolf; Kirch, Konrad; Nickel, Heinz: *Darstellende Geometrie für Ingenieure*, 17. edition, München 2007.

18 Grüßinger, Ralf; Kästner, Volker; Scholl, Andreas (eds.): *Pergamon. Yadegar Asisis Panorama der antiken Metropole*, 2011–2012, 2. edition, Berlin 2012.

19 Guski, Rainer: *Wahrnehmen. Ein Lehrbuch*, Stuttgart, Berlin, Cologne 1996.

20 Hammecke, Harald; Kaabran, Ahmet et al.: *Technische Kommunikation. Technisches Zeichnen, darstellende Geometrie, Grundlagen der Gestaltung, Produktdesign*, 4. edition, Munich 2009.

21 Hemmerling, Marco; Tiggemann, Anke: *Digitales Entwerfen. Computer-Aided-Design in Architektur und Innenarchitektur*, Paderborn 2010.

22 Hesser, Wilfried; Hoischen, Hans: *Technisches Zeichnen. Grundlagen, Normen, Beispiele, darstellende Geometrie*, 33. edition, Berlin 2011.

23 Hilpert, Thilo: *Geometrie der Architekturzeichnung. Einführung in Axonometrie und Perspektive nach Leonardo da Vinci, Gerrit Rietveld, Friedrich Weinbrenner, Albrecht Dürer, Le Corbusier, El Lissitzky*, Braunschweig et al. 1988.

24 Jacoby, Helmut: *Architekturdarstellung. Architectural Rendering*, Stuttgart 1971.

25 Jenkins, Eric J.: *Drawn to Design. Analyzing Architecture Through Freehand Drawing*, Basel 2013.

26 Kemp, Martin: *The Science of Art. Optical Themes in Western Art from Brunelleschi to Seurat*, New Haven 1990.

27 Kieven, Elisabeth; Connors, Joseph; Höper, Corinna: *Von Bernini bis Piranesi. Römische Architekturzeichnungen des Barock*, Stuttgart 1993.

28 Knauer, Roland: *Entwerfen und Darstellen. Die Zeichnung als Mittel des architektonischen Entwurfs*, Berlin 1991.

29 Kraft, Simone: Erwin Panofsky: *Die Perspektive als »symbolische Form«. Eine kritische Textanalyse*, Munich, Ravensburg 2005.

30 Kunstbibliothek Berlin: *Von Schinkel bis Mies van der Rohe. Zeichnerische Entwürfe europäischer Baumeister, Raum- und Formgestalter, 1789–1969*, exhibition catalogue, Kunstbibliothek Berlin 1974, New Collection Munich 1975. Westphalian State Museum of Art and Cultural History 1975, Berlin 1974.

31 Leatherbarrow, David; Powell, Helen: *Masterpieces of Architectural Drawing*, New York 1983.

32 Leich, Jean Ferriss: *Architectural Visions*, New York 1980.

33 Leopold, Cornelie: *Geometrische Grundlagen der Architekturdarstellung*, 4. edition, Wiesbaden 2012.

34 Maurer, Golo: *Michelangelo. Die Architekturzeichnungen: Entwurfsprozess und Planungspraxis*, Regensburg 2004.

35 McQuaid, Matilda; Riley, Terence: *Visionen und Utopien. Architekturzeichnungen aus dem Museum of Modern Art*, Munich, New York 2003.

36 Meuser, Natascha: *Architekturzeichnungen. Handbuch und Planungshilfe*, Berlin 2012.

37 Nerdinger, Winfried: *Die Architekturzeichnung. Vom barocken Idealplan zur Axonometrie: Zeichnungen aus der Architektursammlung der Technischen Universität*

München, exhibition catalogue, German Architecture Museum Frankfurt/M. 1985–1986, 2. edition, Munich 1986.

38 Panofsky, Erwin: 'Die Perspektive als »symbolische Form« (1927)'. In: *Aufsätze zu Grundfragen der Kunstwissenschaft*, Darmstadt 1985, p. 99–167.

39 Parramón, José María; Calbó, Muntsa: *Das grosse Buch vom Zeichnen und Malen in der Perspektive. Historische Entwicklung, orthographische Projektion, Theorie und Praxis der Parallel-, Schräg- und Luftperspektive sowie praktische Anwendung der Perspektive beim Zeichnen und Malen*, Stuttgart 1991.

40 Pollio, Vitruvius: *Baukunst*, Munich and Zürich 1987.

41 Prenzel, Rudolf: *Bauzeichnung und Darstellungstechnik. Working and design drawings = Dessin d'architecture et techniques de représentation*, Stuttgart 1978.

42 Riemann, Gottfried; Heese, Christa: *Karl Friedrich Schinkel 1781–1841*, exhibition catalogue, Altes Museum 1981, West Berlin 1985.

43 Rudolph, Paul: *Architekturzeichnungen*, Fribourg 1974.

44 Sanmiguel, David: *Perspektive. Grundlagen des räumlichen Zeichnens (Topp, 6092)*, Stuttgart 2012.

45 Schaarwächter, Georg: *Perspektive für Architekten*, Stuttgart 1964.

46 Schillaci, Fabio: *Architectural Renderings. Construction and Design Manual: History and Theory, Studios and Practices*, Berlin 2009.

47 Schöne, Richard (ed.): *Damianos Schrift über Optik. Mit Auszügen aus Geminos, Griechisch und Deutsch*, Berlin 1897.

48 Schricker, Rudolf: *Darstellungsmethodik. Architektur, Innenarchitektur, Design. Entwicklungen, Experimente*, Stuttgart 1988.

49 Schumann, Friedrich Karl: 'Gestalt und Geschichte' (*Die Gestalt*, Vol. 6), Leipzig 1941.

50 Schweitzer, Bernhard: 'Vom Sinn der Perspektive' (*Die Gestalt*, Vol. 24), Tübingen 1953.

51 Scolari, Massimo: *Oblique Drawing. A History of Anti-Perspective*, London, Cambridge 2012.

52 Scriba, Christoph J.; Schreiber, Peter: *5000 Jahre Geometrie. Geschichte, Kulturen, Menschen*, 3. edition, Berlin 2010.

53 Sondermann, Horst: *Photoshop® in der Architekturgrafik*, Berlin 2009.

54 Störzbach, Gernot: *Architektur zeichnen. Ein Arbeitsbuch zum Selbststudium*, Stuttgart, Berlin, Cologne 2001.

55 Störzbach, Gernot: *Perspektivisch Zeichnen. Grundlagen zur Darstellung des Dreidimensionalen Raums*, Freiburg 2010.

56 Tchoban, Sergei; Barkhofen, *Eva-Maria: Architekturwelten. Sergei Tchoban, Zeichner und Sammler = Architectural Worlds. Sergei Tchoban, Draftsman and Collector*, Berlin 2010.

57 Tiggemann, Anke; Hemmerling, Marco: *Digitales Entwerfen*, Stuttgart 2009.

58 Tönnesmann, Andreas: *Die Freiheit des Betrachtens. Schriften zu Architektur, Kunst und Literatur*, Zürich 2013.

59 Tréhin, Gilles: *Urville*, Chatou 2004.

60 Weisner, Ulrich (ed.): *Zusammenhänge: Der Architekt Gottfried Böhm*, exhibition catalogue, Kunsthalle Bielefeld 1985, Bielefeld 1984.

61 Wels, Peter: *Architekturzeichnungen*, Hamburg 1993.

62 Wilk, Sabrina: *Zeichenlehre für Landschaftsarchitekten. Handbuch und Planungshilfe*, Berlin 2014.

Drawing between History and Digital Innovation
Fabrizio Avella

1 The first evidence of what we call a plan is visible in a drawing on a wall in Catal Höyuk (Turkey), dated between 7200 and 6800 BC.

2 For a detailed description of the Forma Urbis Romae cf. Mario Docci, Diego Maestri, *Storia del rilievo architettonico e urbano*, Laterza, Bari (Italy), 1993.

3 Jean-Nicolas-Louis Durand, *Recueil et Parallele des edifices de Tout Genre, Anciens et Modernes*, 1801, and *Précis des leçons d'architecture données à l'école polytechnique*, Paris (France), 1805.

4 See Carlos Martí Aris, *Le variazioni dell'identità: Il tipo in architettura*, Città Studi, Milan (Italy), 1998 (1. edition, 1990).

5 Building Information Modeling is a system which associates vectorial entities and parametric information (such as composition of the wall, type of profile of a frame or glass, etc. ... to a graphical-numerical data-base that handles both vectorial and parametrical information with the possibility of biunivocal variations.

6 "If the architecture of the Romanesque buildings was of relatively simple design, the Gothic (transparency, logical structure, and geometric ornament) requires a more virtuous and precise design. [...] No previous era, in fact, had tried to achieve a similar correspondence between exterior and interior, and had concatenated together so closely the individual elements of the body of the building by means of axes and frames. [...] It was only through training and using such a graphical method for designing, during the first half of the twelfth century, that it was possible for the architect to develop in the modern sense, fixing designs regardless of their realisation and transmitting them to artisans to carry out the work", in C. L. Frommel, 'Sulla nascita del disegno architettonico', in H. Millon and V. Magnago Lampugnani (ed.), *Rinascimento da Brunelleschi a Michelangelo*, Bompiani, Milan (Italy), 1994, p. 101.

7 Please refer to W. Lotz, 'La rappresentazione degli interni nei disegni architettonici del Rinascimento', in *Studi sull'architettura italiana del Rinascimento*, Electa, Milan (Italy), 1989, (Original title *Studies in the Italian Renaissance*, Massachusetts 1977).

8 "The overall architecture consists of the drawing and construction. Concerning the drawing, its whole purpose and method is to find an exact and satisfactory way to fit together and connect lines and angles, through which the look of the building is fully defined. The function of the drawing is to assign to the buildings and their parts an appropriate location, an exact proportion, a convenient and harmonious order, so that the whole shape of the building rests entirely in the design itself." [Author's translation] In R. Bonelli and P. Portoghesi (eds.), *Leon Battista Alberti, L'Architettura (De re aedificatoria)*, Book I [*Il Disegno*], Polifilo Edizioni, Milan (Italy), 1966, p. 18.

9 R. Bonelli and P. Portoghesi (eds.), *Leon Battista Alberti*, op. cit., Book II [materials], chap. I, p. 98. We recommend a comparison with the perspective method which Bramante used: A. Bruschi, *Bramante*, Laterza, Bari (Italy), 1990, I ed. Thames and Hudson, London (UK), 1973, pp. 13–32.

10 "Even if the architects of the Renaissance were not the first to use the architectural models, they still built them with much more methodology and correctness than any predecessor." [Author's translation] In H. A. Millon, *I modelli architettonici nel Rinascimento*, in H. Millon and V. Magnago Lampugnani, op. cit., p. 19.

Sources

11 "I never tire of recommending what the best architects used to do: thinking and rethinking the work to be undertaken as a whole and the extent of its individual parts, not using only drawings and sketches, but also models made of wood and other material, consulting experts. Only after this examination can we address the cost and supervision of construction." [Author's translation] In R. Bonelli and P. Portoghesi (eds.), *Leon Battista Alberti*, op. cit., Book II [*I materiali*], chap. I, p. 96.

12 "The drawings we possess today, suggest that Antonio da Sangallo the Younger, the youngest apprentice of Raphael in the construction of the St. Peter Basilica, was the first to use orthogonal projections to represent an interior through the section." [Author's translation] In Wolfgang Lotz, *Studies in Italian Renaissance Architecture*, Cambridge, Massachusetts (USA), MIT Press, 1977, op. cit., p. 37.

13 "Before his appointment as coadjutore (close to Raphael during the construction of St. Peter Basilica, A/N), Sangallo had worked on St Peter also as faber lignarius and carpentarius. He is the only major architect of the Renaissance in Rome coming from the ranks of craftsmen, unlike Bramante, Raphael and Peruzzi, who had all started out as painters, Sangallo had not studied perspective during his education. [...] It is probable that Peruzzi, as a painter, considered the orthogonal projections inefficient for the purpose of representation, while Sangallo, a good craftsman, must have immediately grasped the benefits of greater clarity and readability." [Author's translation] Ibid.

14 V. Gregotti, *I materiali dell'architettura*, Feltrinelli, Milan (Italy), 1966, pp. 28–29. [Author's translation]

15 Erwin Panofsky, *La prospettiva come forma simbolica*, Feltrinelli, Milan (Italy), 1995, [original title: *Die Perspektive als "symbolische Form"*, Leipzig – Berlin 1927] I ed. it. Milan (Italy) 1961.

16 Martin Kemp, *La scienza dell'arte, Prospettiva e percezione visiva da Brunelleschi a Seurat*, Gruppo Editoriale Giunti, Florence (Italy), 1994 [original title: *The Science of Art: Optical Themes in Western Art from Brunelleschi to Seurat*, Yale University Press, 1990].

17 Henry Millon, Vittorio Magnago Lampugnani (ed.), *Rinascimento da Brunelleschi a Michelangelo. La rappresentazione dell'architettura*, Bompiani, Milan (Italy), 1994.

18 Thus defined to distinguish it from the perspectiva naturalis, which concerned the technique to render the depth of natural landscapes. Note in this regard Leonardo's theory that required to lighten the hills and decrease the saturation of colour as we move away from the representation framework.

19 Not considering, for the moment, the perspective construction performed by means of optical rooms or other tools. For the use of auxiliary tools for mechanical construction, cf. M. Kemp, *The Science of Art*, op. cit.

20 See the remains of the volute of the angular capitel at the cloister of Santa Maria della Pace, a solution that probably would have horrified Alberti.

21 It is recalled that the distinction between perspective with one or two vanishing points is simply the result of a nomenclature, which can bring, however, ambiguity: the perspective construction always follows the same laws, only the relationships between point of view, plane and objects determine different perspectives.

22 This rule does not actually have a scientific basis, but is determined by experience and not intended as a rigid prescription. We can simply observe that the perspective which covers a visual field determined in this way has a pleasing visual effect, while those with a huge visual field present unpleasant aberrations.

23 "Plans and profiles, generally distinct drawings, merge into a single representation, thus finding – as Lorini said – a graphical, projective and perpetual trick, able to combine formal and metric reliability with a three-dimensional view of the object. [...] The resulting image is similar to a bird's eye view of a model on which it is possible to make measurements and ballistic simulations." [Author's translation] In Domenico Mediati, *L'occhio del mondo. Per una semiotica del punto di vista*, Rubettino Editore, Soveria Mannelli 2008, p. 133.

24 "Thus, the engineer or architect becomes a simple designer of architectural principles of organisation dictated by the commander. The terrain of dialogue must be, therefore, common among the subjects involved in the project [...]. There is thus a need to find methods of representation that, with greater adherence to the forms of real space, provide reliable support to the decisions of princes, troops and gunners." [Author's translation] Ibid.

25 "A house whose walls are not perfectly parallel, and that do not conform to the project, is not less habitable. For the world of machine these inaccuracies are almost always fatal. Are sufficient deformation of a few tenths of a millimeter to make "intolerant" a rotational motion or a microscopic defect in fusion to make explode a cannon. There is therefore no coincidence that the kind of representation, that in 1852 M. H. Meyer called for the first time axonometric projection, has its origin in the world of Mechanica." [Author's translation] In M. Scolari, *Aforismi e considerazioni sul disegno*, in Rassegna (*Rappresentazioni*), Year IV, No. 9 March 1982, Bologna (Italy), p. 79.

26 "Nor are we surprised to see that, when William Farish in 1820 opens the specific studies about axonometric projection (On isometrical Perspective), the first speaker and the addressee is not the world of architecture but that of the machine." Ibid.

27 "The supremacy of the facade, so the dominant architectural expression of the past, is finally set aside thanks to a method of representation that, not proposing a dominant point of view, prefers the control of stereometric definition rather than the decoration of facade [...] The axonometric projection will thus – according to the hypothesis supported by Bois and Reichlin – became a 'symbolic form' for the movements of the early twentieth century avant-garde, a sort of antagonist to the perspective, the vehicle of a changed relationship between space and architecture." [Author's translation] Ibid., p. 170.

28 "There is no doubting the usefulness of an axonometric projection system of representation in the process of defining the architectural form. The dual function – metric definition and volumetric control – gives it a crucial role in different stages of design. In a cultural context such as modernism, in which the architectural language was dominated by stereometry, axonometric projection becomes the primary tool of expression of the architects." [Author's translation] In Domenico Mediati, *L'occhio del mondo. Per una semiotica del punto di vista*, Rubettino Editore, Soveria Mannelli, Catanzaro (Italy), 2008, op. cit., p. 165.

29 "Before the arrival of what is destined to become the medium par excellence of every kind and class of drawings, artists had available, for those works which were to last only parchment, a material which required long and laborious processes of manufacture." [Author's translation] In Anna Maria Petrioli Tofani, 'I materiali e le tecniche', in *AA. VV. Il disegno, forme, tecniche, significati*, Amilcare Pizzi Editore, Milan (Italy) 1991, p. 191.

30 "The decline of parchment can be said to begin at the end of the fourteenth century, and within fifty years it had been supplanted by paper in virtually every sector of use." [Author's translation] Ibid., p. 193.

31 "When you look in its general outlines in historical perspective, we see that the diffusion of drawing as an artistic object becomes common in the European area only after the middle of the fifteenth century [...]. I believe that it is no exaggeration to say that the availability of this or that type of medium, and especially the introduction and vicissitudes of paper and its diffusion on the European continent, have played a vital role in questions of a conceptual nature, as we have seen." [Author's translation] Ibidem, p. 191.

32 "It is only with the arrival of paper from the East [...] that drawing can be said to enter the stage of history." [Author's translation] Ibid., p. 198.

33 On the symbolic role of the board, De Rubertis writes: "This calls into question just what is and will remain forever in the history the mysterious charm of the line: to express forms through their margin, to allow us to guess the contents by

describing the container, to neglect the object and focus attention on its limit." [Author's translation] In Roberto De Rubertis R., *Il disegno dell'architettura*, Carocci, Rome (Italy), 2002 (I ed. Rome 1994), p. 32.

34   "In the Middle Ages and Renaissance architects showed their preference for the drawing made of lines. The geometric graphic language lends itself to agile and encrypted communication between professionals of the construction process." Ibid., p. 213.

35   "The drawings of facades of Palladian buildings are pen on paper, in order to accurately measure the relationship between architectural members as well as to offer the right level of schematisation necessary for woodcut." [Author's translation] Ibidem.

36   "The editions of Renaissance treatises found in woodcut illustrations were a particularly appropriate system to obtain the desired images. The ideal of a universal harmony in architecture and the need for essential and simple images. [...] The technique of carving poses technical limits to the quality and quantity of the lines, preventing the transposition of the effects of shade and grain of the materials. The images so made present architectures without body, without colour, without material, they are scientific images, representations of ideas to support the idea." [Author's translation] Ibidem, p. 223.

37   The perceptual experience enables us to receive information due to differences between the parties in shadow and illuminated parts of an object: "We could not otherwise estimate, as humans, the distance that separates us from the objects if light did not illuminate them and project shadows, thus suggesting to us the idea of a three-dimensional perception." [Author's translation] In Agostino De Rosa, 'Tutta la luce del mondo', in *XY Dimensioni del disegno*, Rome (Italy), 2005, Volume 9, p. 63.

38   The calculation of the shade net is obtained through the technique of ray tracing, and the nuances of shadows can be achieved by engines that calculate the global illumination, which calculates not only the incidence effects of rays projected from the light source but also from their reflection on these surfaces, according to an algorithm that calculates the light absorbed and reflected.

39   Gouache is a type of tempera made brighter by the addition of pigments such as chalk or white lead, and more dense by mixing with Arabic gum.

40   The grain, which is necessary to reveal aspects of materials such as concrete, plaster and rough material is obtained in relief through operations of bumping or displacement, in which a map of light or dark pixels is interpreted by associating to light colours the parts in relief and to dark colours the hollowed parts. The reaction to light rays determines the illusion of shading holes and of increasing brightness of the parts in relief.

41   The texture is a raster image that is associated with one or more sides of a polygonal model.

42   On the notion of the iconic and mimesis in drawing please refer to Roberto de Rubertis, 'Il disegno iconico', in *Roberto de Rubertis*, op. cit.

43   Computer Aided Manufacturing, Computer Numerical Control.

44   This essay does not address the implications of digital design on the genesis of shape, as this is too broad a topic and unrelated to the immediate objective. Cf. the essay by Livio Sacchi, 'Il digitale: un bilancio', in *Ikhnos, Analisi grafica e storia della rappresentazione*, Lombardi editore, Syracuse (Italy), 2008.

45   One of the themes of the film by Wim Wenders, released in 1991, was the issues relating to testing a visor, initially aims show pictures to a blind mother of the protagonist. Viewing virtual images progressively leads other people to detach from reality.

46   Franco Rella said: "Men have traced lines, expressed words, have constructed codes and composed figures, to give meaning to what, at first sight, was as confused as a tangled and impenetrable forest." In Franco Rella, 'Immagini e figure del pensiero', in *Rassegna (Rappresentazioni)*, Year IV, No. 9, March 1982, Editrice C.I.P.I.A., Bologna (Italy), p. 75.

The *Deutsche Nationalbibliothek* lists this publication in the *Deutschen Nationalbibliografie*; detailed bibliographic data are available at *http://dnb.d-nb.de* abrufbar.

ISBN 978-3-86922-414-5 (Hardcover)
ISBN 978-3-86922-451-0 (Softcover)

© 2015 by DOM publishers, Berlin
www.dom-publishers.com

This work is subject to copyright. All rights are reserved, whether the whole part of the material is concerned, specifically the rights of translation, reprinting, recitation, broadcasting, reproduction on microfilms or in other ways, and storage or processing in data bases. Sources and owners of rights are stated to the best of our knowledge, please signal any we may have omitted.

Translation
Peter & Clark – Multilingual Communications S.A, Luxembourg
Clarice Knowles

Editorial Assistance
Inka Humann

Design
Atelier Kraut

Printing
Tiger Printing (Hong Kong) Co., Ltd.
www.tigerprinting.hk